JESUS LOVES JAPAN

JESUS LOVES JAPAN

RETURN MIGRATION AND
GLOBAL PENTECOSTALISM
IN A BRAZILIAN DIASPORA

SUMA IKEUCHI

STANFORD UNIVERSITY PRESS ∎ STANFORD, CALIFORNIA

Stanford University Press
Stanford, California

Printed in the United States of America on acid-free, archival-quality paper

Library of Congress Cataloging-in-Publication Data

Names: Ikeuchi, Suma, 1985– author.
Title: Jesus loves Japan : return migration and global pentecostalism in a Brazilian diaspora / Suma Ikeuchi.
Description: Stanford, California : Stanford University Press, 2019. | Includes bibliographical references and index.
Identifiers: LCCN 2018041613 | ISBN 9781503607965 (cloth : alk. paper) | ISBN 9781503609341 (pbk.) | ISBN 9781503609358 (ebook)
Subjects: LCSH: Pentecostalism—Japan. | Return migration—Japan. | Brazilians—Japan—Religion. | Brazilians—Japan—Ethnic identity. | Japan—Emigration and immigration—Religious aspects—Pentecostal churches. | Brazil—Emigration and immigration—Religious aspects—Pentecostal churches.
Classification: LCC BR1644.5.J3 I34 2019 | DDC 275.2/083—dc23
LC record available at https://lccn.loc.gov/2018041613

Cover design: George Kirkpatrick
Typeset by Westchester Publishing Services in 10/14 Minion Pro

Dedicated to the Memories of
Hisako Ikeuchi
Tatsuo Ikeuchi
Teruyuki Ikeuchi
Kayako Shiba
Tamaki Shiba
Yasumasa Shiba
Yasutoshi Shiba

CONTENTS

ILLUSTRATIONS

ACKNOWLEDGMENTS

This book has benefited from the support of many people over the years, and I would like to thank them here mainly in a chronological order. My parents, Yumi and Yoshiaki Ikeuchi, have always been incredibly supportive. Born into a working-class family coping with the postwar poverty in Japan, my father in particular believed that education was "the only kind of investment whose fruit no one can take away from you." My siblings, Maya Kōno and Yūsuke Ikeuchi, have also been a consistent source of support, especially during the transition period after I moved to the United States. Migration comes with its costs, however, and I missed some funerals of my close relatives in the following years. So this book is dedicated to my kin who have crossed over to the realm of ancestors.

The Iwakuni Foundation for Scholarship funded my undergraduate study at Hokkaido University in Japan. Shūichi Iwakuni and Toshihisa Yokota, the then and current presidents of the foundation, respectively, treated me as an intellectual equal and challenged me in stimulating ways during the annual events for scholarship recipients. Many faculty at Hokkaido University had enduring effects on the development of my young mind. They include Naoya Itō, Hiroto Koga, and Takami Kuwayama. Tomohiko Ōhira was the bedrock of my formative years at the university; I thrived thanks to his vibrant teaching and warm guidance. The Support Program for Long-Term Study Abroad from the Ministry of Education, Culture, Sports, Science, and Technology in Japan made it possible for me to pursue my master's study in the United States with its generous national scholarship. The faculty in the Anthropology Department at Brandeis University warmly welcomed and patiently mentored me as I clumsily made my entrance into American higher education. Special thanks go to Sarah Lamb and Ellen Schattschneider for guiding me with intellectual rigor and unwavering psychological support.

People I met and worked with at Emory University have helped me grow the ideas in this book with their sustained and stimulating intellectual encouragement. Chikako Ozawa-de Silva gave me the best advice I could ever ask for. She has helped me think deeply about the relationship between culture, religion, and the self while being incredibly generous with her time, energy, and emotional support. From Bradd Shore, I received the best training in psychological anthropology and learned how to analyze cultural diversity in nuanced ways. His playful sense of humor and deep appreciation of ethnographic prose always made our conversations enriching. Jeffrey Lesser, a historian of Brazil, complemented the anthropological perspective with his insistence on the need to situate current events within historical processes. His advice was always spot-on, whether it was about scholarly analysis or academic career.

The generous support from many organizations and institutions made possible the research for this book. I am grateful to the Kathryn Davis Fellowship for Peace, Department of Anthropology at Emory, and Wenner-Gren Foundation (Grant Number 8746) for funding the preparatory and main phases of the ethnographic project. The Nanzan Institute for Religion and Culture, led by Michiaki Okuyama at the time, kindly offered me an intellectual home where I could discuss my findings during the fieldwork in Japan. The University of Alabama's Publisher-in-Residence Program, directed by George F. Thompson, later helped me navigate the process of writing a book. Lastly, the Social Science Research Council gave me the opportunity to spend a summer as fellow-in-residence at the University of Göttingen's Transregional and Global Studies Platform, where I could finish the book manuscript.

Most importantly, it was the people in Toyota and other cities in the Aichi Prefecture that made this research possible. I feel deeply grateful and indebted to Cid Carneiro, who generously opened up the community at Missão Apoio Toyota to an outsider like myself. All the other informants in Aichi—many of whom I had the honor to call friends—appear on the following pages under pseudonyms for the protection of privacy. I therefore cannot directly thank them here, but their generosity and kindness were beyond words. The time and stories they shared with me are now an inextricable part of my own journey. Deus abençoe cada um de vocês.

This book also owes a great deal to the conviviality and intellectual stimulation I received from my colleagues in the Religious Studies Department at the University of Alabama. They warmly welcomed me, an ethnographer trained in anthropology, into their vibrant intellectual community and encouraged me to push my work in new directions. Special thanks go to Russell McCutcheon and Steven Ramey, who supported me as the department chair and faculty mentor, respectively. At my newest institutional home, the School of the Art Institute of Chicago (SAIC), I benefit from the exciting company of diverse interdisciplinary scholars in the Department of Liberal Arts. I thank my colleagues for welcoming my work into the mix and inspiring me to think outside the box. I am fortunate to have such a creative and supportive environment as my academic base.

I would also like to thank friends and colleagues who have read sections of manuscript drafts and have otherwise offered support over the years: Michael Altman, James Bielo, Peter Brown, Julia Cassaniti, Moyukh Chatterjee, Jenny Chio, Cati Coe, Jennifer Cole, Simon Coleman, Dan Coppeto, Betty Dickey, William Dressler, Isaac Gagné, Marysia Galbraith, Casey Golomski, Glen Goodman, Aubrey Graham, Anna Grimshaw, Hemangini Gupta, Claire-Marie Hefner, James Hoesterey, So Hoshino, Shigehiro Ikegami, Angelo Ishi, Jin-Heon Jung, Bonnie Kaiser, Victor Hugo Kebbe, Bruce Knauft, Daniel Linger, Nathan Loewen, Edward Lowe, Tanya Luhrmann, Wolfram Manzenreiter, Cecília Mariz, Gordon Mathews, Lora McDonald, Laura McTighe, Koichi Mori, Ryo Morimoto, Karen Nakamura, Valentina Napolitano, Michael Peletz, Kristin Phillips, Kwame Phillips, Devaka Premawardhana, Sonya Pritzker, Dario Paulo Barrera Rivera, Nathaniel Roberts, Joel Robbins, Jennifer Robertson, Thomas Rogers, Joshua Hotaka Roth, Srirupa Roy, Sonia Ryang, Don Seeman, Stephen Selka, Rafael Shoji, Sydney Silverstein, Merinda Simmons, Mark Smith, Domingos Souza, Marvin Sterling, Vaia Touna, Lesley Jo Weaver, Sarah LeBaron von Baeyer, Carol Worthman, and Masanobu Yamada.

I am grateful to my editor at Stanford University Press, Marcela Maxfield, for believing in this project and effectively handling the review and production process. Special thanks also go to Olivia Bartz and Faith Wilson Stein. The comments provided by the two anonymous reviewers improved the final manuscript so much that I feel bad to be unable to directly thank them. I would also like to make clear that some parts of the book are derived from or based on three of my previously published works. These two articles are available online at http://www.tandfonline.com/ and copyrighted by Taylor & Francis: "Back to the Present" in *Ethnos* (Vol. 82, Issue 4, 2017, doi: 10.1080/00141844.2015.1107610) and "From Ethnic Religion to Generative Selves" in *Contemporary Japan* (Vol. 29,

Issue 2, 2017, doi: 10.1080/18692729.2017.1351046). The third article, "Accompanied Self," was published in *Ethos* by the American Anthropological Association (Vol. 45, Issue 1, 2017, doi: 10.1111/etho.12156). I thank these journals for permitting me to build on the published materials.

Finally, my deepest gratitude goes to Jamie Nicolas Witter for his love, patience, and selfless support over the years. Many migrants told me during the research for this book that home is where you make it, and he makes me feel at home no matter where we are.

PROLOGUE

Along the Big Question Mark

"Wake up!" I shouted to myself as I shook my head like a soaked dog getting out of water. Refocusing my gaze on the dark road ahead, I tightened my grip on the steering wheel. Just thirty more minutes, I told myself. Stay awake for just thirty more minutes and I can collapse into my bed. It was almost one o' clock in the morning, and I was on my way home from a one-on-one Bible study with Sara, a young migrant in her twenties who was a member of the Brazilian Pentecostal denomination that I was researching. Like most Brazilians in Japan, she was a factory worker with a long shift. On this particular day, her Japanese boss asked her to work three extra hours to meet the daily production quota, which is why she could leave her factory only at nine in the evening.

"Thank you for waiting! My body stunk from sweating, so I had to go home to take a quick shower," Sara said as she bustled into the fast food restaurant where I was waiting close to ten o'clock. We usually met at Saizeriya, a chain restaurant that Sara liked, because it was close to her workplace in Kariya. It was a forty-five-minute drive from Toyota, where I lived during fieldwork. We started the Bible study as she ate her late dinner. "Today we are going to learn about opening our hearts to Jesus," Sara said as she wiped pizza sauce from her fingers. "Now, I'm not sure how you Japanese people think about this, but God knows what you think and how you feel all the time. You understand?"

Realizing that she was waiting for my response after a few seconds, I hesitantly opened my mouth. "Um, do I understand?"

"Yes, do you believe that God is always in your heart?"

"Um . . . Sara, you know I'm not Christian, at least not yet. We talked about this."

"Well, but it's God's plan that you chose to study our churches. There is no such thing as coincidence! You want to learn about the Word of God, don't you?" Sara said with a glowing smile that showed little sign of exhaustion from her eleven-hour work at the assembly line that day.

"Yes," I admitted hesitantly, "I'm here to learn." I was starting to realize through such exchanges that there was little room for the detached observer in my fieldwork among Brazilian Pentecostal converts in Japan. Since I could not be a fully immersed participant, either, in terms of what my informants called faith, my principle in dealing with my ambiguous insider/outsider status was honesty to the degree that it was appropriate. "Well," I blurted, "if I can be frank, Sara, I think it's a little bit strange."

"Oh?"

"When you say God is with you anytime, anywhere . . . does that mean someone is by my side even when I'm sitting on a toilet? That feels . . . weird."

Sara blinked and then burst out laughing. "It's not like that, Suma! God is a gentleman!"

By the time Sara and I hugged and said good night to each other, it was past midnight. I started driving, following the familiar signs for Route 155. Japan National Route 155 starts in Tokoname, Aichi, and continues counterclockwise in a large circle around the prefectural capital of Nagoya until it ends in Yatomi, Aichi. On the map, it is shaped almost perfectly like a question mark, with the Chūbu Centrair International Airport located in the bottom dot. The airport on the artificial island serves as the entry point for most Brazilian migrants in the area, as well as the exit point for those who decided that their time in Japan was up. From Tokoname, where the airport is located, Route 155 stretches northward, eastward, and then westward, connecting many manufacturing cities in Aichi: Chita, Kariya, Chiryū, Toyota, and Komaki, to name a few. Toyota, located roughly halfway on the route, is home to the headquarters of the multinational automobile company, Toyota Motor Corporation. During my time there, I heard many residents comment matter-of-factly that the city was the powerful company's *jōkamachi*—a "castle town" whose virtual ruler was not in the city hall but in the headquarters building. In fact, it is the city that was named after the company, not the other way around. In 1959, then Koromo City passed a bill to officially change its name to Toyota City, making a gesture of appreciation to the corporation that brought in jobs, investments, and tax revenue.

My car had passed the city limit of Toyota, and soon enough I was driving on the part of Route 155 called Toyota Bypass, which was elevated to go over a vast Toyota plant. On both sides, I could see fields of gray steel buildings below, lit by colorful artificial lights and pumping out fuming smoke into the dark midnight sky. I wondered how many auto parts made by migrants such as Sara were transforming into brand-new cars at that moment. I also wondered absent-mindedly how many Brazilian workers were on the night shift that night inside the factories that stood along the road.

Route 155, the big question mark. It was the artery of my fieldwork, bringing me to new places, people, and ideas. It led me to interviews in neighboring cities, to weekend barbecue parties on the seashore, and to new churches that my informants thought I should visit. Funny, I thought to myself, I'm chasing down the answers to my questions along this huge question mark. It hit me then that maybe it was not just me, the ethnographer, who was looking for some answers on this road. Some migrants came here in search of answers to their lives, typically what they called "the better future." To other migrants, such as Sara, the answer was now Jesus Christ, and their churches dotted the cities connected by the route. Many of us were on this big question mark, with our destinations uncertain and our quests unfinished.

The bypass ended and my car glided down, passing a large roadside sign that read "Welcome to Toyota, the City of Cars." "Almost there," I muttered to myself. "Almost home."

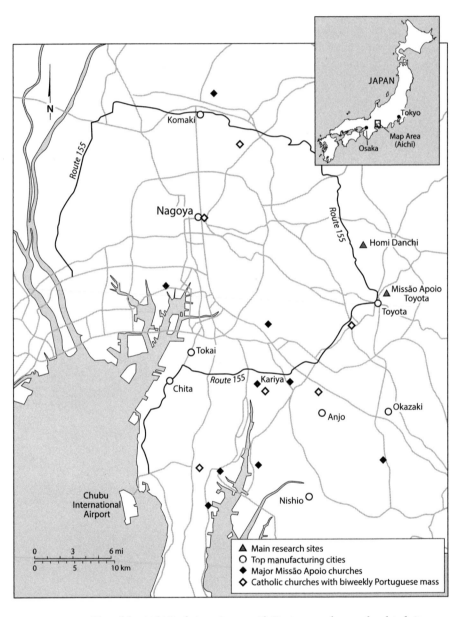

FIGURE 1. Map of the Aichi Prefecture, Japan, with Route 155 and research-related sites.

JESUS LOVES JAPAN

Part One

BEGINNINGS

PILGRIMS IN THE STRANGE HOMELAND

Opening: "Walk in Reverence During Your Pilgrimage"

"Brothers and sisters, this week I spent many days contemplating on the question of being a *peregrino* in this land." Presbyter Bruno addressed the roughly two hundred congregants who gathered for a Sunday afternoon service at Missão Apoio Toyota Pentecostal Church.[1] The majority of the attendants were *Nikkei*—or Japanese Brazilian—migrants who secured their "long-term resident" visas in Japan by proving that they were, at least partially, of Japanese descent. Having opened his sermon with a passage from 1 Peter 1:17, which advises to "walk in reverence during the time of your pilgrimage," the presbyter was inviting the congregation to dwell on the meaning of being a peregrino, or sojourner in a strange land.[2]

The room—its ceiling too low to be called a hall but still the size of a spacious classroom—was quiet except for occasional babbles from a dozen toddlers fidgeting in the arms of their parents, who were seated in rows of white plastic chairs facing the pulpit. Dark red curtains, covering the front and sidewalls from ceiling to floor, enclosed the congregants and added a touch of solemnness to the place. But the attire of most attendants was casual—T-shirts, shorts, caps, and ragged jeans—save a handful in leadership roles who always dressed formally for service. Standing between an electric organ and a drum set on the slightly elevated front stage, Presbyter Bruno looked crisp in a navy blue suit with a light yellow tie.

"No one in this nation can understand this better than us foreign *dekasseguis*—Brazilians, Peruvians, and Bolivians," he observed by listing the major migrant groups who have benefited from Japan's ancestry-based visa. *Dekasegi*, which means seasonal labor migration in Japanese, has transformed into *dekassegui* in Portuguese to refer to Japanese descendants who move to Japan for work. The presbyter's father was one of such dekasseguis, a second-generation Nikkei born and raised in Paraná, Brazil, who migrated with his family in 1996 to save money for a new house. He was seventeen years old when his father took him halfway around the globe to their supposed ancestral homeland.

"I, for one, principally because of my *cara de japonês* [Japanese face] like many of you here, I am Japanese in Brazil." Presbyter Bruno continued to reminisce about his experiences as a Nikkei. "Wherever I'd go, [I'd hear people say] 'Hey *japa*, can't you open those tiny eyes, *japa!*'" Many congregants, who may have received similar treatments in Brazil, laughed out loud. Smiling and nodding, he added, "So when my father decided [to migrate], I thought, 'Well good, now I'm going to Japan.' I arrived, then the Japanese here told me, 'Hey, gaijin [foreigner]!'" The crowd laughed and cheered again. His story of being betwixt and between, dramatized for preaching, was striking a chord with his audience who had also been living with multiple ethnic identities. He continued, "Where are we from, really? We are Japanese, we are Brazilian, and we become sort of lost, you see, in our identity." Presbyter Bruno then returned to the theme of being a peregrino:

> But when the Bible tells us to stay firm, to walk in reverence during our *peregrinação* [pilgrimage], this leads us, this afternoon, to examine certain things in our life. Because when we speak of a peregrino, . . . he can't count on the things of the world [*coisas do mundo*]. He can't accumulate too much baggage. . . .
>
> I remember the day when my father left for Brazil. I had to go and help him with his move, but after two, three days, we still couldn't finish it. There were so many things, brothers and sisters, too many things indeed, which he had accumulated in his fifteen years here in Japan. . . .
>
> But a peregrino cannot be tied down by the things of this world. He cannot gather many things for himself, because the time will come when he realizes that he doesn't belong in that land, and he has to move to another place.

In the sermon, he likens the life in flux of Nikkei Brazilians to the travels of early disciples in foreign lands in biblical times. By blurring the temporal and geographical lines between the two, he links the transiency of migrant life to the transiency of worldly life itself. Migrant converts' transnational mobility thus turns into an ethical proclivity to inhabit the world as pilgrims.

Morality of Mobility

Movement does not merely entail a physical change of locations but also amounts to a temporal, affective, and moral act. Mobility is thus fraught with aspirations, anxieties, and ambiguities. "Going forward," for example, invokes advance, progress, and modernity. The synonyms for "going back," in contrast, include recede, revert, and regress, all of which connote decline and degeneration. But going back does not always equal becoming backward. "Return" can evoke a complex web of emotions with a claim for one's roots, image of pure original state, and nostalgia for the primordial past. Without a sense of destination or place to return to, movement can turn into a "wander," which can entail an uprooted state of aimless roaming or a liberated mobile subject unconfined by boundaries.

Presbyter Bruno's narrative attests to the entanglement of mobility in moral implications. He acknowledges the difficulty many Nikkei Brazilians experienced in establishing a firm sense of national belonging in both Brazil and Japan. Notably, he does not characterize either his migration to Japan or his father's move back to Brazil as a "return" in his sermon. Instead, he describes such movements as "going" (*ir*) and "leaving" (*sair*), effectively refraining from assigning a point of origin to either country. This issue of uncertain national origin translates into a question of ambiguous identity: "Where are we from, really?" Presbyter Bruno, however, does not end on a pessimistic note. Instead of framing the perceived loss of identity as a failure to become fully integrated national citizens, he renders it as an opportunity to cultivate new subjectivities as sojourners in pilgrimage. Just as a peregrino of God must not dwell in the world of material desire, a migrant convert must not cling to the material things accumulated in one place. Ultimately, he seems to suggest, a Christian migrant is a peregrino not just in foreign countries but also in worldly life itself. The sermon generatively interprets sojourn in a foreign land—or *peregrinação*—as a form of ethical mobility consisting in purposeful rootlessness.

Presbyter Bruno's evocation of diaspora as pilgrimage blurs the line be-tween migratory and religious movements, thereby defying the ontological separation between the two. To him and many of his audience, migration and religion do not necessarily constitute two separate phenomena but instead one unified process of subject formation as a sojourner en route. A pilgrim is therefore away from home in a dual sense—far from the ethnic homeland and the celestial home at once. This double diasporic consciousness amplifies the ethical reverberation between the longing for the lost homeland and the yearning for the presence of God. "The empowering paradox of diaspora is that dwelling *here* assumes a solidarity and connection *there*," James Clifford wrote regarding "the axis of origin and return" that constitutes the backbone of homeward subjectivity.[3] This elsewhere—an imagined locus of origin where the return to wholeness becomes possible—does not need be a single place; it can simultaneously encompass an ethnonational homeland and an eschato-logical destination.

Morality of mobility refers to the fundamental interworking of migrant mo-bility and religious sensibility in the reformation of subjectivity among itiner-ants in diaspora.[4] In its Christian mode, the morality of mobility finds its roots in various moments of loss: the Fall as the loss of innocence, the Tower of Babel as the loss of unified humanity, and the Crucifixion as the loss of the savior in flesh. It is not surprising for a mythology so conspicuously defined by loss to fixate on origin, its restoration, and even its immanence. But origin lost and found is never pristine but ever a mediated one, no matter how potent the il-lusion of immediacy. Matthew Engelke described this necessity of mediation as the problem of presence, or "how a religious subject defines and claims to construct a relationship with the divine through the investment of authority and meaning in certain words, actions, and objects."[5] As it turns out, the prob-lem of presence is equally pressing for a diasporic subject, as the memory of homeland is always mediated by an evolving set of narratives, rituals, and things. Possible mediums for the sustenance of home are endless, ranging from a quick online message to an annual ethnic festival. Also among them are re-ligious rhetoric, practices, and networks, which can incite dynamic homeward orientation among migrants. The morality of mobility thus points to the dual mediation at work in the making of itinerant subjectivity, with the relation-ship with the divine on the one hand and the memory of homeland on the other. Peregrino is an apt name for this sojourning subject defined by loss, out of Eden and far from home, still en route toward imagined origins.

The morality of mobility is not an abstract idea but an ethnographic reality to Nikkei Brazilian Pentecostal migrants. They are descendants of Japanese immigrants in Brazil who have "returned" to Japan and converted to Pentecostal Christianity once there. As transnational migrants with a century-old history of diaspora, they craft their selves by weaving together multiple national belongings, ethnoracial identities, and potential homelands. The sources of their generative self-making, however, are not limited to ethnic and national rhetoric. As participants in the global Pentecostal movements, they also claim a belonging in "the Kingdom of God," which supposedly transcends man-made ethnonational boundaries—the world where they have faced persistent racism due to their ambiguous hyphenated identity. As such, the lives of Nikkei Brazilian Pentecostals in Japan are shaped by multiple origin myths—national, cultural, and theological. Myth in this context does not signify a domain of archived imaginary tales but instead refers to a set of narratives that people live, so intensely and compellingly, to bring forth real-world consequences.

In 1990, the Japanese government introduced a new type of visa for "long-term residents." Often dubbed the *Nikkei-jin* (Japanese descendant) visa, it is available to foreigners of Japanese descent up to the third generation. The same logic that governs Japan's *jus sanguinis* citizenship law determines the boundary of Nikkei-jin visa beneficiaries. The right to settlement is conferred virtually as the right of blood. At the same time, the legal system also implies that the "Japanese blood" becomes diluted over time; this is why fourth-generation descendants do not qualify for the visa. Clearly, the national ideology that underpinned the implementation of the new visa recognizes only one point of origin, which is when Japanese nationals left the country. This preemigration original state, the source of any acknowledgeable Japaneseness in the subsequent generations born abroad, cannot be replicated—even when many offspring of third-generation Nikkei migrants are today raised in Japan from birth. Japan's consanguineous myth thus locates the origin of national identity in the primordial unity of race, culture, and spirit, which arose within the geographical bounds of Japan. Although this origin story of "Japanese blood" places Nikkei foreigners on the perimeters of national kinship, their moral entitlement to belonging remains contested due to their ethnoracial ambiguity.

For Nikkei Brazilians who actually migrated to Japan by obtaining the visa, the emigration of their Japanese ancestors seldom constitutes the starting point of their life stories. Many say they do not know where their grandparents came from in Japan, and some openly admit that they do not care. Very few travel to the place of their ancestral roots, even when they could contact living relatives there. This is partly because they are so-called labor migrants who decided to come to Japan primarily to save money, send remittances, and then go home to Brazil. The majority are second- and third-generation Nikkeis who were born and raised in places like São Paulo, Paraná, and Pará. Predominantly, Nikkei migrants themselves do not view their movement to Japan as a return to the country of origin. Instead, many speak about their eventual return to Brazil, planned or fantasized: "Of course I want to go home. I was born there!" Brazil, which received waves of Japanese immigrants in the first two-thirds of the twentieth century, confers citizenship on the basis of place of birth. It is *terra natal* or "land of birth" that is valorized in the rhetoric of national belonging. Furthermore, Brazil has long upheld *mestiçagem*, or "racial mixture," as an important aspect of national identity.[6] Despite the fact that they have often been perceived as the unassimilable Oriental Other, once in Japan many Nikkeis look back to their natal country as the irrefutable homeland. Thus, the primary locus of their authentic identity—and hence origin—now lies in Brazil, where the myth of *mestiçagem* constitutes the centerpiece of national identity. To many, the projected return to Brazil starts to gain moral significance, at once as the craved end to the discrimination they face as vulnerable foreign laborers and as a return to secure belonging in nationhood.

The relationship between "Japanese blood" and "Brazilian birth" is ambivalent to say the least, and negotiation of identities is a daily task for many Nikkei Brazilians in Japan. For those who converted to Pentecostalism that has flourished among migrant communities, however, yet another origin myth takes hold. Pentecostalism is a charismatic Christian movement that places particular emphasis on the direct and personal experience of God through the gifts of the Holy Spirit. On the individual scale, the most defining aspects of Pentecostal identity are attributed to the redemption story of conversion: "I was lost but now I am saved." On the scriptural scale, the Pentecostal myth locates the origin of the current human state at various moments of loss, revival, and suspension: the crucifixion of Jesus, his resurrection, and the Second Coming. By fusing personal experiences with biblical themes, Nikkei converts learn a third way to narrate their origin stories, this time not as national subjects but as *crentes* (believers or born-again Christians). Set in the grand narrative landscape of loss and revival, the Pentecostal conception of time can also help converts defy the temporal scales of modern nation-states.[7] Importantly, Pentecostals often evoke the rhetoric of moral universalism with their origin myth; it is ideally open to anyone regardless of citizenship, ethnicity, bloodline, or place of birth.

Living in Japan as Nikkei Brazilian Pentecostal migrants entails negotiating between the ethical ramifications of three origin myths sketched out above—of Japanese blood, Brazilian birth, and transnational God. I will explore how migrant converts comprehend, combine, and at times contest such myths that shape their ever-shifting boundaries of the self. Where do they think they are "from," when national citizenship, ethnic identity, and religious subjectivity are predicated on diverging origin stories? What happens when the right to mobility rests on the ability to embody state-sanctioned origin? How do their projects of return in turn affect the moral contours of citizenship, belonging, and diaspora?

At the Crossroads of Global Currents

The lives of Nikkei Brazilian Pentecostals in Japan unfold at the intersection of two growing trends in contemporary globalization. The first is the state-sanctioned "return" of diasporic populations. Over the past several decades, nations such as Japan, China, India, and South Korea have implemented legal structures that facilitate the migration of foreign citizens deemed to possess enduring ties to national kinship.[8] This Asian trend shows that nationalism today is more about selective reordering of mobile subjects into tiers of desirables and undesirables and less about a strict fixing of national citizenry—what Aihwa Ong called "flexible citizenship."[9] The regime of return has produced potential beneficiaries around the globe, attracting Chinese Canadians to Hong Kong, Indian Americans to Bangalore, and Japanese Brazilians to Toyota.[10] It has had a particularly visible impact on the shape of Japanese diaspora in the Americas by prompting many descendants to "return."[11] Roughly thirty years after the introduction of the "long-term resident" visa, which enabled the mass migration of Nikkeis, there are roughly 196,800 Brazilian nationals living in Japan today. Although Nikkeis benefit from the visa policy that gives preferential treatment to foreigners of Japanese descent, they often experience subtle and not-so-subtle racism due to their ambiguous quasi-Japanese status. The Japanese majority often expects a special proclivity for smooth assimilation from Nikkei foreigners due to the supposed shared blood but, of course, Nikkei Brazilians are culturally and linguistically Brazilian. The stress they feel from this forced cultural conformity is further exacerbated by the fact that the majority work as unskilled dispatch laborers—the kind of workforce that Japanese mainstream society often regards as disposable. As there already exist two detailed ethnographic monographs by Takeyuki Tsuda and Joshua Roth on the work conditions of Nikkei Brazilians in Japan, this book does not focus on the topic of labor.[12] My labor-related findings mostly repeat and confirm their observations about the discriminatory treatment that foreign migrants often receive as a result of their race, ethnicity, and part-time status. The emphasis will instead be on the intersection of return migration and religious revivalism, which brings me to the next point.

The second relevant global movement comprises the transnational Pentecostal networks. Pentecostalism has been the fastest-growing branch of global Christianity over the past several decades, particularly in sub-Saharan Africa and Latin America. Brazil, for instance, has seen a fourfold increase in its Pentecostal population over the last forty years from 5 percent to 22 percent, becoming one of the epicenters of global Pentecostalism in the South.[13] Although the Christian renewalist movements have been less pronounced in Asia, Pentecostalism has generated many points of contention precisely due to its embattled minority status.[14] Japan has historically persecuted and suppressed Christianity as a foreign religion, and as a result, Christians make up only 1 percent of its population today. Yet this is the cultural context in which many Nikkei migrants have been converting to Pentecostalism since the early 1990s. The flourishing of Pentecostalism among the "return" migrants indicates that it exerts a particular appeal in their postmigration life in the strange ancestral homeland.

This book offers a rare window into the lives of the people who inhabit the crossroads of Asian return migration and Latin American Pentecostalism in transnational Japan. To date, the study of return migration says surprisingly little about the role of religion and scholars continue to explore the complexity of return primarily in ethnoracial terms.[15] I counterbalance this conventional analytical primacy of the "ethnic lens" by drawing on the insights from the anthropology of Christianity.[16] Return migration is an intensely political process that hinges on the intimate work of self-making on the part of its participants. An analysis of Pentecostal conversion among return migrants consequently needs to pay equal attention to the political and psychological dimensions of religious life—two dimensions that are in fact inseparable to start with. I take my framework of moral mobility to represent such a psychopolitical approach to religion on the move. This synthetic perspective can elucidate why Pentecostalism has flourished among people like Nikkei Brazilian migrants, who inhabit some of the most fluid and contested boundaries in this age of globalization.

An ethnography illustrates the particular to illuminate the universal; it recounts a specific cultural life as a lens to magnify something overarching and fundamental about the human condition. Although this one is based on my immersive fieldwork in a single region in Japan, the global currents that brought forth the people who fill the following pages extend far beyond the nation's territorial borders and run through many other countries and continents of the world.

JAPANESE BLOOD, BRAZILIAN BIRTH, AND TRANSNATIONAL GOD

Rooting for Brazil from the Other Side of the World

"Being a *crente* is like having a second job," Sergio said reassuringly from the passenger's seat as I yawned at the wheel. I quickly shut my mouth and gave him an embarrassed smile. It was 4:30 A.M. and we had been up all night. The first two gatherings that we attended were indeed for *crentes*, or "believers." The home group meeting, which took place weekly on Friday night, started at around 10 P.M. and lasted for two hours. Some attendants then carpooled to a nearby mountain, where several dozen church members held a weekly *vigília* (vigil, or late-night prayer meeting). It went on until past 3 A.M. Normally, I would then drive Sergio and some other friends back and then go home myself to collapse into bed. But this day was special. The 2014 FIFA World Cup was in progress on the other side of the world in Brazil. Those who wanted to watch their national team play in the live-broadcasted quarterfinals against Colombia had to be up before dawn at 5 A.M. on July 5 to root for their distant homeland. As I drove to a nearby park, I wondered if the Brazilian players, who must be warming up for the game in Florianópolis, felt this dedicated support that came halfway around the globe from Japan—the country with the third largest Brazilian expatriate community in the world after the United States and Paraguay.

I parked my car in the empty parking lot of Suigen Park, where we had been told to meet with the others who went home first to bring the TV, electric generator, and wireless video transmitter. It was obviously not their first time to have an outdoor TV viewing gathering, and they seemed to know what they were doing. Sergio and I got out of the car to breathe some fresh morning air. Although it was still dark, the rim of the mountains at a distance was beginning to turn whitish yellow. Birds were starting to chirp, signaling the immanent beginning of a new morning. "Oh, my body feels like I've just come out of *yakin* [night shift]," Sergio said as he laughed, stretching with his hands on the lower back of his waist. "I used to do it a lot when I was younger, when I wanted to save a lot of money to return to Brazil quickly. Thank God I don't do it anymore; it breaks your body!" We sat down on a nearby bench to wait, sipping the warm coffee we had bought at a 7-Eleven on our way to the park. Sergio was a Nikkei in his late thirties who had been living in Japan for over a decade. Like most Brazilian migrants, he had intended to work in Japan "for a year or two" but ended up staying much longer. His wife, who attended the same home group gathering with him, usually skipped the vigil to go home for their nine-year-old daughter, who was born in Japan.

"By the way, my daughter said something funny the other day, Suma," Sergio giggled.

"Oh. What did she say?"

"She said, 'Otōsan, nande burajiru ōen suru? Nihon wa?' [Daddy, why do you root for Brazil? What about Japan?]" He repeated his daughter's remark in Japanese, mimicking her critical tone. We both laughed. Unlike Sergio and his wife, who both grew up in Mato Grosso do Sul and spoke only basic Japanese, their daughter preferred speaking in Japanese, especially after she started attending a local Japanese elementary school. He continued, "I explained to her that I am Brazilian, but I'm not sure if she really got it." Then, straightening his back a little, Sergio added, "I've never felt Japanese in my life anyway, you see. Only my grandfather was Japanese, and I never knew him. Everyone else in my family is Brazilian. I had no contact with Japanese culture in my small town, you know, there was no Japanese community there. . . . It wasn't like São Paulo." I nodded. Compared with São Paulo or Paraná, Sergio's home state in Brazil had fewer Japanese communities, and it sounded like he did not grow up in any of them.

"So, you are sansei [third-generation] but you never felt Japanese?"

"No, not at all," Sergio shook his head. "I don't look Japanese either, right? I'm *mestiço* [mixed-race] with *índio* [indigenous], *negro* [black], *português* [Portuguese], and *japonês* [Japanese]. . . . A huge mix. I don't look Japanese.

Sometimes people think my wife is the Japanese one, you know, who got us the visa, because I'm too *preto* [dark]."

"But your wife is not Nikkei," I interjected.

"No! She is Brazilian. But she is *mais branquinha* [lighter-skinned], so people think that. On paper I am sansei, but I feel like a *yonsei* [fourth-generation]! I'm not Japanese. I'm *não sei*, that's right, I'm não sei." We chuckled. To call oneself não sei was something of an insider joke among the Nikkei migrants whom I met. Punning with the word *sei* ("generation" in Japanese and "I know" in Portuguese), Sergio defied the necessity for generational identity by playfully declaring that he belonged to the "I-don't-know" generation.

"We are all não sei in some way, aren't we?" I quipped.

"For sure," Sergio smiled, "We don't really know who we truly are—except maybe God. Only God knows."

A large van appeared on the road before us and then pulled into the parking lot, blinding us for a second with its bright headlights. "Finally!" Sergio stood up, waving at the car. "It's almost five. They are late!" I stood up, too, feeling the morning dew on grass wetting my toes in sandals. The van's door slid open and five or six people jumped out from the back seats, all looking tired and excited at once. "C'mon, *gente* [folks], let's set this up quickly!" Sergio called animatedly, striding around the van toward the back trunk. "The game is about to start!"

The Past in the Present

The ethnographer always arrives late. The life of the people among whom she lives had started long before her arrival and will continue beyond her provisional stay. Her job is to retrieve something whole from this necessarily partial picture that emerges from fieldwork, especially because no study can be exhaustive in the literal sense of the word. Yet, some moments are powerful enough to pull her back to contemplate once again this fact: the human drama that she now participates in had begun years and decades before her timid appearance. What went on before is still going on in this moment. The past is in the present.

To me, the early morning before the Brazil-Colombia quarterfinals that I spent with Sergio in the crisp air before dawn was one of such moments. What unfolded was certainly not contained inside Suigen Park in Toyota City, or within July 5, 2014. No, it went beyond and back. To begin, why are there so many Brazilian migrants of Japanese ancestry like Sergio in Japan today? Why are there a large number of Japanese descendants in Brazil in the first place? Why is generational distinction so entrenched in their identities, so much so that some defiantly joke that they belong to the "I-don't-know" generation? Why is "looking Japanese" so important, and how does ethnoracial ambiguity shape their life in Japan? Why do some migrants like Sergio convert to Pentecostalism and regard it as their "second job," which becomes so important that they stay up all night praying? Last but not least, why do they root for Brazil instead of Japan when the latter could also be their homeland?

The stories that can answer these questions begin in Santos, Brazil, in 1908. By starting with the history of the people with whom I spent over a year, I will show that they do not constitute an independent cultural entity but instead a flexible knot in the ever-dynamic process of identity making. To this day, anthropology often fails to historicize the objects of its study, which leads to the conflation of politico-historical processes with psychocultural differences. Such a lack of historical contextualization has a consequence for the study of migration. A present-centered frame of reference often ends up depicting mobility as something new and exceptional that disrupts the hitherto fixed relationship between territory, culture, and identity.[1] But the tacit dualism between stasis and motion that lurks in such a framework is untenable as migrant identities are borne out of their historical interactions with various regimes of mobility.

Asian "Whites": Immigration to Brazil

Japanese immigration to Brazil started in 1908 with the arrival of *Kosato-maru*, a ship that carried 781 Japanese passengers. By 1941, roughly 189,000 Japanese nationals had entered the country.[2] Having abolished centuries-old slavery in 1888, the ruling class of early twentieth-century Brazil was keenly interested in securing a new supply of labor for plantation fields. Many Brazilian elites viewed the new migrant group from Asia as an ideal substitute for European immigrants, who often protested poor working conditions. An effort to place the newcomers in a social category equal to their European counterparts was therefore palpable from the outset. J. Amândio Sobral, São Paulo's inspector of agriculture, met the first group of Japanese migrants as they disembarked from *Kosato-maru* at the port of Santos in São Paulo and wrote a report on his first impressions. Most of the immigrants were literate; they did not seem poor; they wore European clothes made in Japanese factories; the living quarters of *Kosato-maru*, in which they had traveled for three months, were absolutely clean, and so were their clothes and bodies. Sobral concluded, "The race is very different, but it is not inferior."[3]

Japanese migrants entered Brazilian society at a time when its elites often conflated national development with what they considered as racial progress. Brazil received more African slaves than any other nation in the Americas. When a large number of free blacks became part of its citizenry in the late nineteenth century, nationalist thinkers had to reconcile the large presence of nonwhite population with the prevailing ideology of white superiority at the time. The answer was so-called *branqueamento* (whitening). The whitening ideology posited that by *mestiçagem* (interracial mixing), the white race and its superior civilization would eventually prevail by absorbing positive qualities of other races, and blacks and Indians would gradually disappear.[4] It is important to remember, however, that the Brazilian notions of race seldom appealed to strict biological determinism; the equivalent of the "one-drop rule" did not exist in Brazil. Whitening was as much a cultural and class-based concept as a phenotypic and biological one: "By maximizing their contact with individuals who were more advanced culturally [darker people could whiten]. One of the easiest channels was intermarriage. Miscegenation, therefore, was seen as regenerative, if not biologically, at least in terms of culture contacts."[5]

The first large-scale influx of migrants from the Far East stimulated the nation's preoccupation with race and progress in an ambiguous way. Phenotypically, Japanese were not white. Additionally, the Brazilian majority often deemed the Asian newcomers unassimilable due to what the majority viewed as an alien culture incompatible with the national ethos. The alleged lack of assimilability meant that Japanese could slow down—and worse yet, halt—the whitening process. At the same time, many elites were willing to place Japanese migrants in the racial category of "white," since whiteness involved not only phenotypic traits but also cultural qualities. With the victory in the Russo-Japanese War in 1905, Japan was quickly solidifying its international status as an industrialized First World nation. In the eyes of many Brazilian officials, then, Japanese were whiter (read: more civilized) than blacks and hence more desirable. As Sobral observed, the "race" was "not inferior." The Japanese were, however, also Asian (read: too foreign), and the risk of exclusion from national belonging was ever present.

At the rural plantations where the majority initially engaged in agricultural labor, Japanese migrants soon turned out to be as unwilling to suffer bad treatment as their European counterparts. The establishment of Japanese *colônias*, or rural farming communities subsidized by Japanese firms, alleviated some of the harsh work conditions. Japanese migrants' economic and social status in Brazilian society rose steadily, primarily in the area of agriculture. Over time, many nisei (second-generation) and sansei (third-generation) Nikkeis— born and raised in Brazil—started to leave rural *colônias* for urban areas in pursuit of better social, economic, and educational opportunities. This rural-urban migration and economic ascension of Nikkeis eventually yielded the model minority stereotype, as many successfully climbed the social ladder to become educated professional urbanites.[6] The rate of interethnic marriage also increased among the younger generations who, unlike older migrants, considered themselves primarily Brazilian. The Brazilian majority, however, continued to conflate "Nikkei Brazilian" with "Japanese"—a tendency evidenced by the usage of the Portuguese word *japonês* that, to this day, encompasses both Brazilian nationals of Japanese descent and Japanese nationals living in Japan. Today, Brazil is home to roughly 1.4 million Nikkeis—the largest Japanese-descent population in the world outside of Japan.[7]

The Movements of Gods and Ancestors Between Homelands

The ways in which Japanese migrants practiced their religions in early twentieth-century Brazil reflected a number of social and political forces that shaped their lives. For instance, the Japanese Ministry of Foreign Affairs prohibited missionaries—with the exception of Catholic priests—from going to Brazil from 1918 until the end of World War II.[8] Even major Japanese religions such as Buddhism and Shinto were not exempt from the ban. Shinto, which literally means "way of gods," is a name for various ritual practices dedicated to a multitude of deities and spirits in Japan. Beginning in the late nineteenth century, this ostensible "indigenous religion" of Japan underwent a modern transformation as it fused with political forces such as emperorship and imperialism to coalesce into State Shinto—the dominant ideology of the nation. The Japanese government's official gesture to discourage the proselytization of Japanese religions in Brazil, even the one with hegemonic political influence back home, shows its eagerness to respond to the pressure for assimilation from the Brazilian majority. Not only was there little protest from the migrants themselves against this policy, the popular opinion among the Japanese in Brazil often supported its rationale, which was the maintenance of amicable international relations. "Since Catholicism is the de facto official religion of Brazil, any propagation of other religions should be restrained," read one editorial published in 1932 in *Burajiru Jihō*, an influential Japanese-language newspaper in São Paulo. It continued: "We the Japanese, who are to emigrate more and more to Brazil and who consequently have to promote goodwill between the two countries, Japan and Brazil, . . . must be all the more careful not to make the Brazilians suspicious and anxious about religious matters."[9]

In addition to the government-led determent, there are several other reasons why Japanese communities in Brazil saw few organized religious activities before 1950 (with the exception of Catholicism). The dominant Japanese kinship system prescribed the worship of ancestral spirits as the right and duty of the head of household (*ie*), conventionally the eldest son. Since the majority of male migrants were not the eldest and hence free from the cultural expectation to partake in the care of the dead, the communal demand for ritual experts in this area—traditionally Buddhist monks—was not strong.[10] The common understanding was that they had left their ancestors in someone else's care in Japan during their stay in Brazil. The continuation of ancestor veneration was thus unimportant to the degree that Japanese migrants viewed their life in the nation as provisional. In the early days of immigration, when the majority intended to return one day, they had little reason to locally reestablish the social networks necessary to practice Buddhist rites for ancestors.

Furthermore, the sway of State Shinto—which to most Japanese represented civil ethics rather than religious doctrines at the time—lessened the communal need for explicit "religion."[11] Most prewar migrants were educated during the decades immediately preceding the World War II, when public institutions firmly enforced State Shinto. They reproduced some of such social structures in Brazil, most notably Japanese schools, where students continued to perform the core rituals of State Shinto, such as the recitation of Imperial Rescript on Education. In fact, "the Japanese school in Brazil served as the spiritual center of the community, lent some religious atmosphere with its practices of emperor worship, and consequently became in a sense a community shrine of the *uji gami* [tutelary deity] type. It was sacred."[12]

The veneration of emperor also shaped Japanese identity in diaspora. Unlike the commemoration of ancestors based on the unit of household or local clan, the rituals for the emperor could serve as a symbolic nexus of emerging Japanese ethnicity, which many migrants were experiencing more strongly than ever as they lived among the Brazilian majority. During World War II, however, the Brazilian government banned the teaching of the Japanese language, which severely restricted the role Japanese schools had been playing in the migrant communities. Since Brazil joined the Allies, the Brazilian majority's antipathy toward the "resident enemy aliens" within its national boundary grew day by day. In response, many secret societies linked to the emperor veneration arose and garnered wide support among alienated Japanese and Nikkei communities, promoting ultranationalism.[13]

Japan's surrender in August 1945 shook the foundation of emperor veneration in Brazil but did not quite destroy it. Although the defeat proved the fallacy of imperial invincibility, some factions of Japanese communities in Brazil refused to accept this fact by claiming that the Allies had fabricated the news to deceive them. A powerful secret society called Shindō Renmei ("League of the Subjects' Path" in Japanese) led such ultranationalist movements in postwar Brazil. Some members went as far as to physically attack other Japanese and Nikkeis who accepted the news of defeat, murdering sixteen people and destroying many more farms.[14] The secret societies eventually lost their momentum in the early 1950s as Nikkeis began to migrate to urban cities en masse, leaving their rural agricultural communities behind.

Japan's defeat also corroded the collective belief in return among the Japanese and Nikkeis in Brazil. Most assumed that the war destroyed their homeland permanently, or at least in a way that made their return impossible during their lifetime. Japan was indeed in bad shape, as the postwar migration of fifty thousand Japanese to Brazil—which continued until the early 1970s—can attest.[15] It is during these immediate postwar years that the turn to permanent residency became definitive. Brazil was, and had to be, their new home. Although this shift caused a great deal of anxiety among many first-generation Japanese immigrants, it was not such a shocking decision for the growing nisei and sansei Nikkeis.

The end of Shinto nationalism accelerated Nikkei conversion to Catholicism, especially among the younger generations who were ascending to urban middle class.[16] Many first-generation immigrants encouraged their offspring to pursue this option as a strategy to enhance social opportunities. In many cases, however, conversion to Catholicism did not entail a total abandonment of Japanese ritual practices. Multiple religious identities were common. It is important to keep this pattern in mind, because Nikkei communities witnessed a revival of Japanese religions—such as Buddhism and New Religions—during the postwar period.

The widespread decision for permanent residency in Brazil ignited the migration of gods and ancestors from Japan. Now that the likelihood of return was null, many migrants deemed it necessary to move the center of ancestral rites from Japan to Brazil.[17] The postwar influx of Japanese migrants—especially from Okinawa under the U.S. occupation—also fueled the revival of ancestral veneration. Many migrants, both prewar and postwar, regarded the accompaniment of their ancestors indispensable for the true completion of their immigration process. The move of ancestral spirits in turn affirmed their determination to reestablish their kinship-based ritual complex in their new homeland. Takashi Maeyama wrote in 1972, "Today those who have decided definitely to reside permanently in Brazil sometimes say, 'We are ancestors,' or 'We, the immigrants, will be the ancestors in Brazil.'"[18]

Statistical data reflect the history of migration and religion among Nikkei Brazilians that I have briefly sketched out. Among those who self-identified as Asian in the 2010 Census, the ratio of Buddhists was higher than that among the general Brazilian population (3.65 percent compared to 0.12 percent).[19] "New oriental religions," which include various Japanese New Religions that started actively proselytizing in Brazil after the war, was 1.06 percent among Asian Brazilians compared with 0.08 percent among general Brazilian citizens. Although the majority of Asian Brazilians were Catholic (59.91 percent), the number was still lower than that of the general population (64.62 percent). Pentecostal Christians constituted a minority among Asian Brazilians at 13.76 percent compared with 16.06 percent among Brazilians as a whole.[20]

Brazil and the Growth of Pentecostalism in the South

In the 1970s, just as the last wave of Japanese immigration faded out, Brazil's religious landscape was beginning to undergo a profound transformation: the rapid growth of Pentecostal and charismatic Christianity accompanied by the decline of the Roman Catholic Church. Between 1970 and 2010, the ratio of Catholics shrank drastically from roughly 92 to 65 percent of the population. During the same period, Protestantism experienced a fourfold growth from 5 to 22 percent, mainly due to the expansion of Pentecostal and charismatic groups.[21] The "explosion" of Pentecostalism surprised many observers because "Pentecostalism is the first mass religion in Latin America to definitively reject the Catholic institutional hegemony over the religious field."[22] Although its constituency today consists of people from diverse class backgrounds, Pentecostalism in Brazil—and Latin America in general—has grown the most prominently among the poor in urban peripheries.[23] It is important to note that the expansion of Pentecostalism has not been unique to Brazil or Latin America. On the contrary, it has been the fastest-growing branch of Global Christianity in the last several decades, especially in sub-Saharan Africa, Oceania, and Latin America. Today, approximately 27 percent of Christians in the world are charismatic or Pentecostal, the majority of whom reside in the Global South.[24]

Brazil, the most populous nation in Latin America, is arguably one of the epicenters of Global Pentecostalism in the Southern Hemisphere today. The exponential growth of Brazilian Pentecostalism has not been contained within its national borders.[25] Besides other Latin American countries, the networks of Brazilian denominations such as the Universal Church of the Kingdom of God ("Universal" for short below) have extended to Mozambique, Portugal, the United States, and Japan.[26] Pentecostal networks are able to address pressing local concerns while maintaining their global connectedness. For example, in the United States, where Brazilian expats often feel as if they were an "invisible minority" overshadowed by Spanish-speaking Latinos, Pentecostal churches provide a distinct space where they can be Brazilian.[27] Likewise, Pentecostal movements in Japan also respond to a set of social issues and concerns among Brazilian communities there.

Foreigners in the Ancestral Homeland: "Return" to Japan

In 1990, the Japanese government modified the Immigration Control and Refugee Recognition Act and introduced a new type of visa for "long-term residents" (*teijūsha*). Often dubbed *Nikkei-jin* (Japanese descendant) visa, it is available to foreigners of Japanese descent up to the third generation with no restrictions on their gainful activities in Japan. To many Japanese officials, the change offered a "balanced" solution to the chronic problem of manual labor shortage in the manufacturing industry of their aging country; Nikkei foreigners appeared to be a quasi-Japanese, racially correct, and thus conveniently nonthreatening labor force that could provide a flexible and low-cost manpower to the struggling industrial sectors. Given the dire state of inflation-plagued Brazilian economy at the time, many nisei and sansei Nikkeis started migrating on this visa, oftentimes with their spouses and minor children, who were permitted to accompany them. The Brazilian population in Japan peaked at roughly 317,000 in 2007—more than a twentyfold increase from 1989 that quickly pushed them up to the third-largest group of foreigners in the country.[28] They concentrate in the prefectures with developed manufacturing industries, such as Aichi, Shizuoka, Mie, and Gunma, since the majority settled where the jobs were.

Migration to Japan entailed a significant change in social context, which in turn triggered a drastic shift in migrants' ethnic self-images. In Brazil, Nikkeis enjoy a model minority status today, as many are relatively well educated and of middle-class background. In Japan, however, the overwhelming majority took up jobs in unskilled manual labor in places such as automotive assembly plants and food processing facilities. Like other foreign laborers, many work in factories that are shunned by Japanese as "3 K"—*kitsui* (strenuous), *kiken* (dangerous), and *kitanai* (dirty). Due to the considerable gap in wage standards between the two nations, Nikkeis could earn several times more as factory workers in Japan than as white-collar professionals in Brazil. It was not a shocking sight during the 1990s to spot Nikkei lawyers assembling auto parts on factory floors in cities with large Brazilian populations such as Ōizumi, Hamamatsu, and Toyota.[29] The inability to speak fluent Japanese also barred most Nikkei migrants from pursuing more desirable work options in Japan. Staffing agencies called *empreiteira* or *haken gaisha* typically work as intermediaries between migrant workers and Japanese factories, making it virtually unnecessary for Brazilians to learn Japanese. As providers of outsourced flexible labor managed by external recruitment agencies, migrant workers may work full-time at the same factory for years without full benefits or job security. Many Nikkeis consequently come to feel that the ethnic prestige they (used to) embody in Brazil disappears in the Japanese context—ironically, in the homeland of their ancestors.

On weekdays and even on some weekends, many Brazilian workers shuttle between clockwork factories and small apartments—"like mindless robots," as some told me. Rare days off—albeit unpaid, as most are wage earners—add some much-needed color to the life that many perceive as dull and monotonous. Some drive to nearby cities to visit their relatives who also migrated, rekindling and reaffirming the human bonds that the factory labor robs them of; others travel to regional cities for their shops, restaurants, and nightclubs to enjoy a taste of urban life often missing from Japan's industrial areas that are predominantly suburban and semirural; yet others spend time in Brazilian supermarkets, more leisurely than after-work visits on weekday evenings, to pick out the perfect meat for their *churrasco* barbecue parties. In summer, Brazilians become frequent visitors of the beaches, riverbanks, and lakesides known as prime locations for *churrasco*. Although the loss of model minority status that they once enjoyed in Brazil can be quite humiliating, they are resiliently building their lives in Japan, resolute not to let factory labor completely consume their identities.

Moreover, migration to Japan delivered what they could never achieve in Brazil: unequivocal Brazilian identity. As a marginalized minority among the Japanese majority, many Nikkeis feel—and are perceived as—unquestionably Brazilian for the first time in their lives.[30] Many who never danced *samba* in São Paulo start to do so once in Ōizumi; some who never cooked *feijoada*—the national dish of Brazil—in Mogi das Cruzes learn to do so in Toyohashi so that they can bring it to local Brazilian events; others who never really appreciated *Bossa Nova* in Maringá start to listen more attentively, as if to absorb a new identity, in Hamamatsu. Thus, contrary to the common scholarly designation of this migratory movement as an "ethnic return," few Nikkeis themselves actually experience their migration to Japan as a return.[31] Rather, many describe it as an unsettling encounter with racial discrimination, both subtle and blatant, based on their "un-Japanese" phenotype (for *mestiços*) and mannerism (for all Nikkeis). At the same time, this moment of rude awakening also opened up a new space for their ever-evolving identities, including the possibility of becoming simply "Brazilian" without a hyphen.

The Japanese officials did not see Nikkei Brazilians as uncontested ethnic returnees, either. Although the legal definition of Nikkei-jin certainly constructs potential migrants as partially Japanese, the recognition of relative proximity to national kinship never guaranteed complete national belonging. This is evidenced by a series of policies the Japanese government implemented in response to the 2008 global financial crisis. The sudden recession hit migrant workers with little job security the hardest. While the unemployment rate among Japanese nationals in 2009 was 5.6 percent, it rose to a staggering 40 percent among the Brazilian workers in the surveyed areas of the country.[32] Fired without notice and unable to find other employment, many had no option but to leave the country for Brazil. The exodus of Nikkeis accelerated when the Japanese government announced the implementation of the "support program to those unemployed of Japanese descent wishing to return to their home country [*nikkei-jin kikoku shien jigyō*]." From April 2009 until March 2010, unemployed Nikkeis and their dependents could receive three hundred thousand and two hundred thousand yen (roughly $3,000 and $2,000), respectively, for the cost of one-way travel to Brazil on the condition that they would not enter Japan again on the Nikkei-jin visa "for a while." By the end of 2009, roughly one-fourth of Brazilian residents in Japan had left. Many Japan-born Brazilian youth "returned" to their "home" country for the first time during this period, adding yet another layer to the complex history of Nikkei diaspora. Although Japan lifted the ban on reentry in 2013 with some restrictions, the size of the Brazilian population never recovered to the pre-2008 level.

Today, there are roughly 196,800 Brazilian nationals in Japan, forming the fifth largest group of foreign residents after the Chinese, Korean, Filipino, and Vietnamese.[33] The legal system permits each long-term resident to migrate with his or her spouse and dependents, whether they qualify as Nikkei-jin or not. This has led to the diverse ethnic and racial profile of Brazilian residents. A family of five, for instance, can have a sansei Nikkei mother (the primary visa holder), non-Nikkei father, and three mestiço children. Things become slightly more complicated for the yonsei (fourth-generation Nikkei), many of whom were born in Japan or brought to Japan as a child. They may feel quite Japanese, but in legal terms, they are foreigners who would not even qualify for the Nikkei-jin visa themselves. Although the Japanese government started accepting a small number of yonsei Nikkeis under the "special activities" (tokutei katsudō) visa in July 2018, their activities in Japan are much more restricted and monitored compared with the freedom accorded by the Nikkei-jin visa.[34]

As the growing presence of Japan-born youth shows, the life of Nikkei Brazilian migrants in Japan did not turn out to be as temporary as many had expected it to be when they first arrived. In fact, the majority holds permanent resident visas instead of long-term resident visas today. Approximately 60 percent of Brazilians in Japan are permanent residents, as opposed to roughly 30 percent who are long-term residents.[35] Clearly, their life in Japan is not as fleeting as many continue to see it to be.[36] Whether they will eventually ascend to middle and upper classes in Japanese society, as their Japanese and Nikkei ancestors did in Brazil decades earlier, is still open to debate. Unlike Japanese migrants in early twentieth-century Brazil, Brazilian migrants in twenty-first-century Japan lack solid governmental support from their home country, sufficient socioeconomic capital, and birthright citizenship. Factory work is still the dominant means of making a living. A small number of Brazilian youth, however, are starting to receive college degrees and climb up the social ladder—slowly but steadily.

Encounter with God in the Ancestral Homeland

Just as Japanese migrants brought Buddhism, Shinto, and Japanese New Religions to Brazil, Brazilian migrants carried with them a number of religious practices from Brazil to Japan.[37] Out of all such transnational religious networks extending from Brazil, Pentecostalism has likely seen the most prominent growth among the migrant communities in Japan. In 2008, sociologist Rafael Shoji identified 147 Brazilian Pentecostal churches in Japan, which made up 47 percent—almost half—of all the sites of worship offering Portuguese services in the country. In comparison, roughly 26 percent of such places belonged to Japanese New Religions and 20 percent were Catholic churches; only 4 percent were traditional Buddhist temples.[38] Although the number of churches does not directly reflect the number of followers, my ethnographic findings confirm the significance of his study. In Toyota City, for example, there was one Catholic church at the time of my fieldwork. Since the church's father was Korean, it held biweekly mass for Brazilian parishioners by inviting a priest who could speak Portuguese (a professor of religious studies from Portugal at a nearby university who was also a certified Catholic priest). From what I could see, roughly two hundred people would regularly attend Portuguese mass. The two Pentecostal churches that I knew of in Toyota had roughly four hundred fifty and two hundred Brazilian members, respectively. Almost all of the members attended the weekly Sunday service led by Brazilian pastors.[39] These sociological and ethnographic findings indicate that Pentecostalism has likely grown significantly in the context of Japan—especially in light of Brazil's census data from 2010, in which roughly 14 percent of Asian Brazilians were Pentecostal, while 60 percent were Catholic.[40]

The case of Missão Apoio, the second-largest Brazil-derived Protestant denomination in Japan, can illuminate how this Pentecostal expansion took place.[41] Its non-Nikkei Brazilian cofounders arrived in Japan in 1991 on the Nikkei-jin visas granted to their Nikkei wives. Although they initially arrived as labor migrants without the intention of proselytization, they soon realized that there was a severe lack of communal support for the Nikkei migrants and their families, who often felt isolated, marginalized, and discriminated in Japan. Putting their prior pastoral experience from Brazil into use, they founded a new Pentecostal denomination in 1993 with the help of their equally devout Christian spouses and named it "Support Mission" in Portuguese—Missão Apoio. This brief overview shows that the key actors in the development of

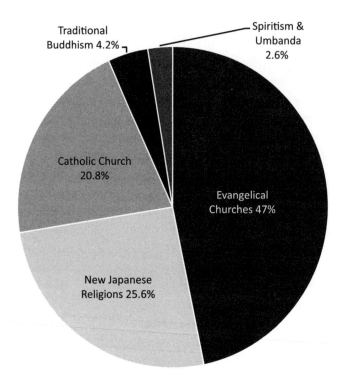

FIGURE 2. Sites of worship offering Portuguese service in Japan. Source: Shoji 2014, p. 37. Reprinted with permission. Note: In the original pie chart, the total percentage adds up to 100.2%.

Pentecostal networks in Japan were the minority of Nikkeis who were already converts prior to their "return." Through kinship, their Nikkei status could often enable the migration of non-Nikkei Pentecostal leaders from Brazil. That being said, the majority of congregants today report to have converted to Pentecostalism after their arrival in Japan—roughly 70 percent of the surveyed members at Missão Apoio Toyota, for instance. As the founders themselves acknowledge in their narrative, the sociopolitical context teeming with racial discrimination and labor exploitation likely has a lot to do with the phenomenon of postmigration mass conversion. In many cases, the Pentecostal church continues to be the only place where Brazilian migrants can congregate with others like themselves without the gaze of the Japanese majority.

The mass exodus of Brazilian migrants during the 2008 financial crisis, however, changed these dynamics for good. Having realized that they cannot expect to grow indefinitely only within the bounds of Brazilian communities, today Pentecostal churches are adopting an increasingly transethnic rhetoric to attract more members from the Japanese majority. The emerging effort for active proselytization in Japan seems to boost a sense of moral superiority among many migrant converts.[42] Although they may be stereotyped as a "backward" Brazilian minority in economic and class-based terms, they can reenvision themselves as a "forward" Christian minority in spiritual terms. Moreover, the cultivation of a new religious identity enables them to claim Japan as a place to be, not on the basis of Japanese ancestry but as conveyors of morality and godliness in a non-Christian "pagan" land.

Evangelization of the Japanese majority, however, has turned out to be challenging to say the least. Not only is Japanese mainstream society overwhelmingly Buddhist and Shintoist, it historically banned Christianity from 1614 until 1873 and continued to suppress the Christian minority into the early twentieth century.[43] There is little explicit antipathy toward Christianity in today's Japan, but its continued association with foreignness and Otherness persists. Christians—Catholics and Protestants combined—currently make up only 1 percent of the Japanese population.[44] But the outlook on evangelization among many Brazilian migrant converts remains youthful and optimistic.

Fieldwork

Aichi is the fourth most populous prefecture located in central Japan, known for its manufacturing sector and the capital of car industry in Japan: Toyota City, my main research site. The first social domain of my fieldwork was therefore the city's factories. As Toyota is home to the headquarters of Toyota Motor Corporation, there are hundreds of automotive plants there, the majority of which being the subsidiaries of Toyota. The auto industry gives rise to a significant demand for a flexible labor force in and around the city. It is not a coincidence, then, that Aichi Prefecture holds the largest Brazilian population in Japan at roughly 51,200.[45] I worked at two different factories in Toyota for five months in total between 2013 and 2014. As there already exist detailed ethnographic works on the labor conditions among Nikkei Brazilians in Japan, this book does not primarily focus on the topic of factory work.[46] My firsthand labor experience, however, helped me understand the power dynamics that saturated the workplace of my informants and enabled me to ask informed questions during interviews.

The second main site of fieldwork was a residential neighborhood with a large concentration of migrants. One of the largest Brazilian enclaves in Japan, a partially subsidized housing project called Homi Danchi, is located in Toyota.[47] In 2014, more than half of the city's 5,120 Brazilians—2,746 of them—lived in the Homi District with 3,717 Japanese neighbors.[48] By living in Homi Danchi, I could insert myself into the reciprocal web of home visits among its Brazilian residents. Since most congregants at Missão Apoio Toyota lived in Homi Danchi, home visits provided me with another occasion to interact with the same people in a different, more private, context. Over the course of fieldwork, they invited me to numerous activities including coffees, dinners, baby showers, birthday parties, soccer viewing gatherings, and funerals, all of which took place in my informants' homes or at the Homi communal center.

The third—and primary—social field comprised local Pentecostal churches that belong to a denomination called Missão Apoio. Although I regularly drove to other Missão Apoio churches in the region, I focused most of my fieldwork effort on the congregation in Toyota. With roughly five hundred members, Missão Apoio Toyota was one of the largest Pentecostal churches in the region, located fifteen minutes away from Homi Danchi by car. The physical structure of the church was the shape of a rectangular box, with just one story and a flat reddish brown roof, resembling the archetypical form of convenience stores ubiquitous in Japan. Congregants would park their cars on the adjacent dirt lot and walk around to the front entrance with sliding glass doors on the wider side of the building that faced the road. Structurally, there were few marks from the outside that signaled that this beige building was a church, save one simple cross attached to the roof and "Igreja Evangélica" written in red paint on one side.

I visited Missão Apoio Toyota for the first time during the summer of 2012. Pastor Cid Carneiro, with whom I had previously spoken on the phone, came to Toyota Station to pick me up. One of his first questions was whether I was Nikkei Brazilian myself, to which I gave a firm no. "Interesting," he said as he drove. "There are many youngsters at my church who speak Portuguese with an accent like yours." Since some Japan-raised Brazilian youth speak Japanese as their first language today, it is not surprising that their Portuguese would also be affected by Japanese phonetics. His next guess was that I was Japanese American—probably because I told him that I was a doctoral student at an American university. I again said no, and explained that I was a Japanese living in the United States.

"Então você é japonesa japonesa mesmo?" (So you are really Japanese Japanese?)

"Uh, sure," I answered after a second of hesitation as I had never heard the phrase *japonesa japonesa* before. As it turned out, I ended up clarifying my new identity—*japonesa japonesa*—a dozen more times that day as I interacted with Nikkei Brazilians for the first time in my life. With Pastor Cid's permission, I returned again in August 2013 for a yearlong fieldwork.

According to the results of the survey I administered at the church, roughly 80 percent of the Brazilian members at Missão Apoio Toyota self-identified as Nikkei and 20 percent did not.[49] Almost all of the non-Nikkei Brazilians were spouses or ex-spouses of Nikkeis, who first entered Japan on their partners' long-term resident visas. Among the Nikkei congregants, roughly 20 percent self-identified as nisei (second generation), 65 percent as sansei (third generation), and 10 percent as yonsei (fourth generation). The gender distribution was equal, with the number of women only slightly larger than that of men. The congregation was overall young, with roughly 90 percent of members in their forties or younger. The overwhelming majority worked in factories and belonged to the contingent labor force with little job security.

I participated in everything I was allowed to attend as a nonconvert outsider, which included Bible study group, Sunday worship, home group gathering, night prayer session, street evangelization, fundraising party at church, and so on. In addition to numerous lengthy conversations that took place organically during participant observation, I also conducted sixty-three interviews in total. I initially attempted to conduct semistructured interviews by preparing a set of questions, but my informants' eagerness to inquire my identity often changed the format into a more open one. Most Pentecostal subjects started by interviewing me about my ethno-national identity and religious affiliation. Those who already knew that I was from a Buddhist family would instead start by checking on my spiritual progress: "So, have you had any experiences with God yet?" The Japanese neighbors, coworkers, and teachers whom I interviewed were equally curious. I often had to clarify why I could speak Portuguese and appeared somewhat Americanized when I was—borrowing one informant's words—"really, actually, 100 percent Japanese with no foreigners in the family lineage."

Just like the interview structure, the categories that I had initially imposed on my subjects also became more fluid over time. In the beginning, I had planned to recruit an equal number of participants from each racial and generational group—five interviews with "second-generation non-*mestiço* Nikkeis*," for instance. A shortcoming of such a rigid approach quickly became clear upon interviewing a woman whom I call Mimi. When I asked her if she identified as a Nikkei, she responded yes and clarified that she was a sansei. "But I don't look very Japanese, right?" she said as she laughed. "Only my father is Japanese, that's why. Some descendants look like you, Suma, but there are many who don't look very Japanese because of *mestiçagem*. You know Cibeli? She doesn't look Japanese but she is actually Nikkei!"

It took me a few seconds to respond. I had actually interviewed Cibeli the previous week, and she was adamant that she was *not* a Nikkei: "I'm just Brazilian—I mean, European ancestors. My husband is the one who got us the visa."

When I asked Mimi if Cibeli had told her that she was Nikkei, she answered no and added, "But her friends told me. People know these things, you see." Such exchanges quickly taught me that people—especially those in my ethnographic settings—cannot always be what they claim to be themselves. Identity walks a fine line between volition and perception, which is constantly shifting. I became particularly careful with preexisting categories after this revelation and learned to take them with a grain of salt. In theory, it was possible for "non-Nikkei" Cibeli to have "Nikkei" experiences since many assumed her to be one.

The opposite is equally true, as Sergio's story at the beginning of this chapter shows. Although the legal system categorized him as a sansei Nikkei, he denied having Japanese identity on the basis that no one saw him as such, even in Brazil. In fact, he joked that he actually felt like a yonsei, who would not qualify for the Nikkei-jin visa. With his next joke about being of an "I-don't-know generation (*sou não sei*)," Sergio further defied, playfully but poignantly, the reified generational categories the migration policy imprinted on him. The pun sheds light on the ideological work that goes into the conceptual foundation of migrant "generation."[50] The myth of Japanese blood legally obliges Nikkeis to identify their emigrant ancestors as the original kin and count each descendent cohort thereafter as the second and third reproduction. It presents generation as a hereditary and natural fact. But if Sergio's subtly rebellious joke makes anything clear, it is the reality that generation is a social and political construct. Just like race, ethnicity, and nationhood, generation can also be imagined.[51] I therefore understand generation to be a "historically grounded conception" shaped by the predominant social, legal, and political patterns that surround transnational migrants.[52]

Juxtaposing Sergio with Bruno from Chapter 1, who spoke about being called a *japa* in Brazil, illuminates the incredible breadth of subjectivities that the term Nikkei encompasses. In a sense, this identifying label conceals as much as it reveals. Perhaps it is the case that "the very term 'Japanese Brazilians' conjures up a group that does not necessarily, in any existentially or analytically significant form, exist."[53] Although I will use such categories as "Japanese," "Brazilian," and "Pentecostal" throughout this book, I do so gingerly with an awareness that they do not refer to any preexisting essences but instead actively constitute such qualities in relation to one another.

Susan Harding once wrote that a non-Christian fieldworker among born-again Christians often works at the "psychic intersection between born-again and un-born-again languages and worlds."[54] In my case, I had not just one but two of such crossroads: between born-again and un-born-again, on the one hand, and between Brazilian and Japanese, on the other. In hindsight, it was these multiple borderlands that defined the tenor of my fieldwork. Rather than a so-called native anthropologist, I was an ethnographer on the edge—of nativeness, of foreignness, and of belonging. In spirit, then, this book is about boundaries and crossroads, and not about one society, one people, or one culture, as there was no "one single" anything about the people I spent a year with.

Part Two

SUSPENDED

3

PUTTING ASIDE LIVING

"We Are in Japan but We Don't Live Here"

"Before we finish the service, today I have a special favor to ask you," Pastor Cid said to the congregation as the instrumental music by the church band faded out and the collective prayer session came to a close. He beckoned me toward the pulpit. I stood up from my chair in one of the back rows and walked up to the front of the room. "This is Suma, an anthropologist—right, Suma, *antropóloga*?—from the United States who is studying the Pentecostal churches among dekasseguis in Japan." I smiled, feeling quite awkward. Somehow the church space felt a little larger with rows of congregants curiously gazing at me. Pastor Cid continued, "She has a survey she wants you to fill out. So if you have some time, please stay here and fill it out to help her." I made a slight bow to his direction to thank him. He was one of the extremely few Brazilians whom I met who did not migrate on the Nikkei-jin visa. Neither he nor his spouse was Nikkei. They came to Japan on the "religious activities" visa, which imposes more restrictions on the recipients' gainful activities. Despite the resultant financial difficulties, Pastor Cid founded and had been leading Missão Apoio Toyota for close to two decades.

Some stood up and left, but most remained in their seats and graciously accepted a pen and a two-page questionnaire. Conversations filled the room as people spoke to one another to confirm the answers. "Hey, honey, when did we come to Japan? 1995?"

"Ah . . . Wasn't it 1994?"

One woman beckoned me and asked if I wanted her to fill one out when her husband was already doing so.

"Yes, but only if you want to."

She looked down on her baby, peacefully sleeping in her arms, and responded, "I don't think I can write now, but my answers are pretty much the same as his, ok?" I nodded. I should take these results with a grain of salt, I told myself as I walked away from her. Various factors, such as whether one happens to be holding an infant, can determine the likelihood of response. It was clear that survey findings in themselves could not present a complete picture. I had to contextualize them with the help of ethnography.

I went through the responses the following week. Most results, such as the roughly equal ratio of men and women in the makeup of membership, confirmed my prior observations. But the most illuminating discovery came from the scribbles in the margins—something that none of the printed questions explicitly asked. Among some thirty-five items on the survey I created, there was the following question: "When did you first come to Japan in order to work and/or to live here? [___ years ago, or in the year ___]." It asked when the respondent came to Japan, excluding brief trips and visits. As I compiled the answers, however, I realized that many people crossed out "live" and circled "work" instead of or in addition to answering the year of their arrival. Some even scribbled next to the question: "I don't live here. I came here to work" (Não estou aqui para morar, vim para trabalhar só). I had included the phrase "and/or to live here" with younger Brazilians in mind, who were too little to work when they were first brought to Japan. But the juxtaposition of "work" and "live" invited an unexpected input from older migrants. The majority of the people who circled "work"—roughly 11 percent of all respondents—were men who arrived in Japan in their early adulthood.[1]

But why does life stop in Japan? Or, to put it more specifically, how does the line between life and work become so divisive that some migrants felt compelled to cross out "to live" on the survey? To answer these questions, I am going to elucidate the evolving relationship between mobility and temporality among Nikkei Brazilians.

Twice a Minority

Takeshi, a thirty-six-year-old sansei migrant from Pará, first came to Japan in 1992 at the age of fourteen with his Nikkei father and Afro-Brazilian mother. He was a friendly and intelligent man who enjoyed reading books. Perhaps not surprisingly, he felt frustrated that manual factory labor was not fulfilling his intellectual potential. In fact, he deeply regretted not having tried harder to finish his education. His parents, who believed their stay in Japan would be just for a year or two, did not strongly insist on his going to Japanese school. Since he found the Japanese language daunting, his attendance soon became intermittent. Takeshi had no solid schooling beyond the eighth grade. His parents never returned to Brazil and his widowed mother still lived in Japan at the time of my fieldwork.

When I asked for an interview, Takeshi suggested that we meet at a coffee shop near the church. His home was too cluttered at the time, he explained, because his wife had just given birth to their second son. Consequently, one of the first icebreaker questions I asked when we sat down at the coffee shop was about the name of his newborn. "His name is Davi Hikaru," Takeshi beamed. "Davi is a king in the Bible, and it's also a common Brazilian name. Hikaru is his Japanese name, and it means light." Curious, I asked if he had two names as well.

"Yes, my Brazilian name is João."

"So why do you go by Takeshi rather than João?" I asked.

"Well, I'm just more used to Takeshi. Growing up in Pará, all of my friends called me Takeshi. I was one of the few Japanese friends they had." He shrugged and added, "I was Japanese in Brazil, you see. And it's a Japanese name."

Judging that this was probably a good segue, I asked him to tell me about his family in Brazil. "Let's see . . . It's my grandparents on my father's side that came to Brazil. My Japanese grandfather, he was a soldier."

"Soldier? Of what kind?"

"I'm not sure; I actually don't know him well because he was already dead when I was born. But there was a photo of him up on the wall in the living room. In black and white, really old photo. He is in a Japanese soldier's uniform, really upright, serious. My father told me that he was from Fukushima and was a soldier before coming to Brazil."

"Oh, Fukushima, that's up in the north, really cold," I responded.

"I have no idea," Takeshi said, and he laughed, scratching his head. "I've never been to Fukushima. But yeah, my grandfather is from there, I heard."

Soon enough, the interview moved on to the topic of his own migration. When I asked if Japan was different from Brazil, he nodded deeply and started describing "the principal difference" between the two nations:

> In Brazil, Japanese Brazilians are treated mostly in relation to the Japanese nation—because we look alike, you know. It's a great pride of the Japanese race. . . . Not all are successful, but the majority of descendants there are very educated and hardworking. So they ended up creating a culture and an aura around descendants. . . .
>
> This is not the case here in Japan. Those people who were none of these things all came here! [Bursts out laughing.] Here it is the opposite. Who is polite, educated, civilized and industrious here? It's the opposite! We commit petty crimes, get into fights all the time, and are lazy. People who are violent, and steal. This is the principal difference that I see. . . . Here, suddenly your culture is lower. The ideals, society, life, and future that shaped you and trained you, they all fail.

Takeshi's words echo a predominant sense of class downgrade that permeates the migrant communities—the disappearance of "great pride of the Japanese race" and the loss of ethnic "aura," as Takeshi put it. Some Nikkei migrants talk about it bitterly with a frown, others calmly with a shrug, and those like Takeshi with a resilient laughter. He is in no way the only one who sees their social status in Japan as suffering and humiliating, compared with the positive qualities they (used to) embody in Brazil. Luana, a forty-nine-year-old Nikkei who had been living in Japan for twenty-three years, similarly observed, "In Brazil, we are such positive people—intelligent, polite, diligent. They joke, 'Want to get into USP (University of São Paulo)? Kill a Japanese and you have a spot!' [Laughs.] Here, it's nothing like that at all." Such remarks suggest that although Nikkeis have been a minority in both Brazil and Japan, how they have been so differs dramatically between the two countries.

The "Modern" Minority in Brazil

In the discussion of Nikkei identities in Brazil, of paramount importance are the popular images of the Japanese nation in the country. Japan, a rare non-Western economic power since the late nineteenth century, often impressed Brazilian elites who were striving to modernize their nation but had yet to succeed. Social discourses in Brazil such as advertisements have often emphasized Japan's positive attributes—high technology, modernity, and First World status. Within this real and imagined geography of progress, the Japanese diaspora within Brazil's own territory—specifically Nikkeis in São Paulo—took on a powerful symbolic meaning. They were "Brazilians of future."[2] Nikkeis had thus become a "modern" minority, a symbol of the country's promised progress. Their actual upward mobility and economic success fueled this kind of public imagination. At the same time, Nikkeis in Brazil were also a marginalized minority because of their stereotyped irrationality, hypertraditional character, and presumed inability to assimilate.[3] On either side of this good Japanese/bad Japanese dichotomy, the Brazilian majority presupposed a primordial bond between Nikkeis and Japan.

It is clear that presumed blood ties alone did not make the Japanese nation home for the Japanese diasporic population in Brazil. Rather, Japan had to be the home for Nikkeis because they did not belong to the present in Brazil. They instead represented both the future (i.e., hypermodernity) and the past (i.e., hypertradition) of Brazil, and Japan was their home away—both spatially and temporally. As Takeshi put it, Japan was "a great pride of the Japanese race" and those with Japanese ancestral ties were reputed to embody great "culture" and ethnic "aura." When Nikkei migrants like Takeshi relate that they *were* Japanese in Brazil, they often do so with a pang of nostalgia because being *japonês* carried a plethora of positive modern meanings.

However, the level of formal education among migrant converts at Missão Apoio Toyota was actually not as high as the stereotypical image of professional cosmopolitan Nikkeis in Brazil. My survey data show that roughly 90 percent of respondents had the equivalent of a high school diploma or less. Approximately 10 percent reported to have progressed to college or beyond (including those who did not complete the degree), which is not higher than the ratio of college graduates in the general Brazilian population.[4] The number is definitely lower than the ratio of college degree holders among Nikkei Brazilians in urban São Paulo (the place with a strong discursive tie to the image of Nikkeis as a modern minority), which was 56 percent in 2008.[5] Thus, my informants in Toyota did not themselves embody all the positive stereotypical traits of Nikkeis, but most of them still felt that migration had spoiled the protective "aura" of ethnic prestige. Takeshi's own limited formal education did not stop him from depicting Nikkeis in general as well educated and well respected. This pattern attests to the emotional sway that the ideal ethnic self-image exerts upon migrants, especially when they perceive their good social standing to be lost.

The discursive formation of Nikkei identities in Brazil, especially the image of Japan as a hypermodern nation that imprints similarly modern qualities on Japanese descendants abroad, prepared a stage for the profound shock of "homecoming" in the 1990s and 2000s. Nikkeis who migrated to Japan were surprised to find out that they did not arrive at the futuristic nation to which they believed they would belong. Marcelo, another Nikkei migrant in his forties, related the following story when I asked him what his experience was like when he first arrived in Japan:

So I came in 1990 by myself and arrived in Narita. This guy from my staffing agency was waiting for me at the airport, and he put me in a van and started driving to the company's dorm.[6] I was looking out from the windows, and said, "What is this?" He was like, "What do you mean?"

I said, "Where are all the modern buildings with bright colorful neon signs? Where are all the cars and people in good clothes?" [Laughs.] Because, you see, all I saw from the van was just vegetable fields and rice paddies, and worse yet, I smelt an odor of . . . some kind of livestock. I was like, "What's going on? Japan is supposed to be a country of the First World [país do Primeiro Mundo]." Big cities, high technology . . . You know. Then the guy laughed and said I had to go to Tokyo to see those things. It was a huge shock. In Brazil, we believe that the whole Japan is like that, like Tokyo.

Speaking about his arrival in Japan, Marcelo reveals the images of Japan widespread in Brazil: metropolitan, advanced, forward, modern, and First World. His "huge shock" is more temporal than cultural, for it was not his customs that were challenged but the sense of time he had long projected onto Japan. In a sense, he had a "time shock." As the migrants' image of Japan thus began to shift, their own ethnic self-image also started to transform in the new context.

The "Backward" Minority in Japan

Upon migration, the majority of Nikkeis took up jobs in Japan's industrial areas such as Gunma, Shizuoka, Mie, and Aichi. As Nikkei Brazilians were now perceived as unskilled migrant laborers, which in many cases they actually were, their social status suffered great humiliation—ironically, in the land of their ancestors where their "Japanese ethnic aura" is supposed to originate. In this new social context, Nikkei subjectivity experienced a dramatic shift from

"Japanese" educated professionals to "Brazilian" unskilled laborers. And with this new identity emerged a host of new stereotypes that began to haunt them—negative images ranging from low-class crudeness to criminal delinquency. As Takeshi put it, "We commit petty crimes, get into fights all the time, and are lazy. People who are violent, and steal."

It is crucial to acknowledge the significant influence of the neoliberal labor system on such images. For instance, Brazilian workers routinely lament "working so much" at the same time as characterizing themselves as "lazy people." This may seem contradictory, but actually makes sense in the context of their wage labor. Many do work long hours because they have to (due to their weak position at the workplace) or want to (because it is the only way to enhance income in the time-based wage system). Either way, long working hours are the result of their marginalized position in the labor market. This awareness fuels a sense of resentment among many migrant workers, which in turn leads to low morale: "I don't want to work. I feel so lazy." The same labor system also incentivizes temporary workers to constantly look for other jobs that pay better per hour, even just by one yen. As a result, many end up hopping from one factory to another, generating a reputation that Brazilians are opportunistic, reluctant to commit, and too idle to persist at one place for the greater good. From another viewpoint, of course, it is the factories dependent on dispensable contingent employees that are reluctant to commit to hardworking foreign workers. Nonetheless, some Nikkei laborers resort to such ethnic stereotypes to explain their own actions. For example, Keita—an eighteen-year-old Nikkei youngster—told me that he was "Brazilian after all" when he quit his job for the third time in a year. "I can't work like an ant day after day at one place. Maybe I lack perseverance because of my Latin nature" (Ore ikkasho de kotsukotsu toka muri dayo. Raten kishitsu de konjō nai no kana). In my observation, the phenomenon of job fluidity (and, of course, insecurity) among Nikkeis has more to do with the broader labor structure than their ethnic nature. But many Japanese—and some Brazilians themselves—conflate these economically driven processes with supposedly preexisting racial characteristics.

Like Keita, many migrant youth born and raised in Japan made similar comments about Brazilianness, despite the fact that they had never lived in Brazil. One day, I was walking back to my apartment building with a group of Brazilian adolescents who lived in Homi Danchi after teaching a Japanese class at a local nongovernmental organization. At one point, I noticed that Fernando and

Yoshiki—two fifteen-year-old boys—were talking about Brazil. "It's a country of thieves and drug dealers," Fernando said.

Yoshiki, nodding with juvenile giggles, responded, "That's right man, that's true."

I asked how they knew these things and offered a modest counterperspective: "You know Brazil is going to host the World Cup this year. It can be a really cool place."

They looked at me and laughed in unison. "Ah *sensei* [teacher], but that's what they say! Brazil is a country of hooligans and burglars."

"Who are 'they'?"

"The people [*as pessoas*]. People around me. Haven't you watched the TV, *sensei*? Gangs with guns shooting at the police, guys with covered faces destroying shops on the street? That's my country!" As they kept on laughing, I thought to myself that they had most likely seen the media images from the military police's "pacification" of *favelas* and a fragment of participants in the 2013 mass public demonstrations that resorted to violent vandalism. Since I did not ask what kind of television programs their families watched at home, it is unclear whether they received these images from Japanese media, Brazilian networks available in Japan such as Globo, or both. Either way, such negative representations affect how Japan-born Brazilian youth come to envision the "homeland" they have never seen with their own eyes.

Thus, negative media images of Brazil exacerbate the sense of ethnic downgrade from a modern Asian minority to a backward Latino minority. As Takeshi put it, their "culture" suddenly becomes "lower" in Japan. This perceived demotion of their culture in turn affects their ethnic and racial self-images in negative ways. Many simply lament or shrug off this demeaning transition, but some Brazilian migrants make conscious effort to rebuild their social reputation in Japan. Fumio Shimamura is one of such people, who appeared on the December 2013 issue of *Alternativa*, a free magazine in Portuguese read widely among Brazilians in Japan. In an article titled "I Want to Help Brazilians Have a Decent Life," Shimamura expressed his sense of duty as the only Brazilian public accountant certified to practice in Japan: "I hope that one day the reputation of Nikkei Brazilians will be equal to that which the Japanese had in Brazil."[7] Ironically, Shimamura's aspiration still hinges upon the tacit consensus that the social status of Nikkei Brazilians in Japan is in no way comparable to that of Nikkeis in Brazil.

In sum, Nikkei migrants slowly realize that, as dispensable foreign laborers stereotyped for laziness, delinquency, and criminality, they do not quite

belong in Japan's future. This recognition in turn intensifies their desire for
return to Brazil.

Return as a Place of Hope: Future in Brazil

In Brazil, the migration of Nikkei Brazilians to Japan is often called *movimento
dekassegui* (movement of temporary workers). True to the term, many migrants
arrived in Japan with the intention of returning to Brazil in a few years after
saving as much money as possible. They were usually prepared to sacrifice com-
fort for the sake of procuring a better middle-class future for their return to
Brazil. What they initially tolerated as temporary discomfort, however, quickly
turned into a perpetual state as "several years" became five, ten, and even
twenty. Some migrants have returned to Brazil to achieve the goals they set out
for, never returning to Japan again. But those who continue to live in Japan
are oftentimes still under the spell of perpetual temporariness. Some migrants who became critical of this psychological tendency call it an "illusion
of return" (*ilusão de voltar*). André, who successfully landed a job as an interpreter with his hard-learned Japanese, told me about his fellow migrants: "They'd
better stop it. It's an illusion. They say they will return next year, but they
never do. Some have lived here for ten years and don't know a single word of
Japanese."

The illusion of return is an ingenious way to characterize how migrants deal
with the perpetual temporariness of life. It captures the power the idea of return exerts in their minds not as a realistic and concrete action to be carried
out but as a fantastic and faraway plan to be fantasized about. Artur, for example, talked about return in the following way:

> I am from Rio, you know Rio? Lots of beaches, beautiful. See that? [He turns
> on his iPhone to show photos of beautiful turquoise-blue ocean.] My house is
> just a few kilometers away from this place. [His thirteen-year-old son peeks in,
> smiles, and says he wants to live there.] I know, son. [I ask if his son has lived
> in Rio.] What? No, he was born and raised here in Toyota. I will return, you
> know, it's just that it's a beautiful place with no jobs. So I will save money and
> return.

For many migrants, return becomes not an act they actually plan for but a place
in mind where they can safely store future desires. In a similar vein, Caroline
Brettel observed the ideological importance of "emigrar para voltar" (emigrate to return) in the history of Portuguese migration. Even when physical

return does not materialize, this mind-set proved psychologically protective since "this maintenance of an intention to return alongside the postponement of actual return is a way of dealing with the insecure environment abroad, where the position of the migrant is very much at the mercy of fluctuations in the international economic system."[8]

As it turns out, return has captured the hopes and desires of many migrants throughout the history of transatlantic migration. Marcelo Borges discussed the importance of social images attached to return migrants in Portugal in the late nineteenth and early twentieth centuries. Since Brazil was the most popular destination until the mid-twentieth century, *brasileiro* (a Brazilian) became a discursive archetype of a native-born Portuguese who emigrated to Brazil, made it rich, and then returned to Portugal to display his wealth. Even those from the southern region of Portugal who tended to migrate to Argentina often spoke about the *brasileiro* because it "became synonymous with return migrants regardless of their destination."[9] Many Portuguese dreamt about becoming a *brasileiro* even at the same time that they mocked his supposed greed through caricatures. Relatedly, Arnd Schneider wrote about the Italian-Argentinians' yearning for return within the historical context that he characterized as "inversion of roles."[10] When Italians migrated to Buenos Aires before the 1950s, Italy meant poverty and backwardness, whereas America represented progress, wealth, and cosmopolitan status. Yet, over time, Argentina failed to deliver the glory of modern progress to such migrants and their descendants, while Italy successfully industrialized and climbed up to its current First World status. Italian-Argentinians' desire for their ancestral homeland, then, is a bitter craving for the promised future realized elsewhere—ironically, in the land their ancestors left behind.

As these stories of migration show, return often provides a place of hope. In the case of many Brazilian migrants in Japan, the future to return to now lies in Brazil.

Transpacific Gypsies

Even after a decade, two decades, and in many cases acquiring permanent resident visas in Japan, many Brazilian migrants still spoke about returning to Brazil "soon." They would then admit that they had been living in Japan for over a decade or that this was their third time to be working in Japan, usually smiling with a hint of embarrassment. In fact, according to a survey conducted in 2004, almost half of male Brazilian migrants and 40 percent of female Brazilian migrants had previously lived in Japan.[11] For roughly 10 percent of all the respondents, it was their fourth, fifth, or sixth time in the country. Many migrants were critical of circular migration that has become rather common among Brazilians in Japan. For instance, Hélio—a twenty-three-year-old Nikkei Brazilian—once asked me, "So, have you found anything interesting about us yet?" It was after a Sunday evening mass in Portuguese at a Catholic church in a neighboring city of Toyota, and he knew that I was a researcher.

"Well, let me think . . ."

I started to think but Hélio quickly interrupted me by offering his own observation: "Have you noticed that too many of us go back and forth between Brazil and Japan, never becoming firm in our decision to stay in either country? It is a problem." He shook his head. "This is not good." At that moment, the father arrived and he excused himself to go into the confessional.

Researchers of transnationalism have long theorized the ways in which the lives of migrants and those who are related to them are not contained within the borders of nation-states. Steven Vertovec, for instance, used the term *bifocality* to capture the state of transnational life that is simultaneously "here" and "there."[12] Although the bifocal mode of being can be celebrated as something liberating, most Brazilians in Japan view their state in a more critical light. Repeated migration is commonplace yet often frowned upon because it signifies the inability to establish a stable middle-class life in either country. In other words, the number of crossings between the two nations equals the number of failures to arrive at a better future, which was the purpose of migration in the first place. One elderly Nikkei Brazilian man in his fifties summed up this frustration succinctly in the following way: "Nikkeis, it looks like they have a country but they virtually don't. When in Brazil, they are Japanese. When in Japan, they are Brazilian. So we do but it's like we don't have any country. We move around too much, too, never settling down, never knowing how to establish ourselves. We are like gypsies [*ciganos*]."

Most migrants experience the circular movement between Japan and Brazil not as liberating but as crippling, partially because they feel at the mercy of fluctuating global economic forces and shifting national migration policies. Sometimes, they can even perceive mobility as something forced upon them structurally, against their own desire to grow roots.

Living with a Japanese Mask

One phenomenon that attests to the irony of migrants' insistence on the temporariness of their life in Japan is the prevalence of permanent resident visas. In fact, the majority of Brazilian nationals who reside in Japan today hold permanent resident visas instead of long-term resident visas. The trend toward permanent residency, however, cannot be taken at its face value to signify that migrants are settling down in Japan. Granted, a small minority of Brazilians express a strong desire to stay and demonstrate such an intention by sending their children to Japanese schools, saving for children's higher education in Japan, and—for the lucky few—buying houses on mortgage. For the majority of Brazilians in Homi Danchi, however, the permanent resident visa was not a token of permanent life in Japan but another option to enhance their transnational mobility. In fact, migrants can leave Japan more easily with the visa since the required renewal is not as frequent for permanent residents. I have met a handful of Brazilians who explained their decision (or plan) to come back to Japan in relation to the maintenance of their permanent resident visa. Hiroshi, who left Toyota to return to Brazil during my fieldwork, told me, "I'll definitely come back to visit in five years to maintain my permanent resident visa; I don't want to lose it." For many, the visa was not symbolic but rather instrumental, and acquiring one did not discourage them from desiring the return to Brazil.

If not the permanent resident visa, however, there was one procedure that many migrants still resisted as symbolically troubling instead of pursuing it as a pragmatic social strategy: naturalization. The August 2014 issue of *Vitrine*—a popular Portuguese-language free magazine among Brazilian migrants in Japan—featured a special article on this topic, titled "All You Need to Know About Naturalization." It read, "The possibility of becoming a native citizen of the country where one lives, with the same obligations and rights as anyone else, is worth the effort, it's a conquest of freedom from the condition of eternal foreigner."[13] Although the article depicted the procedure as a "conquest of freedom," or something necessary to achieve an equal status to the Japanese majority in Japan, the issue's cover image captured precisely why many migrants still found it troubling. It showed an image of a man—presumably a Nikkei Brazilian—putting on a mask of a Japanese face. His original face is covered and hidden by the clean and yet impassive "Japanese" mask, thus invoking a sense of inauthentic identity. An alternative interpretation is also possible: The man may be about to take off a layer of his face. He is about to reveal the "true Japanese self" that lies beneath, the identity that naturalization brings to its fruition. In Brazil, Japanese ethnicity is often stereotyped as rigid and even robotic, which constitutes the negative flip side of more positive images such as diligence and discipline. Although Nikkeis are similarly perceived to be more serious than non-Asian Brazilians, the common understanding today is that they have successfully combined Japanese and Brazilian qualities, thus becoming at once "industrious" and "creative." This latter reading of the cover image, then, can be more unsettling to Nikkeis, since it visually suggests that the underlying robotic "Japanese" core has always been underneath the "Nikkei/Brazilian" face. Regardless of the variety of possible interpretations, the image is a visual display of common views among Brazilian migrants on what "becoming Japanese" entails: assimilation into the "cold," "robotic," and "mechanical" Japanese society, which may well require acting phony (*falso*)—a quality many Brazilians openly dislike about the Japanese in Japan.

The irony is that non-*mestiço*, or so-called *puro* (pure-blooded), Nikkeis phenotypically resemble the face on the Japanese mask. My informants knew, however, that looking Japanese oftentimes had little to do with being Japanese. Historically, Japan has long defined national identity strictly within the narrow convergence of Japanese blood, language, and culture.[14] Its nationality law is based on jus sanguinis, or the principle of blood, which means immigration does not provide a straightforward path to national belonging. Even after a stream of criticism against the nation's ideology of ethnic homogeneity, it is still virtually impossible to effectively evoke the "unity through diversity" rhetoric in Japanese mainstream discourses.[15] This is in stark contrast to Brazil, where the history of immigration and story of racial mixture possess even a mythic value in the construction of national identity.[16]

To this day, migrant—or *imin*—continues to be a sort of "M-word" in the social context of Japan. Politicians time and again soothe the public that they would do everything in their power to battle the shrinking and aging population before opening the door to even more foreigners.[17] To Nikkei Brazilians, such a social climate is a constant reminder that they can never be "authentically" Japanese, despite their "Japanese blood" that the government in fact acknowledged for their ancestry-based visas. To be sure, the great majority of Brazilians whom I met were emphatic that they were thoroughly Brazilian; they did not want to become Japanese just to fit in. Still, one reason why many

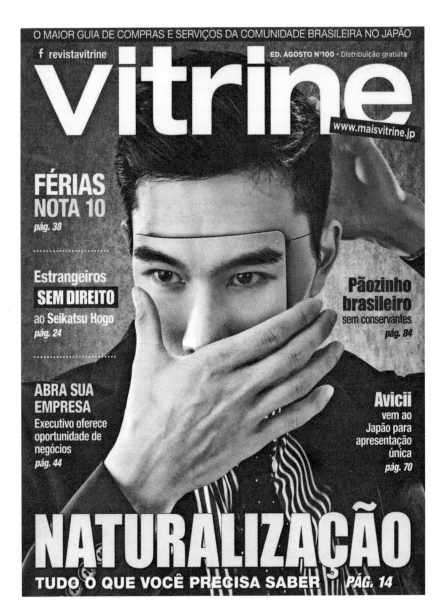

FIGURE 3. "Naturalization: All You Need to Know." Source: *Vitrine*, Issue Number 100. Cover, August 2014.

Brazilians cannot picture a future in Japan is because the country does not offer a tangible vision of such a future for them. The nation's ethnically purist, if not racist, narrative of national identity too often ends up suppressing the diversity such migrants inevitably bring into the society.

No Time to Live

Over time, many Nikkei migrants come to feel suspended between two futures: one in Japan and the other in Brazil. Upon initial migration, they saw how Japan turned out to be anything but the hypermodern First World nation that Nikkei ethnicity had symbolized in Brazil. Thus the migrants did not arrive at the future in Japan where many thought they would belong. Since then, the future for many in turn has rested in Brazil, and many talk about returning there. Unlike the intention of return, however, the materialization of actual return—especially the return to the ideal future—is rare. Some go back and forth between Japan and Brazil multiple times over the years, believing at each crossing that they may finally make it this time to the secure, "better," future. Others—especially the younger generations who have only known Japan—may envision a permanent life in Japan. Currently, however, the dominant rhetoric of Japanese national identity does not provide a clear path for inclusive and uncontested belonging for such ethnically and racially diverse Nikkei Brazilians. Thus, both futures often come to gain a quality of phantasm in migrants' experiences.

If the future becomes difficult to envision, then the present may be what is left as a temporal place to cultivate life. But even the present becomes precarious in migrants' tales. For instance, Takeshi elaborated eloquently on the state of suspended life:

> People went back to Brazil, . . . things went wrong there and they ended up returning here. For one family, looking at each individual family, this has happened at least once. Sometimes twice. Even three times. You come, go, come, go, and then come . . . At a certain moment, one realizes, "Oh my God, I am losing years of my life—because I am depriving myself of living, planning a future that doesn't happen. Is it worth putting aside living [deixar de viver]?"

When I inquired what exactly he meant by deixar de viver, he responded, "There exists a difference between living [viver] and surviving [sobreviver]." He continued:

So when a person lives poorly [i.e., survives], it cannot be considered that he has lived. He simply hasn't lived. That doesn't exist; that's like a negative number because it was bad. A good experience is positive. . . . For me, living is much more than you being there just doing what others want from you. . . .

Or, [*deixar de viver* means] that this person doesn't buy anything because he needs to save money to live the future. A person doesn't go to any place because this would be a waste of money, and he cannot do this if he wants to save money to live the future one day. A person cannot dress well. Because this would waste the money that—he is thinking—should be spent in the future.

"And this future often exists in Brazil?" I asked.

"That's what they plan for themselves," Takeshi answered. Other than "to put aside living," *deixar de viver* more literally means "stop living" or "quit living." Takeshi's narrative fleshes out how life can actually stop in the experiences of migrants as they wait and prepare uncertainly for the future—the future which, as Takeshi aptly observed, often "does not happen." In this context of perpetual temporariness that permeates the migrants' lives, both the future and the present become uncertain. Many sacrifice the pleasure in the present to reach the better future, which, as it turns out, often does not arrive.

Perhaps, then, the past is the place for life. But Nikkei migrants are already there—as descendants of Japanese emigrants in their ancestral homeland, in the nation that their parents and grandparents left behind, in the country where they could possibly find their past ethnic roots. Yet very few make an active effort to explore their ancestral ties to the nation even when they could identify living relatives in Japan. Like Takeshi, who admitted with frank laughter that he had "no idea" what kind of place Fukushima is, most migrants are not keenly interested in such a backward-looking project of return. At the end of the day, what the majority desires is not a nostalgic rediscovery of pristine ancestral past but rather an aspirational reaching out for a better future.

When neither the present nor the future enacts little experiential immediacy, migrants feel trapped, because this robs them of temporal locus for action. The feeling of being in limbo, in turn, leads to the ubiquitous symptom of temporal suffocation that I heard about over and over again during fieldwork: "I don't have time. I work so much. But this is necessary for me to return one day. Someday." The claim that the present does not possess innate experiential immediacy may strike some readers as odd. As Wendy James and David Mills pointed out, however, "the present is of course a convention, a sort of symbolic fiction, in itself."[18] I take fiction to be a synonym for malleable reality, not for fake construct, while acknowledging the need to be cautious with extreme experiential relativism.[19]

The question then is if and how migrants in this context start reconfiguring their temporal realities in ways that do not lead to temporal limbo, which Takeshi characterized as *deixar de viver*. The short answer is yes. For example, an increasing number of Brazilians have been making a conscious decision to "stay" (*permanecer*) and "live" (*morar*) in Japan. They move toward their new vision of future by paying mortgages, by making sustained efforts to learn Japanese, and by consciously sending their offspring to Japanese schools instead of Brazilian ones. I must add, however, that those who can set up long-term future-oriented plans still form a minority among Brazilian migrants at large. The major obstacles are job insecurity, language barriers, and unfamiliarity with Japanese cultural conventions. Although many form casual friendships with their Japanese colleagues at work, such interactions typically do not enhance the sense of embeddedness in Japanese society. This is partially because those Japanese employees who find themselves in the vicinity of migrant workers likewise occupy precarious and marginal positions in Japan's increasingly neoliberal labor system.[20]

Plasticity of Return

Why does life stop in Japan? It is because the forward-looking temporality implicit in the project of migration imposes the postponement of the present life to migrants. Migration is oftentimes an aspirational phenomenon, or "a project of hope," that is "geared toward the future, toward building a new house, investing in more land or other property, ... and generally building the prestige and the future of the house."[21] As Nikkei migrants in Japan struggle to materialize this better future, many begin to feel that they have not lived the present for years and sometimes for decades. In such an aspirational temporality, one must "work" in the present for the sake of better "life" in the future, instead of living the moment. This is why many migrants claim that they are in Japan "not to live but to work." What this phenomenon of temporal suffocation suggests is that life is not an automatic process but instead an active work of temporal enactment.

The experiences of Nikkei Brazilians in Japan illuminate the plasticity of return. A physical trip to the location where one's ancestors grew up often does not automatically constitute a return in one's mind. In other words, return is not a natural event but instead an achievement of convincing self-transformation, which builds the old bond to "homeland" anew. For the majority of Nikkei Brazilians, return was neither achieved nor even intended. Instead, upon their ambiguous arrival in the land of their ancestors, Nikkei Brazilians unwittingly walked into a temporal maze. What they encountered there was not the ancestral past, or the First World future, or the fulfilling present. In response, they learned to put aside living in the hope of reaching another future that should be awaiting them in Brazil once they escape the temporal limbo of migrant labor. But no one could tell for certain when the clock of life would start ticking again.

4

NEITHER HERE NOR THERE

"Welcome to the Favela"

In the evening of June 5, 1999, one van purportedly belonging to a Japanese right-wing nationalist group and roughly fifty motorcycles with riders in biker-gang outfits appeared on the streets of Homi Danchi in Toyota City. Circling around the large housing complex comprising roughly sixty buildings, they repeatedly called out, "Brazilians come out!" (burajirujin detekoi). The provocation came out of the mounted speaker and vibrated through the neighborhood while roughly thirty police officers stood guard. No Brazilian residents came out of their homes. According to a local Japanese newspaper, the intruders were likely looking for a specific group of Brazilian youth with whom they had had a run-in about a week earlier.[1] Nonetheless, the same article situates the incident in the general context of "the emotional animosity" (kanjōteki na shikori) between "the foreigners" (gaikokujin) and "the affiliates of right-wing and biker gang groups" (uyoku bōsōzoku kankeishara) in the area. The rhetoric conflates a fraction of Brazilian residents with the entire foreign community while keeping the nationalists and the outlaws separate from the general Japanese population.

The tension culminated in the arson of a right-wing van parked near Homi Danchi in the late night of the following day, June 6. Both Japanese right-wing group members and Brazilians reacting to the news of arson gathered near the scene, in response to which roughly eighty police officers arrived to keep guard.

Although the situation did not devolve into any violent outburst, the dispatch of prefectural police riot squad (*kenkei kidōtai*) attracted the rare attention of Japanese mainstream media. On June 9, *Yomiuri Shimbun*—one of the most widely read daily newspapers in Japan—published a piece titled "The Dispute Between Brazilians and Right-Wing Extremists."[2] Again, the article's rhetoric juxtaposes the Brazilian residents as a whole with an "extremist" fragment of Japanese society as if to imply that they are both troublesome outsiders. The widely reported "dispute" in 1999 tarnished the image of the neighborhood for years to come.

When I arrived in Toyota City in 2013 to start my yearlong fieldwork, I received multiple warnings about living in Homi Danchi from both Japanese and Brazilian acquaintances. It is messy, dangerous, and unwelcoming, they would say. "Are you sure you can have a balanced picture by studying the Brazilians in Homi Danchi?" One Japanese scholar who had studied Brazilian communities in another city inquired me with a concerned look. A "balanced picture," he seemed to suggest, could only be gleaned from neighborhoods reputed to be more integrated and harmonious. Based on several visits he had made to the housing complex, he also added that Homi Danchi seemed to "have thorns [*toge*] against the surrounding community."

"I'd recommend other *danchis* [housing complexes]," said Gabriel, with whom I had become acquainted during my pilot research a year earlier. He held a degree in law from a university in São Paulo and briefly tried to establish a career as a lawyer in Brazil before migrating to Japan in 1992 due to financial difficulties. He himself lived in a dormitory provided by the auto company he worked for. He continued hesitantly, "It's really crude in Homi, you know. People there don't have culture" (Lá no Homi tem muito barulho né. O pessoal lá não tem cultura). When pressed, he explained that the Brazilians who lived in such an isolated place without real contact with either Japanese or Brazilian culture end up being "neither here nor there" (*nem lá nem cá*). "Especially the young kids who grew up there," he added. "Me, I know I'm Brazilian. I speak Portuguese. I was educated in Brazil. But the youth in Homi don't know who they are—they don't have either culture. That's why they are *nem lá nem cá*."

I was surprised by the fact that many Brazilians—mostly those living outside Homi—spoke of their fellow migrants there in such a generalizing way. But of course, the so-called Brazilian community is not a monolith. It was clear that many migrants—including some who actually lived in Homi Danchi—

perceived the place as occupying the lowest tier of internal social hierarchy. If those who managed to purchase a house are on the top, those who depend on subsidized housing or live in presumably bad neighborhoods are at the bottom. Despite the fact that only some buildings of Homi Danchi were subsidized for families in need, the association of the place with lower-class status seemed to persist.

Roughly two months into my fieldwork, my paperwork finally went through and I signed a lease to live in a small apartment in Building 128 of Homi Danchi. Three days before my planned move-in date, on October 29, 2013, I received a late-night text message from Beatriz, who lived in Building 127. "Have you heard about the jumping off [*tobiori*]?"

"No," I responded. "I was in factory all day. What happened?"

"A Brazilian man living here threw himself off from the top of Building 21, trying to escape the police. He was stealing car parts, you know, and the police were trying to arrest him." I later learned that Frederico Sakamoto, a forty-year-old Nikkei, hesitated for some eight hours on the top of the five-storied building, until he eventually jumped off around nine o'clock at night. The officers from the Aichi Prefectural Police, who had initially come to arrest Sakamoto for motor vehicle theft and visa overstay, spent the whole day persuading him not to commit suicide while surrounded by Japanese and Brazilian residents who gathered at the scene. In the end, he jumped off and hit the area of the ground that was not covered by the mattresses the officers had placed to save him.

Over the next few days, some of my Japanese kin called to dissuade me from moving into Homi Danchi. I was not changing my plan. Most of my Brazilian informants acknowledged Sakamoto's wrongdoing, and although some were sympathetic, many worried about the event's potential impact on the reputation of Nikkei Brazilians. "I believe that things were tough for him and I feel bad for his family," one Nikkei resident of Homi Danchi said. "But things are hard for all of us dekasseguis. Yet most of us don't go around stealing cars. Did he think he could escape the justice forever? Our image just got even worse, thanks to him!" The media coverage of such extreme events helps perpetuate the dominant image of Brazilians in the nation as delinquent, if not crime ridden. In fact, an overview of all the articles on Brazilian migrants published by a major Japanese newspaper (*Asahi Shimbun*) between 1990 and 2008 showed that the most frequent topic was crime (31 percent), followed by "cultural exchange" (11.8 percent).[3] As far as the mainstream Japanese media are concerned, then, Brazilians are either hot-blooded transgressors of law or possessors of unique culture. There is little room for nuanced subjectivity or emotional depth in such depictions of migrants. Stories about the well-known Brazilian enclaves in Japan often come to reflect such dichotomous images of the foreign Other.

A few days after I moved into Homi Danchi, I walked over to Beatriz's apartment in the evening to chat with her over a cup of coffee. I brought a bag of Pilão coffee beans that I had bought at the Brazilian supermarket in Homi called Foxmart. "Oh! You got the expensive stuff for us, thank you!" Beatriz said, smiling. Since most products at Foxmart were overpriced, many Brazilian residents with cars went elsewhere to do grocery shopping unless they needed something that Japanese supermarkets did not carry. Beatriz, a twenty-five-year-old yonsei who grew up in Homi since she was four, asked me in Japanese how much coffee I wanted as she poured water into the coffee maker.

"Not much," I said. "It's getting late and I don't wanna stay up."

"You are so Japanese [*nihonjin dane*]," Beatriz teased. "We Brazilians drink coffee anytime—morning, afternoon, late at night. We're used to it."

As we waited for the coffee to brew, she spoke about how Pastor Cid—who also lived in Homi Danchi at the time—tried to dissuade Sakamoto from throwing himself off during the tense eight hours. "He did what he did in the end, but . . . I wish he had found God." Beatriz quietly poured hot coffee into two mugs. Then, with a mischievous smile on her lips, she added, "Homi is a deep place [*dīpu na basho*], as you can see. Welcome to the *favela* [*favela e yōkoso*]." We both laughed. With its solid concrete structures, perfectly functional infrastructure, and lack of gun or gang violence, Homi Danchi was not exactly a Brazilian shantytown. In fact, Beatriz quickly switched to Portuguese to utter the word *favela*, which perhaps signified the foreignness of such places to herself as someone who grew up mostly in Japan and primarily spoke Japanese. Yet the word captured something vital about the popular image of Homi Danchi in Japanese society as a place for the deviant Brazilian Other—something Beatriz had to confront time after time whenever the media found migrants like Sakamoto. At the same time, some fellow migrants like Gabriel would insist that Homi Danchi was not even Brazilian but instead a cultural limbo of *nem lá nem cá*, where migrants could not authentically be Japanese or Brazilian. To him, Homi was a strange nonplace for people suspended between two cultures.

But are Nikkei Brazilians like Beatriz in Homi Danchi really "neither here nor there"? To investigate what constitutes the pervasive discourse of cultural limbo, I will examine a variety of sources ranging from autobiographic narratives to media representations in this chapter. The rhetoric of in-between identity, although it is commonplace among transnational migrants, must not be taken at face value. This is because such a way of speaking is based on a rather essentialist view of culture, in which different groups are supposed to exist as separate entities with clear boundaries. In other words, the rhetoric of "neither here nor there" assumes that there are clear "here" and "there" to start with, when the line between the two may instead be porous, flexible, and subject to constant negotiation. To claim that some people are between Japan and Brazil is to evoke "methodological nationalism," a framework that takes national units as an analytical given.[4] Yet the narrative of cultural ambiguity and the feeling of contested belonging persist among many migrants—and for a reason. In what follows, I will disentangle the relationship between race, generation, and affect that has come to shape the rhetoric of cultural limbo among Nikkei Brazilians in Japan. My argument will take a diachronic approach; it starts with the stories about migration and family recounted by older migrants and then moves on to the perspectives of younger generations born or raised in Japan.

Out of Sight, Out of Mind: Tales of Lost Families

The Almeidas were a family of six: Luana, a sansei Nikkei mother; Guilherme, a non-Nikkei father whom Luana described as "white" (*branco*); Guilherme's Brazilian mother, whom he brought to Japan a few years earlier due to her deteriorating health; Beatriz, a twenty-five-year-old eldest daughter who arrived in Japan at the age of four; Diego, a twenty-three-year-old son who was two years old when he was brought to Japan; and Sachi, an eight-year-old youngest daughter who was born much later in Japan.

Having migrated in 1993, they had been living in Japan for over two decades at the time of my fieldwork. They were among the small but growing number of migrants in Homi who did not speak of the plan to return to Brazil. This was partly because they owned two apartments there. One unit was for Luana, Guilherme, Sachi, and Guilherme's bedridden mother. The other was for Beatriz and Diego, the two adult children. Although the family lived separately, they frequently visited each other, since the two apartments were only a few blocks away from one another. When I visited Beatriz in the evening for coffee, I would sometimes see her younger sister clinging to her arm as she opened the door for me. Her parents usually left Sachi with Beatriz when they had to go out at night, typically to attend church-related gatherings at Missão Apoio Toyota. Everyone in the Almeida family had undergone water baptism at the church except for Guilherme's elderly mother, who self-identified as Catholic, and Sachi, who was still too young to make her own decision according to the parents.

I visited Luana's apartment in Homi Danchi for an interview one afternoon. She was born in Assaí in the state of Paraná to nisei parents who were, in her words, "children of Japanese with the face of *nihon-jin* [Japanese]." When she was eight, her family moved to the city of São Paulo for the education of her older siblings. Both in Assaí and São Paulo, "there were many [Japanese] descendants" in the neighborhood where her family lived and she remembered various Japanese foods and customs from her childhood: the commemoration of *obon* (Buddhist custom that commemorates the ancestral spirits); *mochi* (rice cakes) her grandparents used to give her as a treat; and *undōkai* (sports day gathering) at the local Japanese association, among other things. Due to this "very Japanese" cultural environment of her childhood, which many of her fellow Nikkei migrants in Homi did not have, she also learned to speak some Japanese when she was still in Brazil. In fact, her maternal grandparents—issei immigrants from Hiroshima—ran a small home school to teach the Japanese language to Nikkei youth in their neighborhood. "When the normal school was over in the afternoon, my parents would round up me, my siblings, and cousins and drag us to the house of *jīchan* [grandpa]. We were like, 'Nooo! We wanna go play! Nooo!'" Luana burst out laughing. Although our interview was in Portuguese, the Japanese phrases she occasionally interjected sounded fluent.

When she was a student at the University of São Paulo, she met and married Guilherme and subsequently left school without graduating to start a family. She jokingly described their first encounter as *amor à primeira batida* (love at first hit) because Guilherme rear-ended her car in a minor traffic accident and later fell in love with her. Although her Nikkei parents initially insisted that she should marry another Nikkei instead of a *brasileiro* (non-Nikkei Brazilian), they eventually came to accept her decision. Guilherme was a high school graduate who ran a small eatery in the city. With the record high inflation rate at the time in Brazil, he was forced to close down his business soon after their marriage. In 1993, they decided to go to Japan to work and save money for a few years "because everyone was doing it back then."

They were not the first ones in Luana's family to migrate. Luana's nisei father had already migrated to Japan by himself one year earlier in 1992. When she started recounting the effect of her father's migration on her family, her face hardened slightly: "My mother had to stay in Brazil because someone had to take care of the renovation of the house with the money he sent from Japan—and over time, there was *afastamento* [estrangement] between them. We began to get used to this situation, that he was always gone. . . . As time went by, more and more afastamento. . . . My father stayed here longer, alone, and my mother there [in Brazil]." When Luana arrived in Japan with her family, she tried to visit her father in Gunma, roughly 250 miles east of Toyota. But he always told her that he was busy. She also noticed that a strange middle-aged woman sometimes answered her calls to her father's home phone. When she brought it up, he explained that he shared a house with a married couple to save more money to send back to Brazil. Luana continued:

> Then one day, he returned to Brazil, he didn't tell my mother, didn't tell my sister, and just showed up at their doorstep. . . . He said, "Because the factory closed down there [in Japan] . . . so I was fired." And he left again to get a job, actually the same one he had before he went to Japan. He took care of a beach house in a nearby coastal city. So he went to live there. And one day, he had something like a seizure and passed away. . . .
>
> When my sister went there to prepare for a funeral, what had happened was, he was with another woman. . . . He had another wife! But my mother never knew; he didn't say a word about it. . . . This woman wanted to receive his pension, because there in Brazil a widow can continue to receive.[5] But my sister said, "Um, I am his daughter. And I have a mother, who is his spouse." The woman became like this [wide open eyes]. She didn't know anything, because they were by themselves here [in Japan]. That's why he didn't want any contact with us—he got himself another wife in Japan.

Luana then went on to describe similar situations she had seen among her Brazilian friends: infidelities, divorces, abandoned children, and so on. "It's tough to be a dekassegui," she sighed. Her story highlighted the distancing effect of migration, both physical and emotional, on family ties.

Luana's story, although it was narrated from her personal viewpoint, reflects some structural patterns that apply more broadly to Brazilian migrants in Japan. A survey conducted by the Brazilian Association of Labor Migrants in 2004, for instance, showed that 43.7 percent of Brazilian men migrated to Japan unaccompanied by their families. Women, in contrast, tended to migrate with family members—spouses, children, and siblings—and only 24.3 percent arrived in Japan alone. Even among married men, 38.2 percent migrated by themselves, but just 19 percent of married women did so.[6] These findings show that gender definitively shapes migratory patterns. One consequence is the prevalence of single-person households among Brazilian migrants in Japan, especially among men. Although they make up roughly 40 percent of the Brazilian households in Japan surveyed by the association, they constitute just 12 percent of all the households in Brazil according to the 2010 Brazil Census.[7] These demographic changes likely exacerbate the sense of afastamento—the feeling of isolation, separation, and alienation from kinship ties.

Seen in this light, Luana's resentment toward her father's infidelity in Japan is embedded in the larger sociological shifts that accompany dekassegui migration. Indeed, the majority of my informants narrated similar stories about what they perceived as "family in crisis." This pervasive impression that migration disintegrates family also echoed in the coverage of dekasseguis in the Brazilian media. For example, a major Brazilian newspaper reported in 2010 that Japan is "a great refuge for those who do not want to provide payment" to spouses and dependents among "Japanese descendants—the dekasseguis."[8] The article framed its observation primarily in legal terms. The Tribunal of Justice of São Paulo—the state with the largest number of Japanese descendants in the country—issued 2,425 letters of request (cartas rogatórias) to Japan in 2005 alone. Of these, 1,122 dealt with alimony, 509 with divorce, 570 with recognition of paternity, and 224 with criminal issues. In roughly 80 percent of the cases, the letters did not reach the addressees in Japan—a situation that the families in Brazil typically interpreted as a sign of irresponsibility and abandonment. Even when migrants received such letters, they could in theory ignore them without any legal repercussions due to the lack of diplomatic agreements on civil and criminal cases between the two governments.[9]

A number of grassroots groups appeared during the 1990s to address such social and legal issues, including the Association of Families Abandoned by Migrant Workers (Associação das Famílias Abandonadas por Dekasseguis). Founded in 1991 to unite "widows and widowers of living partners" (viúvos de companheiros vivos), the association had 300 registered families in 2010.[10] One of the leaders, Djalma Straube, counted himself as one of the "victims" of abandonment. He was living with his Nikkei wife and two mestiça daughters in Brazil when his wife decided to migrate to Japan by herself in 1993. A few years later, however, she stopped sending back remittances, cut off all communications with the family, and effectively went missing in Japan. Five years later in 2000, she suddenly returned to Brazil and filed for a divorce.

There exist no large-scale statistical data on the frequency of divorce and child abandonment, let alone separation and infidelity, specifically among Brazilians living in Japan. Consequently, it is difficult to confirm whether the dominant discourse of "family in crisis" is a numerical reality. My ethnographic findings, however, unambiguously confirm that it was an emotional reality for the migrants, and a rather potent one at that.[11]

Laboring Apart, Growing Apart

Work was another factor my informants frequently brought up when they discussed what they perceived as the prevalent problem of family estrangement in Japan. Many spoke of long and unpredictable working hours as the chief cause of growing emotional distance between spouses as well as between parents and children. Paula was a thirty-one-year-old Nikkei woman who lived with her husband in Homi Danchi. After I taught her some Japanese upon her request (she decided to quit in a month) and we went out several times to have dinner together, we started exchanging text messages on a regular basis. One night, I came across her recent status update on my Facebook wall, which simply read: "Feeling down [sad face]." I typed a quick comment, "I hope you are OK. Hugs." Roughly thirty minutes later, I received an unusually long text message from her in Portuguese:

> Thank you, Suma. God, I sometimes don't know what to do—We Brazilians are here in Japan to work and save money, but our marriage suffers because of this very purpose—work. Last week, Ken [her husband] was asked to work *ni kōtai* [alternating between day shift and night shift every week] and, this week, he is working *yakin* [night shift]. He made it very clear when he started working at this factory that he just wants to do *hirukin* [day shift]. But when the factory really needs it, he can't say no. I asked for *teiji* [regular hours, typically from 8 A.M. until 5 P.M.] at my factory so that I can be home early to fix him a meal before he leaves for work. They said no, this month is really busy and I have to do at least three hours of *zangyō* [extra hours] every day. When I get home around nine, Ken is already gone, and when I get up in the morning and leave for work, he is on his way home. I haven't seen MY OWN [*sic*] husband in a week! What life is this?

Night shift, particularly *ni kōtai* that alternates between day shift and night shift, can be quite taxing to one's health. Since many full-time employees shun it, temporary workers with economic incentive tend to fill the demand, as the wage is typically higher than day shift. Many migrant workers, however, found the irregular working hours challenging to maintain close relationships with their families. This was especially the case with women, who were also burdened with the cultural expectation to serve as domestic caretakers.[12] Paula consequently felt trapped between her two roles: competent migrant worker and nurturing homemaker. Since the common purpose of migration—at least initially—was to save money to bring back to Brazil, many women who had not worked full-time previously came to do so in Japan. As their "temporary" life as migrant laborers became prolonged, however, what many families regarded as a short-term arrangement to enhance savings became more permanent.

Paula complained about the challenge her work posed on her effort to maintain conjugal intimacy. Others expressed the same frustration in regard to the relationship between parents and offspring. Many working parents were concerned that they could not spend enough quality time with their children due to long working hours. For example, Beatriz recounted the following story from her childhood:

> Back then, I didn't see my father at all. I was what, seven or eight, and used to go to bed long before my father would come home from work. I think he came home close to midnight. All my friends were Japanese at school, and my mother spoke some Japanese because she is Nikkei and studied it a little in Brazil. My father, he is white as you know, and didn't speak any Japanese. . . .
>
> One day, he tried to speak with me and I didn't understand what he was trying to say. I looked up at him like, "What is this strange old man saying? I have no clue" [Kono ojisan nani itterundaro zenzen wakannai]. Then he started crying, right then and there, in front of me. I was completely stunned. . . . He was sad, you know, and he told me later that he felt it was his fault. . . . He let that happen, you know.

In this narrative, Beatriz referred to her own father as *kono ojisan*, which means "this strange middle-aged man" in this context. This word choice highlights the widening emotional distance that was growing between her and her father due to the lack of interaction and, to Guilherme's distress, the inability to speak with one another in a common language.

After Luana and Guilherme realized that their daughter was forgetting Portuguese, Luana left her factory work to become a stay-at-home mother and transferred Beatriz to a private Brazilian school. When her Portuguese improved to the intermediate level two years later, Luana then transferred her back to her previous Japanese public school. Luana decided not to resume full-time work and instead started offering Portuguese classes to Japan-raised Brazilian youth in the neighborhood. "Wow, so you are doing something that your own grandfather used to do in Brazil," I commented when Luana showed me the teaching materials she used in her elementary Portuguese language class.

"I guess you are right," Luana said, looking up from the exercise book she was flipping through. "Then no wonder why my students don't do homework! I hated learning Japanese when I was a kid!" We both laughed at this apparent irony. The relationship between cultural identity and linguistic adaptation among children of immigrants is a complicated issue.[13] But how language and generation intersect is slightly more complex in the case of Nikkeis in Japan due to their history of dual diaspora. Luana grew up in a Japanese neighborhood, which gave her the opportunity to learn some Japanese as a child. Guilherme, in contrast, was a non-Nikkei who could not speak Japanese. Beatriz's inability to comprehend Portuguese thus shocked him more strongly, since it foreshadowed the loss of common language between the father and the daughter.

In addition to illuminating how migrants come to regard work as a major cause of emotional estrangement within family, such stories also highlight how gender affects the ways in which they respond to perceived problems. It is Paula, and not her husband, who insisted on leaving work early so that she could prepare meals for him at home. It is Luana, and not Guilherme, who quit factory work to care for their children full-time and ensure that they could speak Portuguese. Thus, the sustenance of "home" in diaspora falls heavily onto women's shoulders, making them feel more sensitive to and responsible for the perceived disintegration of family.

Afastamento: The Culture of Discipline in Question

Conflict, infidelity, divorce, abandonment, loss of intimacy, widening generation gap—these are some of the problems that occupied the minds of Brazilian families in Japan. Although the specifics of such problems varied, I realized over time that my informants seemed to have an overarching affective term for all the issues related to migration—namely, *afastamento*. As the noun form of *afastar* (to distance), the word encompassed the feelings of isolation, estrangement, and alienation from family and kin. Although such an emotive idiom may be common among many migrant groups, Nikkeis seemed to interpret and experience afastamento within a particular historical frame of racialized affects.[14] Racialized affect is a "theoretical lens to highlight racialization and affect as necessarily interconnected, even mutually constituted, political projects."[15] "Latino hot-bloodedness" and "black delinquency" are among the better-known examples of racialized affects. In the case of Nikkei Brazilians in Japan, migrants often viewed afastamento as a turning point in their shifting racialized self-images: It signified the end of "Japanese discipline" that their ethnicity symbolized in Brazil and the beginning of "Brazilian volatility" that their race begins to embody in Japan. This is because afastamento flies in the face of the common stereotypes associated with Nikkeis in Brazil: "the firmer structure and more united family life [*convivência*]," "discipline [*educação*] received at home," and "the gratitude to the family, to the parents, and the ancestors."[16] The idealized picture of "Japanese family" in Brazil is the one of solidarity, mutual respect, and intergenerational unity. Luana herself invoked such a picture-perfect, and somewhat essentialist, image by contrasting it to her non-Nikkei husband's "Brazilian family":

> Guilherme, his Brazilian parents fought a lot. . . . So he grew up believing that, in marriage, happiness did not exist. He used to think, "But what kind of life is this? I don't want a marriage like this." . . . I formed my concept of family differently. . . . My mother was at home with us, and my father would come home to have coffee, and my mother would sit down with him and listen to him. . . . And he would tell her funny stories, and they would laugh together. So the image I have of family is this. "Wow, I want a family like this," you know.

Later in the same interview, I asked Luana if she ever thought she would convert to Pentecostalism before coming to Japan, to which she responded with the following:

> Not at all! [Laughs] It was Guilherme who had all these, um, well . . . We *nihonjin* [Japanese] are raised to be proper. We have this *cultura de educação* [culture of discipline] already. Parents teach us early on, "Don't steal. Don't do wrong things. You'll get hurt if you hurt someone." So this was the teaching among us.

We didn't know the Word of God, but we knew that we had to walk the right path. We had these teachings but nothing of Jesus, you know, in my family.

Here, Luana nostalgically paints a harmonious picture of her childhood family. With the caring stay-at-home mother and respectable father as the bread-winner, her home was a secure place where children could be "raised to be proper" and learn "how to walk the right path." She indicates several times that her non-Nikkei husband's natal family was not as happy or harmonious as hers. In her narrative, his "Brazilian" home figures as a place of constant tension, volatility, and disorder. Interestingly, she even implies that her Japanese "culture of discipline" was something comparable to the Christian "Word of God," suggesting that she and other Nikkeis knew "the right path" even before conversion. Probably because it was her husband who was first drawn to Pentecostalism in Japan, Luana speculates that it was the lack of discipline in his familial background that made him particularly susceptible.

The migration to Japan, however, shook the foundation of this "culture of discipline" that Luana proudly speaks of. Her own father—whom she fondly portrays as a respectable breadwinner in her reminiscence—found "another wife" there. With such firsthand experiences of family disintegration, migrants like Luana found it increasingly difficult to sustain the racialized self-image of "Japanese discipline" in Japan. Instead, the overwhelming sense of afastamento gradually developed a new "culture of disorder" characterized by fights, divorces, abandonments, and delinquent acts—the kind of culture that Luana used to associate with her non-Nikkei "Brazilian" husband's upbringing. The emotive idiom of afastamento thus represented a watershed moment in the history of racialized affects among Nikkeis—from the civilized discipline of Asian whites in Brazil to the volatile disorder of foreign Latinos in Japan. It is ironic that this dramatic shift took place in Japan—the land of ancestors where the idyllic "Japanese family" is supposed to originate.

Learning the "Japanese Way"

What makes the perceived decline of discipline among Nikkei families even more challenging is the difficulty in adapting to Japanese social conventions. The migrants' Japanese coworkers, teachers, classmates, and neighbors often attribute Brazilians' deviance from established norms to the lack of effort to assimilate, if not the lack of "culture" itself.

One well-known area of friction involves the rules about garbage collection. In Japan, there are detailed instructions about how to sort out trash into the burnable, unburnable, and recyclable, including when garbage can be put out on the curb for collection. Trash must be in specific kinds of clear plastic bags that can be purchased for a small price beforehand at supermarkets. Additionally, one must contact a local municipality to make a payment and arrange a collection date to discard a large piece of household furniture such as a couch. These rules can be quite complex, especially for those foreign migrants who recently arrived in the country and cannot understand the Japanese language or customs. The regulations about garbage collection in Brazil are generally more lax. Consequently, some Japanese residents surmise that their Brazilian neighbors have no respect to rules when they repeatedly spot "wrong" trash in "wrong" bags at a "wrong" time at a "wrong" collection site. Some migrants may indeed pay little heed to such practices, especially when their plan of immediate return to Brazil makes them believe that their life in Japan is temporary anyway. Regardless, the so-called trash problem (*gomi mondai*) in neighborhoods with a large number of foreigners such as Homi has received significant media coverage in Japan, reinforcing the stereotype that Brazilians are disorderly.

Things are equally challenging in Japanese schools, which the offspring of working Brazilian migrants started attending en masse beginning in the early 1990s. On top of the language barrier, Brazilian parents also had to deal with a plethora of unfamiliar customs. For example, the two elementary schools in Homi had a practice called *shūdan tōkō*, which required pupils living in the same neighborhood to walk to school in groups by forming lines. Although implemented for security reasons, *shūdan tōkō* also disciplines the bodies of young children by requiring them to stay in lines on their way to school. Deviation generates suspicion. One Japanese school teacher whom I interviewed, for instance, voiced his doubt that a seven-year-old Brazilian pupil in his class, Kenta, may have ADHD. He reasoned that Kenta's inability to stay in the lines during *shūdan tōkō*—which manifested in "erratic" behaviors such as dashing, jumping, and drifting away—could be a sign of his undiagnosed mental illness. I was surprised by his statement, especially because he was one of the rare teachers who were making the effort to learn Portuguese to better serve their foreign pupils. Since I occasionally visited Kenta's family, who lived ten minutes away from my apartment in Homi Danchi, I decided to inquire about the subject with his mother the following week. When I asked her if Kenta had any issues in school, she said she was frustrated with some teachers who thought her son had some mental problems. "He is fine!" She said emphatically. "Yes, he is full of energy, just like any other seven-year-old boy. How is that a mental illness?" She then told me about two mothers whom she knew, one Nikkei Brazilian and the other Nikkei Peruvian, who agreed to medicate their children for ADHD. "It's so sad to see their boys sedated with pills. . . . They used to run around laughing." Although I am unqualified to determine whether Kenta actually had ADHD, he seemed to be an energetic and talkative little boy who loved playing with his friends outside. The story of Kenta shows how some foreign children and their families have difficulty in conforming to the established norms in Japanese school, such as bodily discipline expected in collective activities.[17] And some school officials read such an unconformity as a mental, not cultural, deviance.

Japanese social expectations dictate that mothers must shoulder more work than fathers in ensuring their offspring's well-being in school. One common practice that reflects this culturally inscribed gender role is the preparation of obentō (boxed lunch). Many mothers prepare boxed lunch for their children in nursery, in elementary school, and oftentimes even up to high school to demonstrate their nurturing care. Although some mothers find it fulfilling to express their love by making elaborate boxed meals, the quasi-mandatory nature of this practice also exposes them to the scrutiny of schoolteachers and fellow mothers. As Anne Allison observed: "The making of the obentō is . . . a double-edged sword for women. By relishing its creation . . . , a woman is ensconcing herself in the ritualization and subjectivity (subjection) of being a mother in Japan. She is alienated in the sense that others will dictate, inspect, and manage her work. On the reverse side, however, it is precisely through this work that the woman expresses, identifies, and constitutes herself."[18] The core of middle-class childrearing beliefs in Japan is that "nurture, not nature, is critical in the creation of a successful child."[19] Obentō is among the most cherished mediums to cultivate such "nurture," both physically and emotionally.

Many Brazilian mothers who send their children to Japanese schools cannot meet this culturally endorsed path to proper motherhood due to challenging work schedule, lack of skills, or unfamiliarity with such customs. Beatriz, the daughter of Luana, related the following experience from her childhood:

> The level of obentō that Japanese mothers make is just—unbelievable, you know, on another level. Sausages cut into the shape of octopus, omuraisu that looks like Pikachū, the perfect balance between meat and vegetable in terms of color

and nutrients.[20] . . . So intricate. Can you expect that from a Brazilian mother? Well, not quite. [Laughs.] I always hid my obentō from my friends and ate it as quickly as possible, because I was so embarrassed. Their obentō looked shiny to me, you know. . . .

Once I asked my mother, "Um, I wish I could also bring a cute obentō to school." It was the day of school excursion at East Homi Elementary School. She said OK. The next day, when I opened it at lunchtime, I only saw a huge *omuraisu* with a smiley face drawn on it with ketchup. The smile actually looked distorted and creepy, since it was in my backpack all morning. I sat away from my friends and ate it quickly while hiding it.

Beatriz's story demonstrates how food plays a pivotal role in the negotiation of cultural identity. Her Nikkei "Brazilian" mother could not satisfy her desire to fit into the "Japanese" school by bringing a cute elaborate obentō. Oftentimes, it is school-aged children who feel such tensions more acutely, due to the peer pressure common in their daily environment.

Although some Japanese teachers interpreted Brazilian mothers' apparent unconformity to school customs as unwillingness to provide "appropriate care" for their children, others observed that the seeming failure was due to the different norms in childrearing between Japan and Brazil. This is why some nonprofit organizations in Homi Danchi offered classes on how to prepare obentō. One Sunday during my fieldwork, for example, Torcida—the group that provided Japanese language classes to foreign children in Toyota—invited the parents of its Brazilian students to a two-hour-long obentō class. A dozen mothers (and no fathers, I must add) attended the event. The Japanese instructor, who was a certified dietician, taught the class with the help of an interpreter. She gave instructions on how to cut sausage into the shapes of various animals, how to make rice balls in the shape of Hello Kitty, and how to incorporate small decorating pieces into the lunch box, among other things. At one point, one Nikkei mother exclaimed, "*Meu Deus* [My God], Japanese are so detail-oriented! Why don't we just throw in some rice and meat, and that's it!" Everyone laughed at her playful tone, including the instructor after the interpreter translated it. Such workshops can be quite helpful for Brazilian mothers, but they also reinforce the normative vision of nurturing motherhood in Japan by imprinting it onto foreign women with children. Moreover, it is this kind of moments that made Nikkei women distance themselves further away from their "Japanese" identity as they performed an easygoing and carefree "Brazilian" character.

Thus, many Brazilian mothers struggled to perform the culturally sanctioned gender roles in Japan. This does not necessarily mean that gender relations were more egalitarian in Brazil, where patriarchal values, racial hierarchy, regional differences, and class divides have historically shaped gender norms in an unequal manner.[21] Still, what becomes more pronounced in Japan is a conflict between the purpose of labor migration (i.e., economic accumulation) and the cultural expectation of proper femininity and motherhood (i.e., domestic nurturance). Many migrant women around the globe experience this dilemma, but those in Japan may be particularly susceptible due to the historical entanglement of state and family in the nation. The state-family dyad has long enshrined the triangulation of nurturance, domesticity, and motherhood in modern Japan.[22] To many Brazilian women who work full-time, learning a new cultural idiom of care in such a social context can be a daunting task.

Whether it be dealing with garbage collection, going to school in groups, or preparing obentō, Brazilian migrants struggle to learn the "Japanese way." As many stumble in this process, their "Japanese" identity dissolves even further. What takes hold instead is "Brazilian" self-image and its racialized affects—slackness, volatility, and delinquency, on the one hand, and informality, spontaneity, and easygoingness, on the other.

Lost Generation in Japan?

As the older Nikkei migrants come to feel unambiguously Brazilian, they turn to the younger generations raised primarily in Japan with an ambiguous gaze: If we are now Brazilian, who are these youngsters, many of whom can no longer speak fluent Portuguese? Brazilian or Japanese? As the offspring of nisei and sansei Nikkeis who migrated on the long-term resident visa, the youth are arguably sansei and yonsei Nikkeis. Yet many older migrants do not appeal to this common denominator, "Nikkei," when they speak of the so-called problems that haunt the next generations growing up in Japan. They instead come to see "us" and "them" along the generational lines.

One day, I met with Flávio at a coffee shop near Homi Danchi. The thirty-seven-year-old sansei college graduate from São Paulo was one of the few Nikkei migrants whom I knew who did not work in a factory. Although he had initially done so when he migrated in 1998, he made a living as a freelance consultant at the time of my fieldwork and organized workshops on finances for Brazilian migrants in the Aichi Prefecture and beyond. Since he could not understand Japanese very well, he wanted me to go over some materials he was developing to help Brazilian youth "make healthy life plans." Specifically, he wanted to show the variety of career options in Japan outside of the unskilled manual labor. "Most of these youngsters cannot see their future outside the factory because that's what all the adults in the community do," Flávio sighed. "I want them to know that, if they work hard, they can do much more than that." After listening to me translate some Japanese websites that described which jobs were in demand, he asked me to examine the job aptitude test that he was drafting in Portuguese. "Would this make sense in Japanese? I may need you to translate it into Japanese. Sadly, some of our youth can't read or write Portuguese anymore," he said as he shook his head disapprovingly.

As we were wrapping up the meeting, Daisuke walked into the coffee shop, since he and I were planning to have lunch together. "Oh, great timing," Flávio said, looking up and waving at Daisuke. The two knew each other from the church. "I'll show you just how little Portuguese the young folks can understand." He then asked Daisuke to read some of the questions in the personality assessment section of the job aptitude test—for example, "I enjoy analyzing things." Daisuke stuttered when he pronounced the word *analisar* (analyze). With a smile, Flávio asked if he knew the word's meaning.

"More or less," Daisuke answered. Flávio then suggested I write the Japanese equivalent of the word on the paper. I did, feeling somewhat uncomfortable, as I saw where he was going with it. Daisuke, an eighteen-year-old high school dropout born and raised in Homi, could converse in Japanese fluently, but reading and writing were his weaknesses. Not surprisingly, he could not read the Chinese characters (*kanji*) contained in the word (分析 *bunseki* or "analysis"). When I read the term aloud, however, he immediately nodded with comprehension.

"You see?" Flávio said as he gave me an I-told-you-so look. "The young people in our community can't understand Portuguese well, and sometimes Japanese, either. It is worrying that our next generation is *nem lá nem cá* [neither here nor there], not rooted in any language." I glanced at Daisuke, who sat calmly with a smile next to Flávio. I could not believe Flávio would say such a thing in his presence. Later at our lunch, I asked Daisuke how he felt when adults like Flávio not-too-subtly suggested that he was not really Brazilian. He responded in a mixture of Japanese and Portuguese: "Bom, shōganai tte kanji. Ryōhō desho, ore. É verdade, o que eles falam" (Well, I feel like, what can you do. I am both [Japanese and Brazilian], you see. It's true what they say).

Over the course of my fieldwork, I heard many Brazilian adults raised in Brazil make comments similar to Flávio's. As he eloquently summed up on another occasion, a common concern of older migrants is the "loss of identity" among their offspring:

> I think they [the migrant youth] have a conflict of . . . let's say . . . what culture they belong to, you see. They are neither Brazilian—because they came to Japan at an early age—nor Japanese because they live inside a Brazilian community. So oftentimes, they feel neither Japanese nor Brazilian. They can claim, "I am Brazilian." But they still don't know Brazil, you see, like the job market there. . . . So with all this, I think they end up losing their identity; they don't have identity.

I was always struck by the composure the youth maintained upon being subjected to such blunt remarks that claimed their lack of identity. Most shrugged them off with a nonchalant attitude like Daisuke, indicating just how often they heard such opinions about themselves.

What is ironic about this intergenerational friction is that although older migrants lament "the loss of identity" among the younger generations raised in Japan today, they were on the receiving end of such comments from their Japanese parents and grandparents not so long ago in Brazil. Despite their Japanese families' fear that assimilation would turn them into rootless gaijin (foreigners), Nikkeis born and raised in Brazil learned to skillfully navigate their multiple identities, albeit not without some emotional turmoil. The same is true with the Brazilian youth growing up in Japan today. Despite the rhetoric of "neither here nor there" reinforced by older migrants, many youngsters whom I met could deal confidently with the multiplicity of their identities. This does not mean, however, that they never experienced moments of ambivalence. Some youngsters—especially those who self-identified as mestiço—had to face the ideology of ethnic homogeneity repeatedly as they grew up in Japan.

"I Am Half": Racial Ambivalence of Brazilian Youth in Japan

One night, I was at the Toyota Station with a group of church members who were there for weekly evangelization. Beatriz, addressing Japanese passers-by, started her message in Japanese with the following: "Well, you may wonder who we are—we are Brazilians, Nikkei Brazilians. I myself am *hāfu* [half, or mixed-race]." *Hāfu* is a word Japanese people use to refer to those whom they consider racially mixed. Derived from the English word "half," it points to the Japanese and foreign "halves" of such individuals. Beatriz rarely used the word during our conversations, even when she spoke about the ambivalence she used to feel about her physical appearance. When I asked her later if she really thought of herself as a hāfu, she responded, "Ah, that was just so Japanese people could understand more easily. The only word in Japanese for people like me is hāfu. I myself don't really care about how people may perceive me."

It took Beatriz many years to reach this nonchalant attitude, according to her parents. Luana and Guilherme vividly remembered Beatriz's struggles in school. Guilherme, for instance, recollected an incident when Beatriz was in kindergarten: "Whenever I finished work early, or on my days off, I went [to the kindergarten] to pick her up. I noticed that she didn't run up to me like other kids; it sometimes took a long time to even find her. Even when I—or the teachers there—found her, she was still very quiet and wouldn't come close to me. She was embarrassed by me, you know. She later told my wife, 'Daddy's nose is weird.' She didn't want other kids to see me." As a small child surrounded by Japanese peers, Beatriz was growing increasingly self-conscious about the "non-Japanese" parts of herself and her family. Similarly, Lucas—a twenty-five-year-old Nikkei man who came to Japan at the age of three—told me the following about the year he spent at a local Japanese elementary school. His mother was non-Nikkei and his father was Nikkei.

> Well, my experience at the Japanese school was—just awful. [Laughs.] From day one, I was bullied. They would leave me behind intentionally when all the children in the neighborhood were supposed to go to school together in a group. They would hide my shoes so I couldn't go home. They would call me "*Butajiru-jin* [Brazilian pig]!" To think about it now, it is quite normal for small children to pick on those who looked different—with a face like this [points at his face], I stood out. My Japanese was still very poor, too. But at the time, it hurt me so deeply. I was only a child.

In the end, his parents transferred Lucas to a Brazilian private school because the bullying did not seem to stop.

Brazil has often celebrated racial mixture as the foundation of national identity, while Japan has traditionally viewed it as a disruption to the vision of ethnic homogeneity that should unite the nation. In Japanese, the word closest to the Portuguese term *mestiço* is *hāfu*, which does not focus on the unity of multiple elements but rather highlights the distinctiveness of each of the two "halves"—Japanese and foreign. "Half" individuals are at times coveted for the desirability of their exotic foreignness, especially if they appear to possess "white" features—small round face, big eyes, long legs, pale skin, and so on. For example, many hāfu Japanese work as models in the fashion industry. They can, however, also be ostracized as a perceived threat to the racial purity that is the centerpiece of national identity in Japan. This is why mixed-race children can be particularly vulnerable to bullying: they seem to disrupt the social boundary between the Japanese and the foreign.[23] Many mixed-race Brazilian youth become self-conscious of their looks as they grow up in this social context. Although some are greeted with envy for their "ideal" features, others grow to loathe their foreign "half" that seems to set them apart from their Japanese peers. Those few in the latter group who try to conceal their Brazilian identity in the effort to "pass as Japanese" become a frequent topic of conversation among Nikkei migrants: "The son of so-and-so never brings his Japanese friends home because then they would know that he is Brazilian," for instance. Such stories usually elicit gasps, rolling of eyes, or dry laughs from older migrants. They further the widespread perception that family becomes disintegrated in Japan.

Life at the Margin

What constitutes the in-between subjectivity, or the sense of *nem lá nem cá*, among Nikkei Brazilians in Japan? I have discussed its making in three broad steps. First, the "return" migration to the ancestral homeland transformed Nikkei Brazilians from Asian whites to delinquent Latinos. Although Nikkeis enjoy the image of First World discipline—which at times borders on robotic rigidity—in Brazil, they come to internalize the stereotype of Third World volatility—which can encompass fun-loving passion—in Japan. The pervasive sense of afastamento, or estrangement from family ties, fuels the widespread feeling that the "culture of discipline" that Nikkeis once embodied in Brazil is no more. In place of discipline, afastamento gives rise to disorder and delinquency. These shifts demonstrate that affect is a racialized, political, and historical force.[24] Second, Nikkei migrant families struggle to learn Japanese customs such as *shūdan tōkō* and obentō. As they find it challenging to conform to such social conventions, what is left of their Japanese identity further disintegrates and Brazilian subjectivity firmly takes hold vis-à-vis the "rigid and proper" Japanese majority in Japan. The transition from being Japanese to being Brazilian is never complete, but many older Nikkeis come to feel unambiguously Brazilian. Third, the younger generations born or raised in Japan experience an enhanced sense of contested belonging. Even though the Japanese majority considers them to be Brazilian foreigners, many older Nikkei migrants often tell them that they are no longer authentically Brazilian. The Japanese ideology of racial purity, which deems mixed-race persons "half," further renders many migrant youth susceptible to the discourse of "neither here nor there." This does not necessarily mean that all Nikkei youngsters perceive their background as a source of unending cultural dilemma. In reality, many youth are capable of treating their multiple identities as just that—as different aspects of the self—with a rather pragmatic attitude. The rhetoric of *nem lá nem cá*, then, endures not necessarily because it is an emotional reality to all migrants. Rather, it persists because it is borne out of the historical interactions Nikkeis have had over the past century with multiple regimes of mobility, principles of citizenship, and ideologies of race. And it continues to evolve today at the borderlands of ethnicity, nationhood, and belonging.

(emotional) affect vs.
(material) "historical interactions"

Part Three

RENEWED

5

BACK TO THE PRESENT

Encounter with God

Missão Apoio Toyota had a small kitchen and an adjacent eating area that congregants called *cantina missionária* (missionary canteen) behind the main room used for Sunday service. The profit the church made by preparing and selling various Brazilian snacks supported a number of initiatives over the years. During the aftermath of the Great Tōhoku Earthquake in 2011, for example, a handful of congregants drove up to Fukushima to deliver relief goods purchased by the church. The "missionary canteen" seemed to kill two birds with one stone: It financially supported charitable activities while also providing the taste of home. The foods and drinks sold at the canteen were all Brazilian: *pastel* (thin crust pies with assorted fillings), *coxinha* (teardrop-shaped fried dough with shredded chicken meat), *guaraná* (caffeinated soft drink flavored with the seeds of guarana), and so on. My favorite was *feijoada bentō* (boxed lunch with white rice and stew of beans and pork), which congregants prepared on special occasions. It was a marriage of two iconic foods from Japan and Brazil—hot and steamy short-grain Japanese white rice with a warm thick stew reputed to be the Brazilian national dish.[1] If food is an expression of who we are, *feijoada bentō* was no doubt a potent symbol of Nikkei Brazilian identity.

It was at this canteen that I first met Marcelo, a *sansei* in his mid-forties, who regularly helped out in the kitchen. He was a cheerful, talkative, and friendly man. As soon as he found out that I was Japanese, he offered me a *pastel* and a can of *guaraná*. "Here, have some Brazilian food!" When I mumbled with my mouth full that it was delicious, his eyes lit up. He sat next to me and spoke about his life while I finished my drink. He was from a rural part of São Paulo where many Japanese descendants lived. He arrived in Japan in 1990 at the very beginning of dekassegui migration, when there were still few Brazilians in Japan. He could always find jobs easily until the 2008 financial crisis, when he lost his employment and much of his savings. He was unemployed at the moment. He was grateful to the church because he received some financial help in return for his work at the canteen. As we stood up to move to the main room, where the Sunday service was starting, I asked him if I could interview him sometime soon. He nodded with a mischievous grin. "You picked the right person; I have stories to tell!"

He lived in a subsidized housing project in Toyota that was smaller and older than Homi Danchi. I arrived at his apartment in early afternoon. His wife was preparing lunch in the kitchen and his daughter was playing an online game on her phone in the living room. "Sit down on the sofa and make yourself at home," Marcelo said. "We don't have much, but welcome!" He later told me that the apartment was covered by his unemployment insurance. "I worked very hard for the last factory, never saying no when my boss asked me to do *zangyō* [working extra hours]," Marcelo said with a bitter look. "But in the end, they just fired me. They can drop migrant laborers whenever they want. I really want to become *seishain* (full-time employees), but they don't want Brazilians for that."

Marcelo's financial situation at the time of interview would have made him an ideal informant to support the narrative of "coping with poverty," which is widespread in the study of Global Christianity.[2] This explanatory framework, dominant in both academic and popular discourses, explains conversion as a social strategy to enhance access to economic resources. It hints that converts are driven by material deprivation, rather than by their own agency. What he proceeded to tell me that afternoon, however, diverged from such a stereotypical story line. For one thing, he converted to Pentecostalism back in 2005, before the financial crisis robbed him of a steady supply of jobs. Instead of debilitating poverty, Marcelo's conversion narrative started with a vague, almost faint, sense of crisis that haunted him as he went through his daily routine as a migrant laborer in Japan:

Here in Japan, we work so much. In my case, it was normal to have three, even four hours of *zangyō*. Sometimes I'd work from seven in the morning until ten at night. So life turns into a routine of just going back and forth between work and home—factory, home, factory, home. . . . We want to work a lot because we want the money, you know, many want to go back to Brazil. But we have to work as well—sometimes you can't really say no to your boss. So I spent many years just going about my life like that. And you never have time. You don't have time to stop and really think, really feel. I had this emptiness in my heart, you know, but I never really paid attention.

He then described how he initially found the repeated invitation from his Brazilian Pentecostal coworkers for church gatherings annoying because he used to think "*crentes* are all fanatics." Then one day, his wife was diagnosed with breast cancer:

That was . . . hard. Very. I became desperate. I went to a church gathering at my friend's home, I and my wife. Fortunately her surgery went well and she got better. Then she said she didn't want to go any more, but I kept on going. Soon I started going to church, too. Something filled the emptiness in my heart. Then I went to Encounter with God [a three-day prayer camp] . . . Oh! That was great. I felt that I really had the time just for myself and God, to really think about my life, my purpose, His plan for me, you know. So after that, I decided to convert. I found Jesus, finally.

The first thing Marcelo said when prompted to recount how he converted was, "Here in Japan, we work so much." He then described how power dynamics in the factory, heavy workloads, and migrants' focus on economic gain contribute to the exhausting repetitiveness of life. This monotony of life fueled the sense of what Marcelo calls "emptiness in heart," which lasted for years, since he did not have time to "pay attention" to it. His depiction of his preconversion life overlaps greatly with Takeshi's observation about "stop living" (*deixar de viver*) in Chapter 3. That is, migrants often "put aside living" so they can live the better future purportedly awaiting them in Brazil. Mind-numbing routine and suspension of life constituted the basic tone of Marcelo's reality before conversion. Marcelo initially resisted his Pentecostal colleagues' invitations for church gatherings and his own desire to go, as he used to believe that evangelicals were fanatic. He then recounted his wife's cancer as the final push that enabled him to overcome initial reluctance. It is important to note here that the suffering from the illness is not the driving theme of his narrative, nor does the subsequent healing of the disease mark the climax of the story. In fact, he matter-of-factly admitted that his wife simply stopped going to church gatherings soon after her recovery. The experience of the illness, then, is a onetime trigger rather than a long-running undercurrent of the story.

What runs through Marcelo's narrative from the beginning to the end is the numbing monotony of life, which causes him a dull sense of crisis: that he was not stopping to reflect on his life, that life is slipping away like sand between his fingers, and that by merely going through the motions every day, he was risking going through his whole life without experiencing anything. This theme of "no time to live" also provides the moment of catharsis, which happens during the prayer camp called Encounter with God. He stated, "I felt that I really had the time just for myself and God, to really think about my life, my purpose, His plan for me, you know." For Marcelo, his conversion was not propelled by some traumatic suffering such as illness, discrimination, or poverty, although he recounted all of them to some degree in the interview. Rather, what made him susceptible to an "encounter with God" is the feeling of suffocation that time was not allowing him to truly live.

Marcelo's feeling of "no time to live" is far from an isolated idiosyncratic experience but a widespread sentiment among Brazilian workers in Japan. Virtually all working Brazilians—male and female, old and young—told me that they never had time. In the beginning of my fieldwork, this used to baffle me. Why would they convert to Pentecostalism when this means that what little time they had left would now be spent on numerous church activities? Why do so many come to the church at 9:30 P.M. after a long day of work on a Tuesday night to study the Bible, when this likely means a lack of sleep for their already tired bodies? Why do so many show up to Friday night gathering around 9 P.M., when the long-awaited weekend of free time has just started? Why would they actively decide to participate in something that takes away even more of their already scarce time? The answer lies in the elasticity of time itself. In this ethnographic context, time was not just a linear quantifiable construct that simply passed or accumulated. Rather, time stretched, transformed, looped back, and expanded in the moment—and it was Christian practices that often helped migrants experience time in new ways.[3]

Modern Again in Japan?

"What is your work?" Presbyter Guilherme addressed the congregation. A Sunday service was in progress and he was preaching about "the meaning of work" (*o significado de obra*). "*Qual é o seu trabalho?*" He repeated the rhetorical question. After a pause, he continued, "Yes, I know. We work in factories. We assemble auto parts. We make wings for airplanes. We make foods for convenience stores. That's our work, right?" He looked over his audience with a quizzing look and then continued, "But our true job, the most important work of all, it is to be part of God's plan in this nation, brothers and sisters." While he was evoking a common Christian narrative of spiritual calling, the parallel he drew next between spiritual work and factory labor was quite creative. He went on, "You know, our work and God's work are similar in many ways. Have you thought about this before? Just like us who assemble auto parts on the conveyor belt, God is working on us and assembling us so we can be whole, as we move through our life here on earth." He left the pulpit and walked from one side of the room to the other as if there were a moving conveyor belt, with one hand mimicking the motions of assembling auto parts. Many attendants laughed out loud at his gestures, which likely stimulated the muscle memory in their own hands as well.

Having reached the wall, he again turned to the congregation and emphasized, "And *this* is where God does a *kensa* [examination] on us, to make sure that we are spiritually complete for salvation!" Now everyone laughed. It was such a good metaphor. Like *hirukin* (day shift), *yakin* (night shift), and *zangyō* (working extra hours), *kensa* was among the Japanese words related to factory labor that most Brazilian migrants understood regardless of their Japanese language skills. It refers to the final phase of manufacturing when products receive a quality check. Many migrants who had worked in the *kensa* department could tell a handful of horror stories about *huryō* ("no good," which was a shorthand for deficient products). If a worker lets a *huryō* slip through and has it shipped out, he or she could be the target of collective shaming akin to a witch hunt. One informant, for example, told me that he was ordered to write a public "apology letter" for his carelessness to the whole factory after he missed one huryō. The fear of generating huryō was exacerbated by the fact that many factories upheld "zero huryō" as the official goal which, given the human proclivity for mistakes, was virtually impossible to achieve. But God is free of human error, and He would never let a huryō slip through, Presbyter Guilherme seemed to imply. God's *kensa* on the spiritual conveyor belt is impeccable because, as I was told many times, He judges every soul impartially.

"So never forget what your true job is, brothers and sisters," Presbyter Guilherme reiterated in his message. "Your true job is to contribute to the God's great work on this earth, in this nation. The purpose of your life is much, much more than just working in factory and making money. Let's see . . . Have you ever seen a car on the street, or a sandwich at a convenience store, and felt like running up to it thinking, 'Ah, that's what I make in my factory'?" Many congregants shouted "Yes!" while laughing. He seemed to have struck a chord with his audience again. Nodding deeply, he stressed, "*That's* how you should feel in your true work as well. Whatever you see in your daily life, remember that there is God's work in it, and that what you do for God matters. We are all part of God's great plan."

In this sermon, Presbyter Guilherme contrasts two different kinds of work: unskilled wage labor that is all too familiar to many of his audience, on the one hand, and spiritual work that makes converts become part of "God's great plan," on the other. He even uses two different words for each type of "work": *trabalho* for the former and *obra* for the latter. According to him, the spiritual work that contributes to God's *obra* is the "true job" (*trabalho verdadeiro*) of migrant converts. The ingenuity of his sermon lies in the humorous comparisons between factory labor and spiritual work, which appealed to his audience precisely because they usually did not regard the two as "similar" in any way. On the contrary, I often heard congregants who attended church events immediately after work claim half-jokingly, "*Now* my real work starts." Precisely because they viewed *trabalho* and *obra* in oppositional terms, they found it funny to picture God perform *kensa* on the assembly line in heaven. This unexpected comparison also made some Christian concepts—such as God's judgment—more vivid to the audience, most of whom worked as manual laborers.

Presbyter Guilherme's metaphors flavor mundane manual labor with transcendent spiritual interpretations. The message is clear. You may toil on the factory floor for days on end, but that is not who you really are. You are more important than that, and God knows this. That is why your true work belongs to Him. "Never forget what your true job is, brothers and sisters," as he put it. Such rhetoric of spiritual authenticity is commonplace among migrant churches around the globe—Ghanaians and Jamaicans in England, Latin Americans in the United States, and Haitians in French West Indies, to name a few.[4] The studies about these groups have shown that the sense of spiritual advancement eases the pervasive self-perception of economic and cultural underdevelopment among foreign migrants. A similar story line seems to guide Presbyter Guilherme's sermon. They may be dispensable foreign laborers with less status than the Japanese majority in terms of economic and social class, but they are more enlightened and advanced in spiritual realms. Indeed, many converts made critical comments about what they saw as "the Japanese tradition" or "culture," thereby implying that their ideas and practices were more modern, if not morally superior.[5] Such remarks sometimes concerned religious practices in Japan. As Pastor Cid said in one Bible study meeting, "Japanese people make those little houses and believe that their gods can live there. But God cannot stay in physical structures that men built for Him because He is omnipresent." His tone was not accusatory but instead filled with teacherly concern. He was referring to buildings at Shinto shrines that supposedly house objects that embody divine spirits (*goshintai*), which some converts explicitly referred to as a clear case of idolatry. Even those who politely refrained from using the word *idolatry* in my presence made clear that the practice was morally untenable.

Anthropologists of Christianity have commonly analyzed conversion in relation to the theme of modernity—or at least with implications for forward temporal movement. Peter van der Veer, for example, characterized the worldwide growth of Christianity as "conversion to modernities."[6] Along a similar line, Birgit Meyer observed that Pentecostal converts among the Peki Ewe in Ghana embrace Christianity as the promising path to modernity, although conversion comes with an emotional and social price. They must cut themselves off from generations-old obligations to serve their ancestral and lineage gods. Ewe spirits continue to possess converts, and the church translates them as demons that must be exorcised in collective services. Meyer summarized, "Pentecostalism provides a bridge over which it is possible to move back and forth [between Christianity and Ewe religion] and thereby to thematise modernity's ambivalence."[7] Thus, the global growth of Pentecostalism may have been conducive to the spread of modern identity in various parts of the world.[8]

Is the interdependence of conversion and modernity also manifest among Nikkei converts in Japan, who used to represent hypermodernity in Brazil? My findings indeed suggest such implications. Just as Presbyter Guilherme asserted that spiritual work can help converts advance a greater divine cause amid their stagnant factory labor, Pastor Cid implied that Christian knowledge can help converts see the truth about things that the Japanese majority still could not grasp. In spiritual terms, then, Nikkei Brazilian converts were no longer backward. In this vein, conversion to Pentecostalism can be read as a collective endeavor to restore and rebuild in Japan the modern social status they once had in Brazil. In other words, the spiritual advancement to "modern" religious sensibility through conversion can counteract the disappointing failure of material or social progress that their initial project of migration should have realized through upward mobility. They can be modern again in Japan in spiritual, if not in economic, terms.

Return to the Present

But is the desire for the return to modern identity all that there is to the stories of Nikkei migrant converts? Can it explain the powerful emotions that Marcelo experienced when he finally had "the time just for myself and God"? Maybe things are not so simple. In addition to the one geared toward modernity, my findings point to yet another temporality at work. That is, conversion as a return to the present.

Simon Coleman, in his study of charismatic Christians in Sweden, described the coexistence and interrelation of two distinct temporalities.[9] On the one hand, church members "invoke" history by acknowledging the repetitive and mimetic nature of their actions. But they also "make" history by framing their experiences as new events discontinuous from the past and directed toward ultimate salvation. Their emphasis on "right now," Coleman observed, simultaneously engages both perceptions of history and thereby creates a charismatic temporality that dovetails the past and the future, the personal and the collective, and continuity and rupture. It is such a charismatic temporality that sustains "chronic conversion" couched in the succession of renewals in the present.[10] Coleman also pointed out how charismatic actions in the present are effective in enacting future time. Therefore, the focus on the present does not necessarily entail the negligence of the future, but a change in temporal locus of action.

The charismatic temporality of "right now, right here" exerts tremendous appeal to such migrants as Nikkei Brazilians in Japan, who have been suspended between two futures. Tired of the perpetual suspension of life that the planned return to Brazil has imposed upon them, many welcome the charismatic temporality like a fresh breeze of air. "Do you think your life starts again once you return to Brazil?" One longtime church member preached to the congregation one Sunday: "I've heard enough people say, 'I'll start going to church again once I'm back in Brazil. I'll start being a good person again once I'm in Brazil. Right now, I'm busy saving money.' God doesn't work that way. No, with God, it's always right now, right here. God doesn't say, 'Oh, you can start working on yourself next week.' You have to restart your life right now, right here—in Japan." She admonished her fellow migrant converts to stop postponing life until the imagined return to Brazil in the future and instead told them to restart moral renewal "right now" in Japan.

A session from a Bible study course designed by Missão Apoio drives this point home. One night, Sara asked me if I wanted to come to a Bible study group. I accepted her offer, and in the following week, we met at a coffee shop in a neighboring city of Toyota where she lived. As soon as I arrived, I quickly realized it was going to be just Sara and I, although I had been under the impression that it was a group study. She clarified that it was actually a one-on-one Bible study course that her church was developing for those interested in or new to the faith. After we had some back-and-forth about my ambiguous position as a researcher, I decided to accept the opportunity, thanked her for her time, and sat down. After all, it was true that I was "interested in the Bible and curious to learn," as she put it. I quickly found out that the course was designed in part to proselytize Japanese individuals, because the handout Sara gave me was in Japanese, but the one she kept in her hand was in Portuguese. She neither spoke nor read Japanese.

Faithful to the handout, she started our first session by telling a story from the gospel of Mark (Mark 10:46–52). Bartimaeus, a blind beggar in the city of Jericho, hears Jesus Christ and shouts out to him, begging for mercy. When Jesus asks him what he desires, he asks to be cured of blindness, which Jesus grants instantaneously, saying that his faith has healed him. Bartimaeus thereafter follows Jesus along the road. Then Sara moved on to explain the important points of this story, mostly following the bullet points on the prepared material. When it came to the part that discussed "what obstacles Bartimaeus had to overcome to get what he desired," however, she put down the sheet and started telling how she related to the story:

> You see how Bartimaeus overcame his complacency [*comodismo*] and conquered his own pride [*orgulho*]? This is really, really difficult. It's hard to get out of the habit of being satisfied with the routine. It's even harder, for some people, to let go of one's pride, surrender, and just cry out for help.

We Brazilians typically came to Japan to work and earn money. Very quickly, we fall into this spiral of meaningless routine. Home, factory, home, factory, home, factory, party with friends, sleep, home, factory . . . You know, it's really hard to have a sense of purpose in this kind of lifestyle. I hated it. I only liked the weekend when I could party with friends, but even that was empty somehow when I look back now.

But once you accept Jesus, life cannot be a routine any more. Every day is new with Jesus. He fortifies us, and we are renewed like an eagle. But you cannot make this change happen on your own. You need God for real change.

Taken together with other findings discussed in this book so far, I believe it is more than a mere coincidence that the story of Bartimaeus marked the beginning of the ten-week Bible course. In many ways, the biblical character embodies the sense of renewal in the present that many migrants come to crave after years of suspended life in Japan.

The stories of Marcelo and Sara show that migration and conversion are both temporal projects that reshape human life in tandem. As Nancy Munn observed, "In a lived world, spatial and temporal dimensions cannot be disentangled, and the two commingle in various ways."[1] Through temporality, migration and conversion become interlocked in the experiences of migrant converts.

Flowing in the Holy Spirit

Instead of returning to the future through the forward-looking temporality of migration, migrant converts find a way to return to the present through the charismatic temporality of "right now, right here." But it can actually be very difficult to focus on the present, or to rein in one's mind so it will not wander ahead into the future or back into the past. This is especially so for people like Nikkei migrants in Japan, who can look back to their now lost modern status in Brazil or look ahead to the craved "better future" at the end of the migratory journey. When it is so easy to become caught up with the past or the future, how exactly can they return to the present? One obvious pathway consists of discursive messages. As Sara's interpretation of Bartimaeus's healing shows, migrant converts foster a vision of temporal renewal in the present by garnering powerful meanings from sermons, testimonies, and Bible studies.

Another important pathway is prayer. Takie, for example, was known for being quite skilled in the art of prayer among church members. Since I attended the weekly Friday night home gatherings hosted by her and her husband, I saw her pray for and with others many times, and she always seemed absorbed in the practice. Indeed, she related during an interview how she would sometimes lose track of time during prayer: "Sometimes, I come out of prayer and think, 'Wow, it's this late already? I have to start cooking dinner!'" When I asked her to describe the experience in more detail, she responded, "It's like a ball of warm energy getting bigger and bigger inside you. As I keep praying, it swells up and fills me completely from within like a big warm balloon. Then, sometimes, it's like I am not thinking the words anymore, but they are coming out of my mouth like a river. That's when I know that I am flowing in the Holy Spirit [*fluindo no Espírito Santo*]."

With the phrase "flowing in the Holy Spirit," Takie seems to be describing the effects of a mental state called absorption: "the capacity to focus in on the mind's object . . . and to allow that focus to increase while diminishing our attention to the myriad of everyday distractions that accompany the management of normal life."[12] My informants at Missão Apoio frequently related episodes of absorption in prayer, during which one's sense of time becomes more elastic. The majority related stories of absorption during the time they specifically dedicated to prayer, but Sara had an interesting habit that only a handful of other converts shared. She often prayed in her mind as she worked at an assembly line in a factory. "It's the best time to pray, really," she said with a smile.

> Right now, I work on the line for interior panels, you know, the panel that covers your music player in a car. I do only three things on each piece that comes my way on the conveyor belt. [Gestures the three steps.] Simple. Any idiot can do it. [Laughs.] . . .
>
> After a while, I'm not thinking anymore. My hands remember what to do, and if you think, you can't do it anymore. . . . "Where does this piece go?" You can't think that. You take too much time, you disrupt the line, and the *hanchō* [team leader] shouts at you. "Ah! You again! At this rate, we all have to do *zangyō* because of you!" . . . I used to have panic attacks. What do they think I am, a robot? . . .
>
> But then I started to pray—when my mind goes blank, I pray. "Please, God, I want to leave the factory job, my hands hurt." "I know I have to be loving like

you, God, but I hate my boss." Or, "I want to talk to you, God, I really need a boyfriend here—are you listening to me?" [Laughs.] It's the most exquisite experience [*experiência mais gostosa*], I can just talk and talk to Him, and God feels so close there. . . . Sometimes, when I really talk to Him, then next thing you notice, it's already lunch break! It used to feel like a whole day from morning to lunchtime, but with the power of praying time passes so quickly [*pela força da oração o tempo passa bem rapidinho*].

Sara seems to be describing two distinct temporalities here. One is a temporal modality of "clock-time," or quantified time instrumental to the work-discipline of capitalism.[13] The flexible labor system in late capitalism attempts to squeeze the maximum degree of productivity out of unskilled laborers, which makes Sara feel robbed of humanity: "What do they think I am, a robot?" In such an environment, time is a linear construct that is monitored and accumulated because wage is based on the minute-by-minute performance as well as the quantity of time put into labor. This time passes very slowly, as Sara notes, since many workers numb their mind in the present so that they can receive the monetary compensation in the future.

The other modality is the charismatic temporality of absorption in the present. Instead of simply letting her mind "go blank," she activates her imagination to practice prayer, which to many born-again Christians consists in a lively conversation with God.[14] The focus achieved through prayer can make the time stretch and expand in the present. Unlike clock-time, this time is nonlinear and nonquantified. By becoming absorbed in prayer, Sara could transform her time into something more elastic than a steady progression from one second to another. In this regard, charismatic prayer is a technique that mediates a process called temporalization, or a view of time "as a symbolic process continually being produced in everyday practices."[15] To put it more simply, Sara is *making* time instead of just passing it.

Thus, many migrant converts learn to access—and create—the charismatic present of "right now, right here" through absorption in prayer.[16] Given that those with such flow-like experiences often feel rejuvenated, the temporalization of the charismatic present through Pentecostal practices may have some therapeutic effect—especially for those who have not inhabited the experientially immediate "now" for many years.

[handwritten note:] — expansive, productive charismatic temporality — distinct not necessarily from "secular" time but from industrial capitalism's "clock time"

Break from Temporal Suffocation

"Here we are!" Lucia exclaimed, turning around toward the backseats where I was seated with her two teenage sons. "Junya, wake up! Everyone is here—they are waiting for us!" The boys rubbed their eyes and yawned as they sat up from their reclined seats. It was almost midnight. Stepping out of the car, I saw a dozen cars parked on both sides of the narrow mountain road. It indeed seemed that we were the last people to arrive at the *vigília*—the late-night prayer gathering that Missão Apoio Toyota held at a small mountain roughly fifteen minutes away from the church every Friday night. Although I usually drove there myself, I decided to ride with Lucia and her sons that night, since she told me that there was one open seat in her car. "*Paz* [Peace]," a voice greeted us from the darkness—there were no street lights—and I recognized that it was Pastor Cid when he turned on his flashlight. "Ready for a little walk?"

"*Paz*, Pastor, just a second," Lucia answered. "We have to put on mosquito repellent first—they are quite annoying now that it's almost summer."

The group of roughly twenty church members gathered at the trailhead of the short path that led to the mountain top where there was a small clearing. The air was warm and humid, and we could hear frogs croaking in a nearby pond. "Okay, everyone, let's go," Pastor Cid said. We started walking. As usual, he was using a long tree branch that he had picked up from the ground as an improvised cane. He also sang worship songs in Portuguese in his low baritone voice, which reverberated beautifully through the dark forest, as he led the group in the roughly twenty-minute walk. Once we were on the top of the mountain, we formed one large circle for the first collective prayer. When it was over, then it was time for individual prayer. Some found their own spots to pray in the clearing while others went into the forest to look for a more isolated place. Especially in a moonless night, it was mostly through hearing that people could locate each other after the circle disbanded. The darkness soon filled up with voices. Some were loud and expressive, and others were low and meditative. Most were in Portuguese, but some were in Japanese. Many prayed in intelligible words, but some were also speaking in tongues. The prayer session turned into an improvised orchestra of emotive voices, ebbing and flowing in the warm darkness of the summer night. One voice always stood out, and it was Pastor Cid's. He usually started out with an expressive praise of the Father in Heaven that, after a quick crescendo, always turned into full-blown glossolalia. It was as if his voice conducted the supposedly individual prayers, taking the lead in everyone's effort to—as one regular attendant put it—"experience God more intimately." When his voice slowly came down from the climactic fast-pitch utterances to slow and soft muttering, no longer in tongues, other voices followed him to the anticipated closure. I stood still in my spot as the wave of voices gradually simmered down, eventually melting into the chirping of crickets, the rustling of leaves, and the murmur of life in the dark forest—a pregnant pause that lasted only for a few seconds before people started to come out of their respective spots in bushes to gather once again in a large circle.

By the time we walked back to the trailhead and said good night to one another before driving off, it was past 3 A.M. As usual, I was exhausted. So were Lucia's two young sons, who quickly curled up and started sleeping on our way back to Homi Danchi. I sat in the passenger's seat and made small talk with Lucia, but my eyelids were heavy. Since I was not used to such late-night activities, I always found *vigília* rather time consuming and physically tiring. I turned to Lucia, who spoke excitedly about her family's plan to drive to a beach during the summer. "Lucia, can I ask you something?"

"Of course, *querida*, what is it?"

"Um, why do you come to *vigília* every Friday? I mean, it's late and sometimes you feel sleepy, don't you?"

Lucia laughed softly. "Well," she responded, "Here in Japan, we work so much. And I have kids too so I am literally running around all the time. When I come here or go to church activities like Encounter with God, it's just really nice, because I have the time for myself. It's like I can finally breathe." She rolled down the window to let some fresh air into the car. Maybe she did feel sleepy, too. "Factory, home, factory, home, factory . . . You just have this . . . emptiness [*vazio*] in your heart when you live your life like that. That's why I need the time just for me and God. It feels good in that place. I feel truly alive."

When migrant converts speak of having time "just for me and God," they are clearly not referring to clock-time, which saturates their experience of unskilled wage labor. Since the majority tolerate the work-discipline imposed by clock-time to save money and return to Brazil, seeking time outside of work means the pursuit of time that is not spent on the preparation for the future. In other words, they are looking for the time in which they can live the present without postponing or sacrificing it. This other time is the charismatic temporality of immediate present, which converts learn to cultivate through Pentecostal prayer practices.

As I have pointed out above, many Nikkei migrants approach their conversion to Pentecostalism as a move toward modernity, or a restoration of their modern status in Japan. The stories of migrants such as Sara and Lucia, however, demonstrate that there is another experiential aspect to the Pentecostal movement. That is, conversion also mediates a break from the symptom of temporal suffocation. It is a return to the present.

Temporal Tandem

I have thus far elaborated on how migration and conversion hinge upon a set of heterogeneous temporalities and yet become interlocked in the subject formations of migrant converts—the kind of relationship that may be termed a "temporal tandem" of migratory and religious movements. By temporal tandem, I mean a joint production or reconfiguration of time—or temporalization—that simultaneously draws on and drives seemingly disparate and yet closely related projects.

Rijk van Dijk's work on the relationship between migration and religion can illuminate the concept of temporal tandem well. He wrote about the different modalities of time and modes of subjectivity manifest in Pentecostal practices in two contexts: one in the migrants' home country of Ghana and the other in the host Dutch society. In Ghana, leaders at prayer camps emphasize the "breaking" with kinship ties and tradition as well as the move toward individuality by focusing on participants' past sins and the long-term future. In diaspora, in contrast, scrutinizing the past for potential sins becomes taboo so as not to expose the vulnerability of some migrants with painful memories (e.g., illegal status or prostitution). Of particular relevance here is van Dijk's observation about the relationship between conversion and migration:

> Hence, prayer camps introduce the person to transnational and transcultural relations as an emergent stranger; as somebody detached from the bonds with the family, . . . and therefore unconstrained in the attempts to "make it to the West," to "get the papers" and to become prosperous. . . . The prayer camps' discourse promotes a sense of strangerhood that starts at home and serves as a preparation and incubation to what they might expect when they travel to the West.[17]

My research among Pentecostal Brazilians in Japan builds on van Dijk's insight and expands it beyond the case of "strangerhood" in Ghanaian diaspora.

In transnational mobility, conversion and migration often become mutually reinforcing as seemingly disparate temporal modalities commingle to shape migrants' subjectivities in dynamic ways. In this sense, migrant converts experience a temporal tandem. Through temporality, they experience the fundamental interworking of spatial movement and spiritual development.

In the case of Nikkei migrant converts in Japan, the working of temporal tandem is apparent in how the prolonged suspension of life anticipates the charismatic temporality of "right now." Indeed, it is through temporalization that migration and conversion become firmly interlocked to generatively shape the realities of migrant converts. I must also add that temporal tandem works in multidirectional ways. For instance, many migrants, once converted, start to frame migration as a mission driven by higher purpose, for they are to evangelize a modern and yet "pagan" nation such as Japan. In this view, Japan once again becomes the potential future of the migrants, but this time, the future of the worldwide Christian frontier. Other migrants return to Brazil expressing less anxiety and fear of failing to actualize in Brazil the rosy middle-class future. Charismatic rhetoric typically flattens out geographical, temporal, and cultural differences that we often associate with national borders.[18] To Pentecostal migrants, life should be the same—equally difficult and equally rewarding—whether in Japan or Brazil, as long as they are in the presence of God. It is one time—one temporality—that must reign over both countries, which is an endless and continuous succession of renewals in the present.

THE CULTURE OF LOVE

Graduation Ceremony of Love

Love! Love you! Love Forever! No matter where I turned in the room, the word jumped into my eyes. The main room of the church was decorated with colorful flowers and red heart-shaped balloons with "love" in English on them. It was the day of *formatura*, or graduation, for a course called Casados para Sempre that Missão Apoio Toyota's marriage ministry taught twice a year. The leaders encouraged married members to take the course—even with unconverted spouses, if they agreed—to learn how to achieve what the title promised: *casados para sempre*, or "married for life." Participants attended the weekly class for thirteen weeks before receiving the certificate of completion at the graduation ceremony. Roughly fifteen couples joined the first class of 2014 and they were going to be certified as new graduates on this day.

One by one, graduating couples walked into the room with big smiles on their faces. They walked slowly from the back of the room toward the front pulpit on the rolled-out red carpet while the invited guests—mostly friends and families—clapped warmly from both sides. The attires and proceedings of the ceremony were reminiscent of a wedding except that, instead of her father, each woman was escorted by her husband. All were dressed in formal clothes, with men in suit and tie and women in dress and makeup. The program also included a ballroom dance party after the certification ceremony, during which the attendants danced to Brazilian gospel ballads. All the graduates offered their testimonies at some point of the day. "First of all I would like to thank God," they would typically start, "for giving these *ferramentas* [tools] for better marriage through the Word." Then many would elaborate on particular topics that made a strong impression, ranging from the idea that marriage was "a covenant not a contract" to the necessity of forgiveness for one another. "I hope you are standing here today knowing a bit more about the presence of God in our marriage," Presbyter Bruno said during his sermon. "1 John 4:8 tells us that whoever does not love does not know God, for God is love. So every Christian must learn how to love, and this is especially true in our marriage. . . . Marriage is not just about us; no, on the contrary, it's about much more than us. By loving your husband or wife, you are keeping the eternal covenant between men and Christ." He congratulated the graduating couples for their contribution to the Kingdom of God through the hard work they put into their marriage and family. "Family is the building block of God's Kingdom," he stressed, "and by loving, you are being a fierce fighter for God."

The highlight of the graduation ceremony was *confissões de amor* (confessions of love), in which each couple expressed their renewed affection for one another. Again, the enactment of romantic courtship was palpable. The husband would get down on one knee with the wife's hand in his, look up into her eyes, and declare his unwavering love for her. "You are just as beautiful as the day when I first met you, there on the beach in Santos [a port city in the state of São Paulo]," one husband said. "I remember your long dark hair dancing in the wind. . . . You looked so pretty and I couldn't get my eyes off of you. That day was the beginning of our story, written by God. Because deep down in my heart, I knew that I wanted to marry you." The wife, a nisei woman in her late thirties, giggled and glanced at the audience with an embarrassed but happy smile. Everyone was cheering, clapping, whistling, and occasionally shouting teasing words such as "I'm jealous!" I was giggling, too. It was such a playful and joyous moment. It was clear that couples were speaking not just to each other but to the other attendants as well, and in that sense, they were performing love and romance for the rest of us to witness.

Another couple whom I knew walked up to the stage. Takie and Jun, both sansei from the state of Paraná, led the home group that I attended in Homi Danchi. Jun went down on one knee and looked up into Takie's eyes without saying a word for a few seconds. Then he started, "The first time we met, we were both working, weren't we, at Morishita [a nearby automotive factory]. Everyone was so tired and stressed. Nobody was smiling. Nobody was happy.

FIGURE 4. Confession of love at the graduation ceremony of Casados para Sempre (Married for Life) at Missão Apoio Toyota, 2014. Photo courtesy: Luiz Harada and Wilson Narita.

Me, too, I was so irritable and depressed back then; it was before I found Jesus." Jun then reminisced about the organizational change at their workplace that brought him to the same assembly line as hers. "And when I saw you, the whole factory lit up. We were in those ugly uniforms, working and sweating, but *meu amor* (my love), you were so pretty. . . . I may not have realized this right away, but it was very special. God made you for me." Takie, like other women, listened contently with a smile as her husband went on to thank her for being such a great mother for their two children despite all the difficulties of being a dekassegui. "Te amo, minha querida, para sempre" (I love you, my dear, forever), Jun said firmly. "Eu te amo também . . . muito, muito, muito" (I love you, too . . . so, so, so much), Takie responded, choking up in tears.

History of Love

Love constitutes a key emotion in many Christian cultures. From Asia to Africa to the Americas, Christians around the world speak about love, weep tears of love, and act in the name of love. In California, the members of Vineyard churches strive to practice love and compassion through immersive prayer.[1] In Russia, those enrolled in a drug rehabilitation program run by the Orthodox Church try to reconfigure their moral subjectivities through the experience of love.[2] In Brazil, Pentecostal Afro-Brazilians reclaim pride in their black identity by speaking about God's universal love.[3] In Zambia, Christian gay men claim their belonging in the nation by fusing the rhetoric of queer empowerment with the notion of God's unconditional love.[4]

This apparent ubiquity of love leads many believers to think that love is therefore a universal Christian emotion. And the members of Missão Apoio Toyota were no exception. The single most important message from Jesus, many converts would tell me, was love—timeless, transcendent, and transformative. Love consequently served as the central theme in many church events. At the graduation ceremony in the opening scene, for example, love figured as an emotion at once divine and romantic. It was divine because it came from God and cemented their marital union as a covenant. It was romantic because it helped converts become more expressive and affectionate toward their companions. But is this kind of love, which fuses the rhetoric of holiness and the aspiration for romance, as universal as converts claim it to be? Is it possible that love, despite its rhetorical ubiquity among Christians, has particular historical connotations within the cultural settings inhabited by Nikkei converts? Put more simply, what is love and what does it do to Brazilian migrant converts in Japan?

Their claim for the universality of love has some ground in that such a discourse enjoys global circulation today. The trope of romantic courtship and companionate marriage has spread to various parts of the world, making many couples to opt for "modern" love marriage instead of "traditional" arranged marriage.[5] The course Casados para Sempre itself is also a case in point. Casados para Sempre is the Portuguese translation of Married for Life, a seminar developed by American evangelical authors Mike and Marilyn Phillipps back in 1983. Today, the course and textbook of the same title are popular among many evangelical churches around the globe. The Missão Apoio churches in Japan regularly received the shipment of Portuguese-language textbooks from Brazil, where many Pentecostal churches taught the class.[6] Thus, a quick look at the distribution chain of the seminar materials already reveals the transnational connectedness of evangelical and Pentecostal networks, through which the trope of Christian love has been gaining traction in many societies around the world.[7]

Love, however, is inseparable from the everyday politics surrounding gender, race, class, and kinship. In Mozambique, for example, young women participate in the "love therapy [*terapia do amor*]" administered by the Universal Church of the Kingdom of God to strive for companionate marriage that they view as more modern than traditional marriage mediated by kin. They find the therapy attractive because it offers a new way to approach marital union as a relational commitment grounded on interpersonal intimacy between spouses. Love therapy thus provides young upwardly mobile women with space, ideas, and practices to give meaning to their newfound economic independence and social autonomy. It also helps them disentangle themselves from their extended kin and traditional expectations, which many perceive as oppressive.[8] As real as the transnational connections of Pentecostal networks may be, love is not utterly transcendent from the sociopolitical contexts in which Christians live.

At Missão Apoio Toyota, too, love was not detached from the migrants' struggles and aspirations. Jun narrated that love felt all the more powerful in his ugly factory uniform. He felt that love literally "lit up" the gray sterile surroundings that he endured as a migrant laborer. His confession of love points to the necessity to situate love within the political context of Nikkei transnational mobility.

Learning to Love

It smelt delicious. I looked up from the conveyor belt, where I was packaging puddings. A large pile of baked cheesecakes fresh out of the huge oven rolled into the room on a squeaking cart. I quickly looked down just in time to put a sticker on the next pudding, then the next, and then the next. Roughly five of us were working at the line to package the puddings that were going out for local convenience stores in the next delivery truck. The batch we were working on was almost done, so I guessed that my next task was at the small mountain of cheesecakes. The team leader indeed called my name and those of several other workers. I stood next to Camila, a thirty-four-year-old married sansei woman with two little boys, whom I knew from my home group in Homi Danchi. She was a short, plump, and well-humored woman and I enjoyed being around her a lot. Standing side by side, we took out cheesecakes from round steel pans to softly place each one in a large silver tray. "I like this task because you can chat while you work," Camila said. "We don't need to work at the pace of the conveyor belt." I nodded in agreement.

She then started telling me about the last class of Married for Life, which she was taking with her husband. The seminar was unexpectedly good, Camila told me. "I decided to take it simply because Bruno [the presbyter] was so persistent. I was like, 'Fine! I'll take it!' But it's actually good; I feel some real change already."

"For example?" I asked, picking up another pan of cheesecake. Since I could not attend the Married for Life seminars as a single woman, I was always interested to hear stories from the participants. She elaborated:

> The other night, I became very emotional [*emocionada*]. We were supposed to confess anything that we hid or had not told our spouses, because between husband and wife, there can't be any secrets. And . . . João, he started telling me about this one time he cheated on me. I was stunned. I never knew. . . . He was crying so much. I had never seen him cry like that. "I'm sorry, so sorry." At first, I was angry. Apparently this happened when we were dating—if I had known, I would not have married him and had kids! . . .
>
> He says he is so much happier and feels more affectionate toward me now. It's like this stone has been lifted from his heart and now he doesn't have any obstacle to truly love me, you know. Secrets are like rocks that block true intimacy. . . . So it's good that we faced it together, I guess. It was painful, but it was good.

Camila highlighted the emotive force of this experience ("I became very *emocionada*") by recounting her husband's tears, her anger, and her eventual forgiveness. The confession took place during the lesson on intimacy, when each participant was encouraged to recognize one's past sins, repent, and forgive. The textbook assigned in Married for Life draws on the biblical passages about Adam and Eve to explain the rationale behind this practice:

> Genesis 2.25 reveals God's plan and the potential of our life of "One Flesh" as husband and wife. . . . There was no shame or darkness (sin) between them. Imagine oneself completely naked in all the senses—physical, emotional, and spiritual—together with your spouse, without any shame, without any obstacle! . . . "Transparent" in spirit, soul, and body; free to be just themselves, with total openness and sincerity. . . . This is God's plan for your marriage as well.[9]

The Married for Life seminar promotes a marital relationship that is "open" and "transparent" in the "physical, emotional, and spiritual" senses. In such a view, any obstacle to the expression of "true love," including secrets, must be overcome.

The ideal conjugal relationship at Missão Apoio seems to echo the vision of companionate marriage—a marriage in which romantic courtship, mutual sincerity, and emotional intimacy play a pivotal role. People around the globe who have taken to the idea of companionate love have embraced it as a token of modern individuality, oftentimes by contrasting it to "traditional" ways of union such as arranged marriage.[10] This seems to be the case with Brazilian Pentecostal converts as well. My informants often criticized what they saw as the Japanese way of marriage as something morally backward compared with their view of Christian union. A pastor at one Missão Apoio church once told me: "I heard that couples here treat each other like air after years of marriage and they think it's normal. They even have a word for it: *kamen hūhu* ["masked," or inauthentic, marriage]. It's horrible. Marriage is an alliance of love that unites two individuals forever. . . . Japanese couples don't even show love to each other!" He later added, "But younger generations are changing it now, and that's great. Japan is changing in a good way. When I came to Japan fifteen years ago, I didn't see any couple being affectionate [*carinhoso*] toward each other. Last week I saw this young couple kissing at the station, really passionately, you know, they were in love!"[11] Here, the pastor contrasts loveless Japanese marriage and loving Christian relationship. By asserting that "Japan is changing in a good way" with younger generations who are not afraid to express love, he suggests that the Japanese are becoming emotionally more modern, but perhaps not quite as modern as Christians. To the pastor and many converts, then, love was a quintessentially modern affect.

Cold Japanese, Warm Brazilian, and Emotional Pentecostal

Many congregants thus spoke of love as a universal Christian emotion that led converts into modernity. At the same time, they often referred to love as a distinctly Brazilian emotion. To many of my informants, love was apparently a layered construct.

Mayumi, a sansei in her forties from Paraná, offered the following testimony at a home group gathering one night. She began by telling the other attendants where she and her husband had been the previous weekend, on October 12 and 13, 2013. They drove to Kyoto—which is three hours away from Toyota—to attend an event called Empowered 21 All Japan. It was jointly organized by a number of Pentecostal and charismatic churches in Japan and beyond. Roughly a third of the speakers included in the two-day program were from abroad, including Hong Kong, Singapore, the Philippines, and the United States. One of the cofounders of Missão Apoio was among the featured speakers. Mayumi and her husband decided to go after seeing a poster for the event at the church. Mayumi first showed us a short video she had recorded with her iPhone. The phone's camera panned almost 180 degrees from one side of the hall to the other to capture the excited crowd that filled the venue. Many participants were praying aloud fervently to a dramatic tune played by the band on the stage. "Please listen. The people around me were praying in Japanese; it was so emotional," she said. We indeed heard a man's voice, distinct due to his proximity to her phone, uttering words such as *kamisama* (God/god), *kansha shimasu* (I'm grateful), and *idai na ai* (great love). He sobbed as he prayed. When the video was over, she continued:

> I could only make out *kamisama*, but I was moved that Japanese people— Japanese people, I'm telling you [*japoneses mesmo, sabe*]—were praying with so much emotion, shouting, crying, and even jumping. I had never seen that many Japanese filled with the Holy Spirit, filled with faith [*cheio do Espírito Santo, cheio de fé*]. We Brazilians often think that Japanese are cold [*japoneses são frios*], but we are wrong! When the Spirit touches you, they too cannot help but express joy and gratitude.

A few other people who had also attended the event nodded in agreement. Apparently, the sight of expressive Japanese charismatic Christians had made a lasting impression on them. One congregant chimed in, "We sometimes feel that all *crentes* are Brazilian, but that's not true!"

The scene unfolds in two diverging and yet interrelated tropes. On the one hand, Mayumi and others uphold the transcendence of Christian fellowship from ethnic boundaries such as the one between "Japanese" and "Brazilian." This is a rather common claim in the speech genre of Christian testimony. She interprets emotional expressiveness as reflective of the capacity to feel the Holy Spirit, a key quality that mediates charismatic kin-making. By declaring that some Japanese indeed possess such a capacity, she is testifying to the universality of Christian love while simultaneously legitimizing and buttressing the Christian identity of those in the room through her testimony. As Peter Stromberg observed in his study of born-again conversion narrative, many Christian speech genres are "constitutive."[12] That is, they are not mere "factual" accounts of life events but rather transformative mediums that create and fortify Christian subjectivity.

On the other hand, the remarks by Mayumi and her fellow congregants point to the widely shared images of Japanese and Brazilian ethnicities: Japanese are cold and Brazilians are warm (*japoneses são frios; brasileiros são carinhosos*). Statements such as "We Brazilians think that Japanese are cold but we are wrong!" paradoxically indicate that to many migrant converts, the fervent style of Pentecostal worship is something stereotypically un-Japanese. They instead consider it as more compatible with the supposedly Brazilian affects such as *carinho*, which encompasses emotional openness and affective warmth. Despite the frequent attempts to free Pentecostalism from any particular ethnic associations, my informants still let out remarks that subtly contradicted their own claims about God's universality (or universal accessibility, at least).

Affective openness, which shows through embodied practices such as "shouting, crying, and jumping," thus connects Brazilian identity to Pentecostal subjectivity. Japanese people, in contrast, are stereotyped as more reserved and emotionally flat, which makes it surprising whenever some of them act with fervor in public. This triangulation of cold Japanese, warm Brazilian, and emotional Pentecostal led to a widespread perception that, unlike Brazilians or Pentecostals, Japanese were not very loving. Being Pentecostal was affectively in alignment with being Brazilian because the two subjectivities were connected by open expression of intimate emotions. This meant that, in the Pentecostal landscape of emotions, Brazilians were more apt than Japanese to experience love—the marker of modern personhood.

Ancient-Style Modern Women

Thus far I have focused on the modern connotations of love. To the congregants at Missão Apoio Toyota, however, this was only half the story. The other half concerned the ancient quality of love. My informants used the word *ancient* (*antigo*) to refer to the attributes derived from what they saw as the timeless, unchanging, and universal truth authorized by the Bible. To them, love was not just modern but also ancient. These seemingly opposite characteristics seemed to form two sides of the same coin.

Culto para Mulheres, or Worship for Women, was a monthly event at Missão Apoio Toyota, organized and attended just by women. The structure of each gathering was similar to a regular Sunday service: worship songs, messages, testimonies, and sermons. What was different was the fact that it had a particular theme every month. One Saturday evening, I walked into the church to see large letters cut out of cardboard hanging on the front wall behind the pulpit. The words read: *Mulheres Modernas à Moda Antiga* (Ancient-Style Modern Women). That was the theme of the service that night. To the roughly hundred women who gathered, *Pastora* Ester began her sermon with a question: "Some people say that we are not modern because they think we embrace old irrational values. But are we really?" She then listed three definitions of modern women. Modern women take up challenges; they take good care of themselves; they are financially independent. She then argued that many female figures in the Bible embodied many of such attributes. Abigail, for instance, was an intelligent, articulate, and wise woman who protected her husband whenever he was in trouble. She did so while remaining respectful of male authority because she was deeply pious. She met at least the first two definitions of modern women because she faced challenging situations with grace and she took good care of her spiritual health as a godly woman. "Abigail was brave, bright, and humble. She was ancient and modern [Ela era antiga e moderna]. She is a superwoman from the Bible [Ela é uma supermulher da Bíblia]."

The last of her three definitions of modern women, that of financial independence, seemed slightly thornier than the other two as the *pastora* spent more time on it. She assured her audience, many of whom were full-time factory workers, that working hard to help one's family did not go against Christian ideals. "If anything, you should be ready to work just as hard as men to help your family." The *pastora* made it clear, however, that women's labor should always be for the sake of assisting others and never for personal achievement. To her, it was the purpose of work that made women's work Christian or un-Christian. She then told a story about one female congregant to drive her point home:

> A while ago, a sister came up to me, all frustrated. "*Pastora*, my husband is driving me crazy! I work so hard! I do four hours of *zangyō* [extra hours] every day but he does *teiji* [regular hours]. He comes home at five and just sits there doing no house chores. When I come home at ten, exhausted, I have to do all the work at home! He says we don't need to do *zangyō* to survive and it's my choice." . . .
>
> I said, "You don't need to but chose to do *zangyō*? Then it's your responsibility. You are trying to be a man, but earning is men's role. When you try to take that role, something goes wrong in the family. . . . Since many of us work in the factory side by side with men, I see a lot of women trying to be like men.

Do not do it because there won't be any peace at home if you do. . . . If anyone tells you that men and women are just the same and should do the same thing, then think about this: After all, we women are not paid the same amount for the exact same service we provide, right, sisters? [Many women nod deeply.] Right, at so many factories? Men get 1,000 yen per hour and we get 800 yen. Think about it.

The *pastora* advanced a sharp social critique here. She was aware that many nonconverts perceived evangelical churches as antimodern for supposedly promoting outdated and unequal gender roles. In response, she pointed out that the equality between men and women was not always a reality but instead a mere pretense in Japan. Despite the Employment Gender Equality Law (*danjo koyō kikai kintōhō*) that passed in 1985, some companies continued to pay less to women for the same or similar kinds of tasks performed at work. The women at church knew this well from experience. In fact, wage inequality was a fact of life that women still faced in both Brazil and Japan.[13]

The *pastora* thus suggested that the Pentecostal gender roles that she upheld made sense in this state of gender affairs. "Think about it." When the broader social system was implicitly telling them that men and women were not equal, why should they dream otherwise? Was "trying to be like men" a wise choice in such an environment where a level playing field for both genders may be an illusion? She thus implied that Pentecostal gender ideals, which appoint men to the role of breadwinner, were a rational response to the labor condition that continued to be shaped by patriarchal values. The seemingly "ancient" Christian gender roles could be adaptive and sensible in the supposedly "modern" capitalist context. We are modern in our own way, the *pastora* proclaimed: Ancient-Style Modern Women.

Ancient Love

Gender role was a central topic in the Married for Life classes, which advocated for a "complementary" model of marital relationship. The chapter on "*Papéis* [Roles]" in the textbook listed a number of "natural" roles for each spouse. The husband should ideally be a "leader," "provider," "fighter," and "model of God's sovereignty"; the wife's roles included "assistant," "supporter," "administrator," "companion," and "reflection of God's love."[14] The husband leads and the wife accompanies, the textbook affirmed, and that is the way God has intended humans to build family since the beginning of time. The naturalization of male authority is evident here. The women at Missão Apoio Toyota, however, were not stereotypical victims of patriarchy in that they were not servile, submissive, or subjugated. On the contrary, many were energetic, capable, and self-assured. Without the unofficial leadership of women, quite a few church activities would have been difficult or impossible to continue. Although only pastors and presbyters—all men—could give regular sermons, women spoke from the pulpit just as confidently at every service, delivering messages and testimonies. The tacit consensus seemed to be that women could be as active as men as long as they did not publicly challenge male authority.

Why do women, who constitute the numerical majority in Pentecostal movements around the globe, voluntarily embrace overtly patriarchal values? Many researchers of Global Christianity have answered this long-standing question by arguing that Pentecostalism provides a nuanced form of agency to its female participants.[15] Elizabeth Brusco famously analyzed that Pentecostalism works in women's favor by obligating men to marital fidelity and provision for family.[16] She argued that Pentecostalism is a "strategic" women's movement by which they can redirect to the household the income their male partners used to spend on activities associated with machismo—the public performance of aggressive and exaggerated masculinity such as drinking, smoking, and illicit affairs.[17] "Aggression, violence, pride, self-indulgence, and an individualistic orientation in the public sphere are replaced by peace seeking, humility, self-restraint, and a collective orientation and identity within the church and the home."[18] Brusco's study shows that, if not symbolically, women pragmatically benefit from the Christian reconfiguration of gender roles.

To the majority of Brazilian migrants in Japan, the biggest challenge to family life was not necessarily machismo but afastamento, or the sense of estrangement from family and kin. As I detailed in Chapter 4, they felt that labor migration triggered and exacerbated afastamento, which in turn led to loneliness, conflict, infidelity, divorce, and overall disintegration of family. It is perhaps not surprising, then, that many converts felt that the Pentecostal gender roles helped cure the ailment of afastamento and brought families back together. The most common narrative in this regard concerned a "woman who acts like a man," a wayward figure who lost sight of her proper role in her struggle as a migrant worker. Marcela, for instance, had the following to say about "so many women who come to Japan to earn money and forget about family":

They work in factories side by side with men. In most cases they earn as much as men. They have their own money for the first time in their life, in their own bank accounts, every month. . . . They start buying things just for themselves. They start complaining that their husbands are not working as hard as they do. . . . They start acting like decision makers at home. "Do more *zangyō!*" "I worked on Saturday last week; you should do laundry!" . . . I used to be like that. [Laughs.] I wanted to save enough money to go home to Brazil as quickly as possible, so it was all about work, work, work. . . . But then I realized there can't be peace in the family if women compete with men. Men and women have different roles, and we should complement each other, you see.

Marcela still worked full-time at a nearby factory even after taking Married for Life, but she believed that God saved her marriage by teaching the proper roles for husband and wife. Now she did her best not to work extra hours or on weekends so that she could "protect home" by running household chores. By staying home longer, she could also perform a number of tasks her twelve-year-old daughter's school expected from parents (more specifically, mothers). Her Facebook feeds sometimes featured elaborate obentō that she had prepared for her daughter. "I'm getting better! My daughter so happy," read the caption for a photo of boxed lunch with rice balls in the shape of Hello Kitty. She also felt that her husband became more willing to work long hours because he really understood that it was his role to provide for the family. There were fewer fights at home after they took Married for Life, she said.

Especially during the first years in Japan, when the majority of migrants are determined to quickly return to Brazil with enough savings, married couples tend to work equally long hours. In factories, men and women engage in the same kinds of unskilled labor, oftentimes side by side at the same assembly lines, which demonstrates that men and women are not very different in essential ways. Furthermore, many women gain more financial independence from their male partners and start demanding a reassignment of household chores, although most of them continue to serve as the primary domestic caretakers. These changes in the labor, economic, and domestic conditions often stimulated a feeling of anxiety concerning the shifting gender roles, which led many migrants—both male and female—to claim that women were becoming like men. To those who thought that migration—especially the conditions of factory labor—caused afastamento, the perceived disruption of gender roles was part of the problem. In such a context, the Pentecostal gender ideals, reinforced by a community of people who held each other accountable, provided couples with an opportunity to rearrange their marital relationships. Converts thus felt that the patriarchal roles and values, which represented the "ancient" side of Pentecostal love, helped reunite migrant families struggling with afastamento.

Love was a prominent theme not just in Married for Life and Worship for Women. It also dominated the stories from another seminar called Veredas Antigas, which was specifically for parents and children. Again, the invocation of "the ancient" was apparent; *veredas antigas* means "ancient paths" in Portuguese. Missão Apoio Toyota organized the weekend retreat at least once a year to "restore eternal family values" (*restaurar os valores eternos da família*), according to the circulated poster. The church leaders promoted it as an opportunity to heal the "emotional traumas and frustrations" that haunted many migrant families.

On the Sunday following the Veredas Antigas in 2013, one middle-aged woman walked up to the pulpit to share her experience. She started by recollecting her first years in Japan as a teenage daughter of two Nikkei migrants. "I hated my parents. I felt so lonely because they were never at home. They did so much *zangyō* and *yakin* [night shift] to earn more money. There was afastamento in the family." During the retreat, however, she realized how unrealistic her expectations toward her parents had been. She was a mother herself today and she too sometimes had to leave her own child at home while she worked. "This realization humbled me. In this world, only God is perfect. So we must love one another just as He loves all of us." In tears, she begged for forgiveness from her family. Her husband and son walked up to embrace her, softly repeating "Te amo" (I love you). The pastor then invited the whole congregation to pray for the family "so that God's love will fill their hearts." With their hands held together, the family faced the other congregants to receive prayers.

In sum, the ethnographic findings from the various church-led initiatives for "family restoration" demonstrate that to many migrant converts, the ancient and the modern were not antithetical to one another. Quite the opposite. The ancient was firmly embedded within the modern, and the yearning of migrant converts for the timeless truth seemed to only grow at a time of constant mobility and rapid change. In this sense, the ancient love was as much a product of modernity as the modern love. Migrant families thus navigated their tumultuous path to the better future by envisioning a return to the eternal Christian past.

Disorderly Brazilian, Disciplined Japanese, and Righteous Christian

With the vision of ancient love, Nikkei converts strived to recover family solidarity, which was once the hallmark of their "culture of discipline" in Brazil but had been undermined by afastamento in Japan. In this sense, Pentecostal love recuperated something vital of the imagined "Japanese family"—that is, harmonious unity—not in ethnic but in spiritual terms. Love thus offered Nikkeis a way to reclaim their "culture" without resorting to their Japanese ethnicity. Although they used to be the possessors of "Japanese culture" in Brazil, their culture this time—the culture of love—is Christian, and they cultivate it as they live amid the Japanese majority in Japan.

Interestingly, quite a few converts thought that their "Christian culture" made them more compatible with the life in contemporary Japanese society. Vinicius was a nisei man in his thirties who had migrated to Japan at the age of sixteen with his father. When I asked if he felt "Japanese" since he had naturalized more than a decade earlier, he responded in Portuguese: "No, I don't feel Japanese. It's hard. I only know the environment at the factory; that's the only social context that I'm used to. I don't know much else. But at the same time, I'm not really Brazilian either. If I go back to Brazil, people there would find me strange. I don't have the accent of my land [*sotaque da minha terra*] anymore, for example. I have been living here for too long." Although Vinicius felt neither Japanese nor Brazilian, he felt firm and clear about another facet of his self, which was Christian:

> Also, I am a *crente* today. I converted here. So I can't follow certain practices that are very common in Brazil. Like, that crazy *jeitinho* [accomplishing something by circumventing rules and conventions] of Brazilians—people lie and break rules to get what they want, you know. As a *crente*, I can't do it anymore; it's not right. Actually, living as a Christian is easier here since the Japanese are more honest—everything by the book. Japanese follow the rules and respect authority. Generally they have better discipline [*mais educação*], you see.

In this response, Vinicius relates to Japan not in ethnic but in moral terms. He transforms the perceived politeness and honesty of Japanese people into irrefutable markers of their tacit Christianness: "Living as a Christian is easier here since the Japanese are more honest." He then juxtaposes his claim of Japanese politeness with the perceived prevalence of law-bending behaviors (*jeitinho*) in Brazil, arguing that Japan is in fact the right place for righteous Christians. What some Nikkei migrants laugh at as the rigidity of rule-obsessed Japanese thus turns into a desirable ethical trait called honesty to migrant converts such as Vinicius.

Another Nikkei convert, Luana, also spoke during an interview about the modesty and respect of Japanese people. After she criticized what she viewed as the excessive sensuality of Brazilian culture (such as the Carnival), which she thought made it harder for men to live without sinning, she added, "If my Sachi [her eight-year-old daughter] were in Brazil, she would be walking around freely in a tiny top, her belly and legs all bare. So I prefer it here; it's more modest."

It seems that the inherent Christianness that some converts see in Japanese society lends legitimacy to their evolving born-again identity in Japan. This is because a discourse that emphasizes ethical qualities of Japanese people can consequently construct Japan as the right country to live in for Christians concerned with moral righteousness. Coupled with a common sense of a mission to evangelize the non-Christian nation, many migrant converts begin to embrace Japan as a place to be, if not as an uncontested home. The rhetorical triangulation of disorderly Brazilian, disciplined Japanese, and righteous Christian thus helps some migrants to craft a new sense of citizenship in Japan in spiritual terms.[19]

From the Culture of Discipline to the Culture of Love

Although Pentecostal conversion can restore the sense of family solidarity and cultural status to Nikkeis, this new Christian "culture of love" is distinct from their old Japanese "culture of discipline." This is because Christian love, which converts place at the center of their ethical aspiration, adds the element of affective warmth to the supposedly rigid "Japanese culture." Marianne's story can illuminate this point. She was a sansei Nikkei and related her childhood in Brazil as follows:

> When I was young I thought my mother didn't love me. All of my friends at school, their mothers kissed them, hugged them, called them "my little love" [*amorzinho*] and "my pretty thing" [*fofinha*] and everything. I had none of it. . . . I was thirsting for love, but I could not get it, because my parents were very Japanese. They didn't say any warm things to me, didn't hug me, didn't even kiss

each other! When I realized that she didn't know how because of this, you know, this way she grew up, I was so moved. I forgave her. She is only human, you know, that's all she knew, because that's the only culture she grew up in.

She subsequently framed her conversion to Pentecostalism in Japan as a way to overcome the "cold Japanese culture" of her childhood.

Love overcame the potential flaws of "Brazilian culture" as well. Although many Nikkei converts saw some parallel between "Brazilian expressiveness" and "Christian love," they were also quick to add that Brazilians are prone to confounding love with sexuality.[20] Love in Brazil, these Nikkei Pentecostals would observe, is entangled with sensuality, carnality, and sin ("Just look at the Carnival!"). Christian love, in contrast, is holy. In such rhetoric, migrant converts evoked Christian love as a morally higher version of Brazilian love.

To Nikkei migrant converts, then, "family" in the new culture of love thus embodies the best of both worlds—"Brazilian warmth" (*carinho*) and "Japanese discipline" (*educação*). It is at once affectionate and unified, spontaneous and stable. What is more, not only does it combine the positive characteristics of both Japanese and Brazilian affective worlds but it also augments them by drawing upon Christian aspirations. According to migrant converts, "Japanese family" may have been stable, but it was cold and rigid. "Brazilian family" may be more expressive and warm, but it is prone to disorder and dissolution. By merging *carinho* and *educação*, "Christian family" can transcend both "Japanese" and "Brazilian" cultures to constitute the basis for the third, transethnic, culture. In this imaginative landscape of racialized affects that Nikkeis inhabit, Pentecostal love is certainly a "Christian" emotion but also "Japanese" and "Brazilian" in more implicit ways.

I am not suggesting here that the kind of love Nikkei converts experience in the various ethnographic scenes is actually a mere ethnoracial trope. Instead, my argument is that this Christian love is a historical affect, a fruit of more than a century-old transpacific diasporic circuits that have shaped and been shaped by Nikkei migrants. In this sense, I have illuminated the temporal depth of emotion by focusing on the "history of everyday rupture," which points to the "contexts of continued instability and change induced by migration."[21] Creatively drawing on their migratory, racial, and affective histories, migrant converts continue to move toward the culture of love.

Part Four

CONTESTED

7

OF TWO BLOODS

The Japanese Blood and the Blood of Jesus

One Sunday afternoon, I was interviewing Miyako, a sansei woman in her forties, in the communal area of Missão Apoio church in a neighboring city of Toyota that I was visiting. Miyako served the church as a Japanese-Portuguese interpreter and chose to answer most of my questions in her fluent Japanese. Although she could only speak Portuguese when she arrived in Japan at the age of twenty, she made a colossal effort to learn Japanese as she worked full-time in a factory. She spoke eloquently about her childhood in São Paulo, her migration to Japan, her conversion to Pentecostalism, and her marriage to another Nikkei migrant whom she met at the church. When we moved on to the topic of her yonsei children, who were born and raised in Japan, her tone became a little tense:

> In my family's case, my kids here have Japanese faces and names. But Japanese kids still say to them: "You are Brazilian, a foreigner. Get out." "Don't come to this school." "Die." We went through all of that. Utterly, one hundred percent, it's Japanese blood that runs through our veins [*mattaku, hyaku pāsento, nihonjin no chi shika kekkan ni nagaretenai noni*]. I also gave Japanese names to my kids. But they would still say, "We don't need you foreigners." Once, my daughter was bullied. She was pushed, and fell down the stairs. We went through a lot—a lot.

After we spoke more about her concerns for the future of her children, I thanked her for her time and wrapped up the interview because the time for Sunday service was approaching. We moved from the church canteen, where we had been conversing, to the main hall.

It was the day of monthly *santa ceia*, or the Lord's Supper, in which converts consume a piece of bread and a small cup of grape juice that symbolize the body and blood of Christ to reflect on His self-sacrifice. I sat down next to Miyako and listened to worship songs, sermons, and testimonies. Then it was time for *santa ceia*. When the person next to me passed a tray of bread and juice to me, I passed it on to Miyako without touching because I was not a convert. *Santa ceia* made me feel a little nervous since it highlighted the line between converts and nonconverts—or the saved and the unsaved—more starkly than other church activities. I observed everyone around me eat a piece of bread and then drink a cup of juice with a look of deep concentration. Many kept their eyes shut and muttered prayers. After a few minutes, the church band started playing a song called "Alvo Mais que a Neve" ("Whiter than Snow"). One by one, congregants came out of personal prayers to join the collective voice and sang along:

Blessed may be, the Lamb	Bendito seja o Cordeiro
Who on the cross for us suffered	Que na cruz por nós padeceu
Blessed may be, His Blood	Bendito seja o Seu sangue
That for us there He shed	Que por nós ali Ele verteu
Look, washed in that blood	Eis nesse sangue lavados
With such pure white clothing	Com roupas que tão alvas são
The redeemed sinners are	Os pecadores remidos
Already before their God	Que perante seu Deus já estão
Whiter than snow	Alvo mais que a neve
Purer than snow	Alvo mais que a neve
If washed in that blood	Se nesse sangue lavado
I will be whiter than snow	Mais alvo que a neve serei

I was relieved to be able to participate by singing along. Since the congregation at Missão Apoio Toyota also sang "Whiter than Snow" at the monthly Lord's Supper, I knew it almost by heart. I glanced sideways at Miyako, who was singing with her eyes shut and palms open toward the ceiling. "If washed in that blood . . . I will be whiter than snow . . ." There were trails of tears on her cheek.

Kinship, Citizenship, and Religion Through the Lens of "Blood"

Two kinds of blood shape the lives of Nikkei Pentecostals in Japan: the blood of Jesus and the "Japanese blood."[1] On the one hand, the sacrificial blood of Jesus serves as a potent medium of Nikkei Pentecostals' born-again identity and sense of belonging in the Kingdom of God. On the other hand, the fact remains that their Pentecostal churches are flourishing in Japan, which the majority of migrants entered on the ancestry-based visa by proving that they are carriers of "the Japanese blood." Here, then, is an apparent irony: They see themselves as active participants in a transethnic and transnational Pentecostal movement when the legality of their life in the nation—and, by extension, the continuation of their churches—depends on the specific ethnoracial substance. In what follows, I will delve into the tensions surrounding the relationship between the two bloods by exploring the contentious intersection of kinship, citizenship, and nation-state.

Miyako's experience of the "Japanese blood" is ambivalent to say the least. She seems to resent how her children's peers rejected her family's belonging in Japan despite their "fully Japanese" lineage and active effort to integrate: "Utterly, one hundred percent, it's Japanese blood that runs through our veins. I also gave Japanese names to my kids. But they still said, 'We don't need you foreigners.'" Her remark illuminates the ambiguity of the "Japanese blood." It provides the foundation of national identity in Japan and, by extension, underpins the legal recognition of Nikkei foreigners' proximity to the national kinship. At the same time, it is never a total guarantee of national belonging for people like Miyako who do not conform to the narrow definition of Japaneseness as the convergence of "blood," language, and culture.

Her experience of Jesus's blood through rituals and songs, in contrast, seems emotionally fulfilling, even therapeutic. As the lyrics of "Whiter than Snow" suggest, "the blood of the Lamb" plays a central role in the making of Pentecostal culture. It symbolizes selfless sacrifice made by Christ ("Blessed may be, His blood that for us there He shed"), promise of ultimate salvation ("Washed in that blood . . . the redeemed sinners are already before their God"), and desire for moral and spiritual transformation ("If washed in that blood I will be whiter than snow"). The symbolism surrounding Jesus's blood, then, seems to enhance a sense of belonging in the Pentecostal community. But does this mean that—as my informants often told me—"Jesus is the solution to the afflicted world," meaning Jesus can cure the malaise converts experience? In the context of Japan, where the rhetoric of blood has powerfully fused family, nation, and citizenship in its modern time, the story may not be so simple.

Blood is not the essence but a metaphor of kinship, as generations of anthropologists have observed.[2] Yet consanguinity persists as a powerful imagery to demarcate common social belonging. Japan is a country where deep-seated cultural ideas and practices concerning blood abound, and Nikkei migrants' identities are certainly affected by the essentialist notion of "Japanese blood." Pentecostal converts, in contrast, describe the blood of Jesus as a "symbolic" and "supernatural" matter. Not only is it theologically important as the symbol and promise for salvation, it is also a mediator of spiritual kinship: "We are one big family in Jesus Christ."[3] In fact, many important rituals in church life—such as the Lord's Supper—are aimed at producing and sustaining spiritual kinship united in the blood of Jesus. Thus, the focus on the trope of blood can illuminate how the lives of Nikkei Pentecostal migrants in Japan are deeply intertwined with competing and yet coexisting models of belonging: one based on naturalized ethnonational kinship and the other grounded in spiritual kinship that unites "brothers" and "sisters."[4] Their experiences show that kinship is an evolving logic intertwined with multiple sociopolitical forces such as law, nation-state, and religion.[5] Japan's preferential treatment of foreigners of Japanese descent implicitly attributes supposedly innate relatedness to the nation's diasporic populations. The social construction of "return" is therefore the politics of kinship writ large. It is not difficult, then, to imagine that Pentecostal conversion in this context would be greeted with some contestations.

Japan: Blood Endures, Blood Corrupts

In modern Japan, common descent has long been the centerpiece of national identity. The country's political ideologies have deployed blood ties to conflate family and nation, constituting them as mutually reinforcing entities. Amid the national effort for modernization and centralization in the late-nineteenth-century Meiji period, the rhetoric of "family nation-state" (or "national family," *kazoku kokka*) emerged and took hold: "The *kazoku kokka* (family state) was projected as an enduring essence, which provided the state with an elevated iconography of consanguineous unity, enhanced the legitimacy of new economic, social, and political relations, and provided the Japanese people with a new sense of national purpose and identity."[6] The family-state system dictated that the emperor was the benevolent "father," or the "head of the household" (*kachō*) of one big "national family," and the citizens were his "children."[7] He also fulfilled an indispensable role as a chief priest in State Shinto, in which he carried out a set of liturgies as a descendant of mythic lineage that could supposedly be traced back to the first gods of the nation. The ideology of family-state, then, was intimately tied to the nationalization of Shinto—a name given to a disparate mixture of rituals practiced for gods, deities, and spirits in Japan. In this historical context, nation-state, politics, kinship, family, and religion were not separate domains but instead ontologically inseparable, together constituting "the Japanese people."

Blood figured as the powerful, almost mythic, essence in the creation and maintenance of the family-state. Terms such as *minzoku* (people, or ethnic group), which gained large circulation during this period, often conflated "phenotype, geography, culture, spirit, history, and nationhood."[8] Such modern "semantic and semiotic inventions" were later incorporated into the postwar constitution of 1947, which "retained the definition of nationality and citizenship as a right of blood."[9] Although the explicit ideology of family-state ceased with Japan's defeat in World War II, the central significance of blood in the creation of national identity persisted. To this day, "*Jus sanguinis* aligns nationality with kinship; the nation is, by virtue of its shared blood, an enormous family."[10] The demarcation of national belonging as the narrow convergence of language, culture, and "blood" also persists to this day.

Nikkei Brazilians figure ambiguously in this field of discourses on blood and Japaneseness. The long-term resident (or Nikkei-jin) visa that enabled their initial migration to Japan was granted on the basis of descent. This requirement of Japanese ancestry constitutes potential migrants as Japanese, at least partially. Most Nikkei migrants who arrived, however, were born and raised in Latin America and did not embrace the qualities the "Japanese blood" was expected to embody.[11] Although the dominant political ideology in Japan regards the "Japanese blood" as an essence that transcends generations, it also dictates that the blood can become too diluted over time. This is at least the implicit logic behind the restriction of the Nikkei-jin visa only to the children and grandchildren of Japanese emigrants. Many third-generation migrants recount the difficulty that arises if children they are trying to bring to Japan are over eighteen years old.[12] I heard, on more than one occasion, parents exchanging information about visas for their yonsei children: "Have you ever had a difficulty in getting the visa for your son? Mine is almost eighteen and in Brazil. It's a nightmare." The legal boundary of Nikkei-jin primarily falls between the third and the fourth generations. Culturally speaking, however, the line is arbitrary to say the least, especially due to the fact that many yonsei Brazilian youth are born and raised in Japan.

Thus the social construction of "Japanese blood" as an essential and yet perishable substance puts many Nikkei Brazilians in an ambiguous position. Some may have what the Japanese majority views as pure bloodline and Japanese appearance, but not the linguistic and cultural competence. Younger Brazilians may feel native in the Japanese language and culture, but they may still be judged gaijin (foreign) in terms of appearance and legal definition.

To reiterate, the taken-for-granted unity of "Japanese blood" and the Japanese people is a modern "semiotic invention" as well as a cultural "iconography." These terms provide me with clues to develop a semiotic analysis of "Japanese blood" as a mediator of "material kinship."

Material Kinship: Forms of Signification in Japanese Nationalism

Webb Keane characterized forms of signification that are not arbitrary as "material"; for instance, the ebb and flow of the tides form a material sign of cyclical time because the signifier (i.e., the tide) is directly affected by the signified (i.e., the cycle).[13] In this sense, tide is a noncoincidental index of time. Building on such an observation, Keane also highlighted "the social power of naturalization" facilitated by the materiality of signs:

> Indexes do not only presuppose some *prior* causes of which they bear the effects, they may also have *entailments*. . . . The social power of naturalization comes from this: not simply the false reading of indexicals as if they were directly iconic of some prior essential character, but rather the misconstruing of the possible entailments of indexicals—their effects and possibilities—as if they were merely expressing something (such as character) that already exists.[14]

Put more simply, some signs can be construed as indexical and material—and, by extension, innate, natural, and preexistent—even when they are not necessarily "directly iconic of some prior essential character."

I take the "Japanese blood" to be one such sign because its aura of materiality helps naturalize the conflation of nation, family, phenotype, and culture. The "iconography of consanguineous unity" is an ingenious way to characterize this conflation, for it captures the materiality, inviolability, and touch of sacredness that emanate from the sign.[15] It is in this sense that I characterize the social belonging bound by the "Japanese blood" as material kinship. In material kinship, the recognition of arbitrariness between what binds and what is bound is minimized because people learn to perceive the two as one and the same. Furthermore, material kinship tends to foreground the state of *being* kin rather than the process of *becoming* kin, since materiality can make the operation of signification appear as a natural fact. The case study of Nikkei migrants, however, helps expose the nonnatural foundation of the material sign that is the "Japanese blood." Their stories and experiences can serve to disintegrate the domains the sign fuses—nation, culture, "blood," and so on. I now turn to some of such narratives.

Migration: Blood Acts

What the Japanese officials who penned the 1990 Revised Entry Regulation Law may not have fully realized is the malleability of kinship. In many forms of kinship, including the actual ramifications of consanguineous system, blood is often not the defining essence but a flexible actor. The story of Vinicius can illuminate this plasticity of kinship. Vinicius's father was two years old when his family emigrated to Brazil from Okinawa around 1955. Okinawa is the present-day southernmost prefecture of Japan, which comprises hundreds of tropical islands called Ryūkyū Islands. Until the annexation by the Meiji government of Japan in the late nineteenth century, Okinawa maintained political autonomy as Ryūkyū Kingdom. Its culture, including the language, remains distinct to this day.[16] Okinawan emigrants and their descendants in Brazil consequently developed ethnic identity different from—and sometimes opposed to—the rest of Nikkei Brazilians. For instance, they use the Okinawan terms Uchinanchu (Okinawan) and Yamatonchu (mainland Japanese) to refer to Nikkeis of Okinawan descent and of non-Okinawan descent, respectively, even in Brazil.[17] Vinicius's father grew up in one of such Okinawan Nikkei communities in São Paulo. Legally speaking, his father is issei (first generation) and Vinicius is nisei (second generation). When Vinicius came to Japan with his father at the age of sixteen, he filed for naturalization in Japan, knowing that his father's Japanese nationality and his status as a minor made the process easier for him. He had been a Japanese citizen for over fifteen years at the time of interview. His two Japan-born children also have Japanese nationality, but not his wife. Being a fourth-generation Nikkei Brazilian, she would have to go through a more rigorous process if she were to naturalize.

When Vinicius's father met his mother in Brazil, she was already pregnant with him from her previous relationship, but he married her regardless. When Vinicius was born, his father simply registered him as his own son. On paper, Vinicius was impeccably Japanese—in terms of descent and nationality. "It's funny, right?" Vinicius said with a smile, "I *am* Japanese but I have no Japanese blood [*sangue japonês*] in me whatsoever!" Although he had been living in Japan for over a decade, his father quickly went back to Brazil after several years, completely disappointed with his "native" country. Vinicius recounted:

> VINICIUS. Things were tougher for him. At least I have a face of gaijin [foreigner], European too, and tall, so Japanese colleagues were fascinated by me. "*Kakkoī* [cool, handsome]," they would tell me. My father has a Japanese face, but his Japanese was an issue. What he thought was Japanese, because he grew up speaking it in his family, was actually a language of . . . what was it . . .
>
> SUMA. Uchinanchu ["Okinawan" in the language/dialect in Okinawa]?[18]
>
> VINICIUS. Right, Uchinanchu. So he looks Japanese and is Japanese, but when he opened his mouth, people were like, "What is this guy?" He hated it here. So he left after saving money and never came back.

Vinicius's family story challenges the normative assumptions underlying *jus sanguinis* of Japan in three ways. First, Japanese descent—or nationality—does not always equal the continuation of "Japanese blood" per se. Second, the "Japanese blood" does not ensure an affinity for Japan or a grasp on Japanese language and culture. Third, Japanese society is not ethnically homogeneous or seamlessly unified, as the ideology of "Japanese blood" suggests. The voices of historically oppressed minorities such as Koreans, Okinawans, Buraku-min, and Ainu people complicate the dominant narrative of national unity.[19]

Between Two Names: In the "Gray Zone" on the Gradation of Japaneseness

The ideology of "Japanese blood" constructs Nikkei migrants as "quasi-Japanese"—more Japanese than non-Nikkei foreigners but less so than the Japanese majority in Japan. This ambiguous social position in turn leads to a distinct form of discrimination, namely, demanded conformity. As Vinicius's narrative of his father shows, Japanese appearance—or Japanese descent in and of itself—can increase the expectation for assimilation from the Japanese majority.

Many of my Brazilian informants shrugged off the signs of imposed conformity with pragmatic nonchalance. One night, Paula—a thirty-one-year-old Nikkei woman—came over to my apartment in Homi Danchi to have me translate and fill out the forms her company had required her to submit. The procedure was to change her status from temporary worker to full-time employee. As we sat down, she exclaimed, "I'm so happy I'm turning *seishain* [directly employed full-timer]! With this better health care coverage I can finally start planning for a child!" I started filling out the forms, checking with her in Portuguese. When I had finished all the forms, she asked me to write her name on the nametag for her new factory uniform as a full-time employee. Since her registered last name, which appeared on her Japanese driver's license, was Okuda Santos (オクダ・サントス), I was going to write the same name on the nametag. But she stopped me, saying, "You have to write just Okuda, and in *kanji* (奥田)." When I responded in confusion that her registered name in Japan seemed to be in *katakana*, one of the three alphabets of the Japanese language used for people and objects of foreign origin, Paula responded:

> Because I am Nikkei. If you can write your name in *kanji*, that's better. If you are just a temporary employee maybe they don't care that much, but I'm not anymore. Name in *kanji* is better; that looks more Japanese.... If you have Nikkei family names, many factories ask you to write them in *kanji*, you know. This factory is better than before. At my first factory I had to dye my hair black. My hair is naturally brown, and I dye it blonde now; you know, back then, I had to dye it really black, like Japanese.

Puzzled, I asked her if the practice of dyeing hair black to appear more Japanese was common. She responded calmly that it depended on the factory but many of her friends had done so at least once.

A mechanism of inclusion and exclusion is at work in her story, and I call it the gradation of Japaneseness. On this spectrum, Nikkeis often fall into the "gray zone" between the utterly foreign and the purely Japanese. Consequently, they measure and fine-tune their outward Japaneseness according to the context. The social pressure for assimilation increases in the full-time sector of the labor market. This is why Paula felt compelled to foreground her Japanese identity as she shifted from the more marginal temporary labor force to the more stable full-time employment.

The ways in which Vinicius and Paula invoked and enacted their "Japanese blood" attest to both its materiality and its malleability. On the one hand, they intuitively understood the basic tenet of Japanese nationalism: that the "Japanese blood" indexes the unity of phenotype, nation, language, and culture. This is why Vinicius prefixed his story with "It's funny, right?"—because he knew that his biological lineage and appearance did not match the stereotypical image of "the Japanese," but his nationality and social lineage did. Similarly, Paula's strategic performance of her Japanese identity hinged on her firsthand understanding of what is expected of the "Japanese blood"—and therefore of being Nikkei—in Japan. Although Nikkei migrants have an intuitive grasp on the materiality of the "Japanese blood," they treat it not as an inviolable "iconography" but rather as a flexible marker. Paula's fine-tuning of her Japaneseness as an outward expression demonstrates the performativity and malleability of racial identity in people's actual lives.[20] This is also in line with the documented fluidity of racial categories in Brazil, where people tend not to equate race with biological essence; instead, racial identity is a negotiable sum of skin tone, social and economic class, volitional self-presentation, and conventional perception by others.[21] The performance of Japanese race among Nikkeis in Japan may therefore be influenced by their cultural upbringing in Brazil as well.

Many Nikkei migrants perform—and occasionally defy—the "Japanese blood," but those converted to Pentecostalism, in a sense, go a step further. They attempt to transcend material kinship by cultivating another form of relatedness that is "symbolic" and "spiritual."

Pentecostalism: Blood Separates, Blood Unifies

Also referred to as the blood of the Lamb and of eternal covenant, the blood of Jesus has long signified manifold ethical ideals for Christians: self-sacrifice, purification of sins, ultimate salvation, and unbroken relationship with God, to name a few. Consequently, its theological meanings and ritual functions are numerous. Here I focus on one cultural significance of the blood, which is its sanctifying power that separates the converts from the presumably sinful world. One major ritual illuminates this function of the blood well: water baptism (*batismo nas águas*). Missão Apoio Toyota held it once a year in Yahagi River, which runs through the center of the city. Those wishing to participate—and to officially convert—were required to attend a study session prior to the ritual. To the two dozen people who gathered that night, the church leaders explained that water baptism at once meant death and resurrection. "It is like getting a death and birth certificate at the same time," Pastor Cid elaborated:

> It means that you are cut off [*sepultado*] from the world and therefore dead to the world, and to your old self. Then you are born again by being baptized in the blood of Jesus. Now, don't take what I say literally. [Laughs.] The blood of Jesus, for us Christians, is a symbol of life. Thanks to his sacrifice, because of the blood he shed to cleanse our sins and to save us, we can be born again as new creatures united in God.

The blood of Jesus is a "symbolic" (*simbólico*) substance that mediates the rite of passage into born-again life. It is a potent symbol because of its twofold significance, death and rebirth. By symbolizing death to the sinful way of life and rebirth in the new sanctified life, the blood of Jesus marks born-again identity and separates it from what is deemed worldly. In so doing, the blood also separates converts from the way of life centered on "traditional" familial ties.[22] Churchgoers—especially those who converted despite their families' opposition—stressed the primacy of their personal relationship with God over familial obligations. Larissa, for instance, drew on Bible verses to express her feeling toward her parents who followed a religious group called Seichō-no-Ie: "I love and respect my parents, but that does not mean I should blindly obey them when my faith is at stake. As Jesus said, sometimes true family means brothers and sisters in God."[23]

Larissa's remark points to another significance of Jesus's blood in Pentecostal culture: the nexus of spiritual kinship. Perhaps the most common trope in this regard is that "the Church is one family under God." It was, in fact, one of the first things I was repeatedly told as an anthropologist studying the role of migrant church networks: "You know, the church is like a big family. We dekasseguis are often here alone, without families, so church is like a real family to us." There is a grain of truth in such a statement. Many Brazilians indeed left their families in Brazil, and even those who brought families to Japan were still without the support of extended kin network. The church often came to fulfill the role previously taken on by relatives, occupying a more intimate place in the lives of congregants. One long-term member related:

> My friend who converted in Japan has recently returned to Brazil and called me, shocked. She was like, "Aline! *Crentes* here don't spend all day together on the Christmas Day and the New Year's Eve! They spend those days just with their own families and friends! How sad!" I was like, "Of course they don't; they have families there! That's what we do just in Japan." But she misses that, you know, how intimate church feels here in Japan.

Such remarks demonstrate that church networks provide migrant converts with another source of kinship outside of their immediate families. A number of linguistic conventions, both Brazilian and Christian, enhance the sense of intimacy in such new kin relationships. At Missão Apoio Toyota, for instance, congregants referred to God as "Father" (*Pai*) while situating themselves as "children" (*filhos*) dependent on His grace. During conversations, they addressed each other as "brother" (*irmão*) or "sister" (*irmã*). Furthermore, members with age difference frequently used kin terms such as *tio* (uncle), *tia* (auntie), *filho* (son), and *filha* (daughter) while speaking to each other, which is a practice common in Brazil. Together, these linguistic utterances helped create a sense of community where many could feel at home. Some scholars may interpret the human bond sustained by such cultural customs as an example of "fictive kin."[24] The term *fictive kin*, however, implies that the kinships mediated by blood and marriage are innately more real than those facilitated by, say, conversion. Yet marriage can be just as culturally construed as conversion, and so is "blood," as I have demonstrated in my above discussion of the "Japanese blood." I would therefore view the relationships fostered at churches like Missão Apoio Toyota as *another*—not "alternative" or "fictive"—form of kinship. To my informants, this type of kinship figured as spiritual relatedness.

Common metaphors also suggest that church is not only "one big family" but also "one big body." Missão Apoio adopts the so-called cellular vision (*visão celular*), or the strategy of church growth based on small home groups, as its ministerial model. Each cell (*célula*), or home group, strives to have around a dozen members. When a cell grows in size, it splits in half, and each new cell group aims to double the number of members so that it can multiply again. It is a decentralized system that mobilizes lay practitioners' social networks as the chief resource for the church's organizational expansion. In this corporeal idiom, each home—where the weekly *célula* meeting is held—is a "cell" that should multiply to contribute to the growth of the larger "body" that is the church. The family metaphor and body metaphor fuse with one another to enhance the sense of unity among church members. Missão Apoio seems to owe much of its success among the migrant communities in Japan to this cellular system.[25] In Homi Danchi alone, there were dozens of *células* that met on a weekly basis at congregants' homes. No one, not even the pastor, kept track of exactly how many *células* there were, which again demonstrates the decentralized character of Pentecostal organization. Within the organic metaphors of family and body, congregants' social networks turn into the veins through which the blood of Jesus can circulate to nurture the church-family-body.

As the mediator of spiritual family and body, the blood of Jesus frequently appeared in sermons. One day, Pastor Cid delivered a sermon titled "What Is the True Church?" (Qual É a Verdadeira Igreja?). After asking rhetorically what kind of church Jesus would build today, he went on to elucidate, one by one, the four "keys" (*chaves*) of the true church: conquest of death, repentance, evangelization, and Jesus's blood:

> Anyone who is born again is living through His blood. Now, open your Bible—1 Peter, chapter 1, verse 18. . . . Great, now let's read together, until verse 23. Ready?
>
> "For you know that it was not with perishable things such as silver or gold that you were redeemed from the empty way of life handed down to you from your ancestors, but with the precious blood of Christ, a lamb without blemish or defect. . . . For you have been born again, not of perishable seed, but of imperishable, through the living and enduring word of God."
>
> Brothers and sisters, turn to the person next to you and say this: "You are a new creature in the blood of the Lamb!" [The congregants repeat.] Say, "Jesus Christ the Lord united us!" [The congregants repeat.] Amen and amen.

Given the central significance of Jesus's blood in Christian theology, such a message in and of itself is perhaps unremarkable, possibly typical of the genre of preaching. It is when we step back to assess the social context of this sermon that its unique appeal becomes more apparent. That is, the majority of attendants were Nikkei Brazilians who were permitted to migrate to Japan precisely because of their Japanese ancestral lineage. Some themes of the sermon then stand out as particularly pertinent, namely, the contrast between "perishable" matters associated with ancestors and the "imperishable" blood of Jesus and Word of God. Through the active cooperation of attendants, who reaffirmed their Christian identity through mutual vocalization, the pastor valorized, encouraged, and glorified the latter—the blood of Jesus.

The overall message is clear. It is not material heritage from ancestors (silver, gold, and seed) but the transformation through Jesus's sacrificial blood that makes them who they are. In this instance and others, migrant converts often highlighted the separation of spirit and matter, which is a common framework in Protestant cultures.[26] In doing so, they also stressed the higher value of "second spiritual birth" over "first material birth."[27] Such rhetoric facilitated their understanding of spiritual kinship as transcending ethnic, national, and racial boundaries. This boundary-crossing power of spiritual kinship mattered all the more when the other kinship that initially brought them to Japan—the naturalized "Japanese blood"—only offered precarious belonging in the nation.

Spiritual Kinship: Forms of Signification in Pentecostal Community

Arguably, both the "Japanese blood" and Jesus's blood mediate claims for relatedness. Although both serve as signs of kinship in this sense, the primary form of signification for each is distinct. The discourse of "Japanese blood" emphasizes the indexical materiality of the sign and naturalizes the boundary of the Japanese people as a single race. Pentecostal converts, in contrast, invoke Jesus's blood as an explicitly symbolic and immaterial matter, thereby implying that spiritual kinship goes beyond naturalized kinship.

When church leaders warn those unfamiliar with or new to born-again community not to take their words about Jesus's blood "literally," they are implicitly contrasting their understanding of the sign against that of Catholics. Similar to the Pentecostal converts in Brazil, the majority of the members at Missão Apoio Toyota were at least nominally affiliated with the Catholic Church prior to conversion.[28] In Pentecostal semiotic ideology, or "basic assumptions about what signs are and how they function in the world," the materiality of signs in Catholic rituals appears dubious.[29] My Pentecostal informants frequently made critical comments about Catholic practices, ranging from infant baptism to rosary prayer to the Holy Communion, by arguing that they "do not make sense" (não faz sentido). For instance, they would observe that sacramental bread (hostia) cannot literally and materially be the body of Christ.

It symbolically *represents* the body of Christ, they would stress. Their effort to distance themselves from material understandings of signs' effectiveness was manifest in how they conducted the Pentecostal equivalent of the Holy Communion, the Lord's Supper (*santa ceia*). The act of consumption was always preceded by a reading of relevant biblical passages and encouragement from the pastor to sincerely consider whether one deserved to consume the symbols. Without the understanding of articulable meaning invested in the objects and the right intention during the act, converts would say, they would be consuming mere breadcrumbs and grape juice. Unlike material signs that often come to embody meaning in themselves, symbolic signs call forth an intentional and sincere subject for meaning to be realized.

Thus, converts evoked the blood of Jesus explicitly as a symbolic sign. For them, the relationship between the signifier (i.e., Jesus's blood) and the signified (i.e., Christian fellowship) was not a given but in need of conscious and continuous work for it to sustain itself. Indeed, it was a truism among converts to say that no one is born Pentecostal but becomes one. Put otherwise, one must be born again to become born-again. This is in stark contrast to the ideology of the "Japanese blood," which holds that no one can be unequivocally Japanese unless he or she was born Japanese in the first place. Unlike the semiotic relationship between "the Japanese blood" and "the Japanese," the blood of Jesus and "the Christian" are not fused in indexical materiality to constitute a naturalized entity. Instead, converts are urged, in moments ranging from water baptism to the Lord's Supper to daily prayer, to consciously reflect on the symbolic meanings of the signs to reaffirm their identity as Christian. What I refer to as spiritual kinship, hence, diverges from material kinship in its greater presupposition of and reliance on the sincere intentional subject.

Intentionality, interiority, and sincerity have often constituted the sources of the "modern" self in the West as well as in many other parts of the world.[30] It is hardly surprising, then, that Pentecostal converts often position themselves in alignment with "modernity" while downplaying "tradition" as something that must be overcome. In the case of Nikkei Brazilian Pentecostals in Japan, they often put the label of "traditionalist" (*tradicionalista*) on two main groups: other Brazilians who are not born-again (e.g., Catholic) and the non-Christian Japanese majority in Japan. Such a Pentecostal moral narrative of modernity, however, collides with the dominant rhetoric of national identity in modern Japan, which emerged from a model of personhood distinct from that of sincere subject.

The Marriage of the Two Js—Japan and Jesus

In the making of the modern imperial subject in Japanese history, Christians have occupied an ambiguous place. On the one hand, Christianity represented enlightenment, civilization, and Western reason, especially in the late-nineteenth-century zeal for industrialization and modernization. It is during this period that the Christian population in the country saw a small but significant growth, mostly among the educated elites who traveled to Europe and North America. On the other hand, Christianity also signified moral deviance from the Japanese Spirit (*yamato damashī*) due to its presupposed foreign and unpatriotic character. The negative perception of Japanese Christians as the internal Other intensified as the government introduced and consolidated a number of new rituals as part of State Shinto. The political leaders naturalized the fusion of Shinto practices and budding nationalism by claiming that Shinto was a timeless tradition indigenous to Japan since time immemorial, despite the fact that many liturgies were invented during the modern period. Since the emperor, whose lineage could supposedly be traced back to the first gods (*kami*), served as both the head of state and the icon of State Shinto, politics and ethics were necessarily intertwined in the making of modern Japanese subjects. In fact, Japanese leaders did not uphold the separation of church and state in the same way as many Euro-American nations did at the time. They argued that the practice of State Shinto did not involve any "religious beliefs" but instead constituted "civic duties" of all Japanese citizens, a stance that caused many Japanese Christians a moral dilemma.[31]

In 1891, for instance, a Japanese Protestant intellectual Kanzō Uchimura (1861–1930) received a storm of public criticism when he refused to perform a State Shinto ritual. A graduate of Sapporo Agricultural School and Amherst College, Uchimura was baptized by the American Methodist missionary Marriman Colbert Harris during his school years in Japan. Although he was a strong nationalist and supporter of the emperor, he was troubled by the deification of objects that saturated State Shinto rituals. As someone who renounced the worship of gods after Christian conversion, he found the ceremonious sanctification of ritual objects idolatrous. Uchimura recounted what unfolded during his time as a faculty at the First Higher Preparatory School in Tokyo—which later came to be referred to as the "lèse-majesté incident" (*hukei jiken*)—as follows:

After the address of the [principal] and reading of the [Imperial Rescript on Education], the professors and students were asked to go up to the platform one by one, and bow to the Imperial signature affixed to the [rescript], in the manner as we used to bow before our ancestral relics prescribed in the Buddhist and Shintō ceremonies. I was not at all prepared [for] such a strange ceremony, for [it] was the new invention of the [principal] of the school. . . . Hesitating in doubt, I took a safer course for my Christian conscience, and in the august presence of sixty professors (all non-Christians, the two other Christian professors beside myself having absented themselves) and over one thousand students, I took my stand and did not bow. . . . For a week after the ceremony, I received several students and [professors] who came to me, and with all the meekness I could muster . . . I told them also that the good Emperor must have given the [rescript] to his subjects not to be bowed unto, but to be obeyed in our daily walks in life.[32]

In this narrative, Uchimura resists the ritual performance of "civil ethics" by stating that the rescript was "not to be bowed unto, but to be obeyed in our daily walks of life." He thus implies that the "correct" mode of moral cultivation consists not in bodily disciplining through ritual action but instead in continuous and conscious examination of the inner self. That the principal demanded the external behavior (i.e., bowing) and not necessarily the internal sincerity (i.e., conscience) made Uchimura hesitate because, to his sensibility, the two must correspond with each other for the act to be effective.

The non-Christian Japanese officials, however, clearly did not share Uchimura's view because they explicitly positioned State Shinto rituals as something devoid of personal belief. In fact, they argued that anyone could and should participate regardless of his or her inner religious conviction on the ground that such ceremonies did not intervene with the individual's deep interiority. Their strategic emphasis was on public participation and bodily gesture. This downplaying of individual interiority, which justified mandatory participation, did not necessarily mean that the moral transformation that resulted from ritual action was shallow and superficial. Rather, the state capitalized on a vision of ethical personhood different from the individual with sincere interiority—that of disciplined selves, which I will elaborate on in more detail in Chapter 9.

Uchimura was soon removed from his position by the Ministry of Education. Both Shinto and Buddhist figures issued public criticisms against

Uchimura, arguing that Christianity must be un-Japanese in its essence. One of the critics, the philosopher Tetsujirō Inoue (1855–1944), summarized the conflict between the Imperial Rescript and Christian ethics as the incompatibility between "particularistic patriotism" and "indiscriminate universal love."[33] Although Uchimura did not agree with such critics, he nonetheless had to acknowledge the tension between what he called the "two J's": Japan and Jesus. He wrote in 1926: "I love two J's and no third; one is Jesus, and the other is Japan. I do not know which I love more, Jesus or Japan. I am hated by my countrymen for Jesus' sake as Yaso [a Japanese word for "Christian" at the time, which could be pejorative], and I am disliked by foreign missionaries for Japan's sake as national and narrow. No matter; I may lose all my friends, but I cannot lose Jesus and Japan."[34] In fact, much of Uchimura's lifework focused on the reconciliation of the tenuous relationship between his Japanese and Christian identities.

Transethnic "Imperishable" Spiritual Kinship

The sentiment that Christianity is somehow foreign to the so-called Japanese way of life remains pervasive to this day. Despite the long history behind such a perception toward Christianity, some contemporary writers reify it as something derived from the Japanese psyche. Moreover, the Pentecostal insistence on exclusive affiliation further entrenches the line between Pentecostal identity and Japanese identity. All the leaders and most of the members at Missão Apoio Toyota thought that authentic conversion required the renunciation of ancestral memorialization. In the context of contemporary Japan, this Pentecostal expectation for purified religious boundary often meant the discontinuation of Buddhist practices.[35] This stance elicited ambiguous reactions from the few Japanese people who regularly visited the church at the time of my fieldwork.

Yamada-san was a quiet and reserved single man in his late forties with a slight limp. He seemed to genuinely enjoy the friendship with Nikkei Brazilian youth from the church. One night, we struck up a conversation as we sat together listening to the young church members sing worship songs at a street evangelization. "So, how do you find the church?" I asked.

"Oh, it's really great. People are so warm. I feel so welcome," he answered. He then straightened his back and whispered, "But I'm not sure about baptism yet. I mean, I heard during the Bible study that the commemoration of ancestors [*senzo kuyō*] was not compatible with Christian way of life. That makes things difficult. I'm the eldest son and *senzo kuyō* is my duty. I can't imagine how much that would upset my family." The other regular Japanese visitor, Hagino-san, was also unmarried at the time, being a divorcé with two adult children. Like Yamada-san, he also stressed the significance of ancestral commemoration in his daily life. Especially after his mother's death roughly ten years earlier, he had seldom missed a day in tending the Buddhist altar at home with fresh water, rice, and flowers. "I also chant sutras in front of the altar every day. Sutra is the daily food for our ancestors [*okyō wa gosenzosama no gohan*]. So I do this with a lot of care." Hagino-san was more optimistic than Yamada-san about the compatibility of Buddhist and Christian practices because, to him, "both were about love." Although he was aware that the church did not encourage the rituals for ancestral spirits, he still did not think that his love for his deceased mother would be a problem for his budding interest in Christianity.

Thus, the brief overview of Christianity in modern Japan illuminates the still-contested nature of spiritual kinship in this social context. The dominant traditions such as Shinto and Buddhism have historically played a significant role in shaping familial, ethnic, and national kinships. In fact, the "Japanese blood" has served to fuse these different levels of kinship into one singular con-sanguineous unity, initially within the prewar ideology of "family-state." The Pentecostal logic of spiritual kinship inevitably faces some resistance in such a cultural environment insofar as it positions itself as incompatible with and transcendent from material kinship. Yet it is precisely such an immaterial qual-ity of Pentecostal kin-making that appeals to Nikkei migrants, who find themselves at the margin of Japanese national kinship. In this sense, they are striving to achieve through one blood what they could not accomplish with the other blood: uncontested belonging. The irony, of course, is that their legal sta-tus in Japan hinges on the first blood that they attempt to transcend with the second.

There is one more aspect of Jesus's blood particularly pertinent to the next generations of Nikkeis growing up in Japan. The blood of Jesus in Pentecostal semiotic ideology, unlike the "Japanese blood," does not become "diluted" over time because it is an explicitly symbolic sign unattached to material substance. Furthermore, its point of origin in personal history is typically located at the time of conversion, during which one is reborn as a "new creature" in the sac-rificial blood of Jesus Christ. Since the experience of conversion is commonly understood as repeatable—in fact, continual—at any moment of born-again life, spiritual kinship mediated by Jesus's blood is in theory also renewable at any given time. When contrasted with "Japanese blood," the biblical characterization of Jesus's blood as "imperishable" holds some truth in the following sense: By attempting to overcome the materiality of signs and naturalized blood ties, the blood of Jesus gains more power as the mediator of transethnic and transgenerational relatedness. This is an important ramification of spiritual kinship especially for the younger yonsei generations who are coming of age in Japan today. What will happen to them in the future, when the nation's legal system will tell them that their "Japanese blood" has thinned so much that it does not provide even the slightest veil of national belonging? They are of two bloods.

8

ANCESTORS OF GOD

Belief in the Eye of the Beholder

"God told us that our time in Japan is over. Time to return to our country," Luan affirmed with a smile, sipping his after-meal coffee. He had told me over the dinner that he used to drink a lot, but God had cured him of his sinful habit. Now coffee and *guaraná* were all he needed to feel satisfied after a good meal, especially because his fiancée, Kana, cooked each one with "a lot of love."

"Yes, it is time to return!" Kana chimed in from the kitchen where she was doing the dishes. I had offered to help, but she told me to remain at the dining table with Luan because I was a guest. I looked around the dining space again, which was part of the larger living room. The apartment was filled with open moving boxes, which made sense given that their planned move-out date was only a week away. I could see a wide-screen TV, vacuum cleaner, and desktop computer lurking out of thick cardboard boxes of various sizes.

"You are bringing a lot of things back," I commented, pointing at them.

"Oh yes, of course," Luan said, rolling his eyes. "We have to. You won't believe how expensive electronics are in Brazil. In Japan, they are cheaper and better in quality. It doesn't make sense to leave them here. We are bringing the washing machine, too."

"A washing machine? From Japan to Brazil?" I gasped.

Luan and Kana giggled, amused by my shocked expression. "We already bought a plan with lots of space with the moving company—two meters in all the directions—so they'll all fit. We need all of them to start our new life there," Luan explained. They smiled at each other. Their wedding was scheduled several months afterward in Kana's hometown in Paraná, Brazil. "Japan has been great—above all, we now have faith and will bring it back to Brazil to start our new life together with God," Kana said, wiping her wet hands with her apron as she sat down at the dinner table. Judging that it was the right time, I put out a voice recorder and asked if I could start the interview—the original purpose of my visit. They nodded. "Ask anything!" Luan said cheerfully.

The interview lasted for about ninety minutes. When I turned off the recorder, Kana offered another cup of coffee, which I hesitated before accepting because it was already 11 P.M. Taking tiny sips, I waited for a good time to excuse myself to go home as we made small talk. It was then that Kana and Luan started speaking about a "strange" festival in Komaki, a city one hour's drive away from Homi Danchi. The festival had taken place the previous week (on March 15) and they came across its footage online. The Hōnen Festival at Tagata Shrine is best known for its 280 kg (620 pound), 2.5 meter (98 inch)–long wooden phallus. While the wooden phallus is carried around on the street, people try to touch it, as it is the embodiment of harvest, prosperity, and fertility. "*Nossa* [Oh my]! These women flock to the phallus and try really hard to touch it! They believe they can get pregnant that way!" Luan exclaimed. Taken aback by their incredulous expression and critical tone, I asked if they thought such Japanese women actually "believed [*crer*]." "Yes!" they responded in unison. "The way they tried to touch it was intense!"

Right after I left Kana and Luan's place, I sat down on a bench on the street side on my way home, which was only a five-minute walk away. First I jotted down the conversation about the Hōnen Festival on my notebook. "This always happens," I thought to myself, half amused and half frustrated. "They always say the most interesting stuff off-tape!" Then I picked up my cell phone and called a friend who lived in Ichinomiya, a city located right next to Komaki where the festival took place. She and her friends had actually invited me to go to the festival, which I turned down since I had a Japanese class to teach at a local nongovernmental organization that day. Junko answered my call after a few seconds. After apologizing for calling so late and briefly describing the context of the question, I asked if she "believed" in the power of the phallic object that she touched during the event.

"Believe? Believe what? [*shinjiru tte, nan'no koto?*]," she responded. I hesitantly explained if she was convinced of its impregnating power. Junko laughed for a good few seconds. "I touched it but I don't expect to get pregnant! I don't have a boyfriend right now to start with." She then added, "I can't speak for others, but I feel it's not really about believing. Just look at all the foreign tourists who came![1] No one would ask you about what you believe there, that's for sure."

As Junko herself admitted, she "cannot speak for others" and it is not my purpose here to speculate on the inner psychological states of the visitors at the festival. Instead, this ethnographic scene can illuminate how some Pentecostal converts project their own understanding of belief onto non-Christian practices that they witness. In the comments made by Luan and Kana, Japanese Shinto festivals (*matsuri*) figured as a mirror on which their own ideas about what belief did were reflected. To them, participation in ritual (i.e., touching the phallus) and self-aware belief in its meaning (i.e., impregnation) were supposed to be welded together. This is why they deduced that everyone who made an active effort to touch the object must "believe" in its meaning and effect. Their reaction to the ritual, however, reveals more about Pentecostalism than about Japanese religions, as Junko's response implies. Belief may be in the eye of the beholder.

Faith Beyond Belief

In that they were trying to make sense of unfamiliar acts with the familiar categories they knew, Luan and Kana were being lay anthropologists in a foreign land. In their own cultural idiom, the "intense" action they witnessed could not have been explained without the preexisting psychological attitude of "believing in meaning." As it turns out, this formula of belief-to-action-via-meaning has been influential among professional anthropologists who have theorized about culture and religion as well. Clifford Geertz, for instance, characterized belief as a cognitive readiness to find meaning in the otherwise meaningless world: "He who would know must first believe."[2] In his view, belief created the path to knowledge in religion. By stressing the distinction between "common-sensical perspective" and "religious perspective," he also implicitly painted religion as a separate realm that remains beyond the reach of nonbelieving minds unless the entry permit—belief—was obtained.[3]

If Geertz envisioned belief as a profound well of human creativity that made another reality possible, his contemporary Rodney Needham suggested precisely the opposite: He noticed that there was something "empty" about belief in the common English usage of the term. Based on his fieldwork among the Penan in Borneo, he described how his observations eventually came to challenge the category he had long taken for granted. Needham's informants often spoke of Poselong, a preeminent supernatural being that Needham translated as "God" in English. Although he initially surmised that the Penan "believed in their God," he soon came to question his own cultural framework that he had projected onto the people. Although the term *belief* implies a certain psychological interiority, he had to admit that he did not have any "linguistic evidence" about the Penan's "psychic attitude toward the personage [Poselong]." All they did, as far as Needham knew, was to "speak of its existence." Yet he first found it natural to equate external speech with internal state by resorting to the idea of belief.[4]

So, why did Luan and Kana feel compelled to ascribe the Japanese women's action during the Hōnen Festival to their preexisting belief in the phallic object? Neither the Penan nor the Japanese gave the observers the necessary verbal evidence to support the hypothesis of the believing mind. And yet the concept of belief as "a mental state of assent to a proposition already contained in the mind" seems to persist as a powerful explanatory model.[5] Talal Asad famously pointed out that the prioritization of belief in the study of religion is largely due to the legacy of Protestant Christianity that continues to shape both popular and academic discourses about how the human mind functions. He was particularly troubled by the bias toward individual, cognitive, and conscious assent to discrete propositional truths: "Geertz's treatment of religious belief, which lies at the core of his conception of religion, is a modern, privatized Christian one because and to the extent that it emphasizes the priority of belief as a state of mind."[6] In his view, to assume an interiority-oriented posture toward belief, and to make it inseparable from all things religious, is to unwittingly invoke a Protestant scheme of salvation consumed with the individual acceptance of core doctrines. Not all traditions prioritize belief, or such a vision of belief at least, as the core driving force of moral subject formation. He thus called attention to the inadequacy of belief as a cross-cultural category.

What is ironic is that, with the flourishing of Global Christianity today, an increasing number of people outside the West are speaking precisely in the language of internal belief. Brazilian Pentecostals in Japan are among such people. As Luan and Kana exemplify, not only do they speak to the ethnographer with the concept of belief, they also interpret their encounters with the perceived cultural others in the same analytical framework. Clearly, then, the category of belief gains a renewed significance, both theoretically and politically, in such a transnational site of boundary making where "us" and "them" take shape. How do Nikkei Brazilian converts in Japan build and deploy their vision of belief—or *crença*—in the process of subject formation as migrant converts? Does their collective endeavor to cultivate faith (*fé*) really prioritize "belief as a state of mind"? Given that conversion is a painstaking process, what are some of the ambiguities and contestations that the ideal of sincere belief faces in the context of "return" migration in Japan?

Roadmap to Water Baptism

To inquire why Kana and Luan reacted the way they did, I first turn to the Pentecostal ritual that best illustrates the church's official view on the relationship between ritual, meaning, and faith: water baptism, or the baptism in the waters (*batismo nas águas*). Like many other evangelical Christians, my informants generally regarded water baptism as the definitive moment of conversion. Missão Apoio Toyota held it once a year on the riverbank of the Yahagi River, which runs through the center of the city.

The church invested a considerable amount of time and energy to ensure that all the new converts "knew what it meant" to take part in water baptism. Initiates had to be completely sure, the leaders would say, because there was no way to "deconvert" after water baptism. Prospective converts had to go through several steps. Several months prior to the ritual, which was scheduled in August, the leaders of my home group started asking whether anyone unconverted had the intention of participating in the baptism that year. "If you want to be baptized, please come talk to us," they would say, "because you want to make sure you know what you are getting yourself into." Those who were judged ready for water baptism by home group leaders then attended the preparatory study session, which took place roughly two weeks before the ceremony. Pastor Cid lectured on the meaning of conversion every born-again Christian must know, such as the acceptance of Jesus Christ as the savior. In the next step, prospective converts filled out and turned in a form to demonstrate their sincere intention. Aside from basic personal information, the form included items such as "Describe Previous Experiences with God." Finally, the weekend before the day of water baptism, those who had fulfilled all the previous requirements performed the "confession of faith." One by one, prospective converts stood before the whole congregation to give a short speech about their sincere desire to follow Jesus Christ. As the process shows, the church laid out a closely monitored roadmap to the moment of conversion "to make sure everyone understands what the ceremony means," to borrow the pastor's phrase.

In 2014, the water baptism took place on August 12, Tuesday, during a period commonly referred to as *obon yasumi* (*obon* vacation) in Japan. *Obon* is a Japanese Buddhist custom to commemorate the spirits of ancestors who are said to return to the world of the living for roughly three days around August 15. It is customary to travel back to one's hometown and visit the ancestral grave, which is the official reason why many employers grant multiple holidays around obon. The majority of Brazilians in Japan, however, are not Buddhist and the custom of obon does not concern most of them. But the obon vacation is a different matter. It is typically seven days long in the so-called Toyota calendar adopted by the factories that have direct and indirect business relations with the Toyota Motor Corporation.[7] Since most congregants at Missão Apoio Toyota worked in factories that granted the obon vacation based on the calendar, it was virtually a collective weeklong summer vacation for everyone. Some families left for a beach in Southern Aichi, neighboring Mie, or tropical Okinawa as soon as the vacation started. Most of those who remained in Toyota gathered on the riverbank of the Yahagi River to welcome the new members of the church. I arrived barely in time, having just returned from Hyogo that morning after visiting my ancestral graves there the previous weekend. To my relatives who insisted that I should stay longer to show respect to ancestors, I mumbled apologetically that I had research to conduct.

Around noon, those who were going to be baptized—roughly two dozen of them—put on white robes and formed a circle, which was in turn surrounded by all the other attendants. The ceremony started with a reading of biblical passages about the baptism of Jesus Christ by John the Baptist. The microphone went back and forth between Pastor Cid and Lucas, the interpreter, after each verse to provide a bilingual procession. Although the majority of new converts understood only the pastor's words in Portuguese, the younger ones—two of them born in Japan, as far as I knew—likely listened primarily to the interpreter's Japanese translation. After the reading, the pastor reviewed the meaning of water baptism once again. It is a reaffirmation of a life in sanctity separate from the world; it is grounded on your own decision to have a personal relationship with Jesus; it is a moment of death to the old self and rebirth of

FIGURE 5. Two pastors and two initiates who are about to immerse in the water at the Yahagi River, Toyota City. Photo taken by the author during the water baptism in 2014.

the new self. Then, led by the pastors and presbyters, the initiates started down the riverbank toward the water. Due to the typhoon that had just passed, the water was brown and the current was faster than usual. The pastors, the presbyters, and the first initiates to be baptized stepped into the water with caution. "Sister Aline," Pastor Cid started:

> PASTOR. Is it your free and spontaneous will to be baptized?
> ALINE. Yes.
> PASTOR. Do you believe that our Lord Jesus died and resurrected for your sins?
> ALINE. Yes.
> PASTOR. Do you promise to serve and love Him every day of your life?
> ALINE. Yes.
> PASTOR. In the name of the Father, the Son, and the Holy Spirit, I baptize you.

As soon as the pastor finished his last word, he immersed her into the water and then pulled her up with the assistance of a presbyter. The crowd clapped and congratulated her with hallelujahs. Baptism proceeded swiftly from there. The line of initiates became shorter and shorter, and as each new convert got out of the water, family members and friends dashed to embrace his or her soaked body in joy.

The Line Between Bath and Baptism:
Faith as Sincere Belief

The church leaders stressed two interrelated objectives as prospective converts moved through the process of water baptism, from its preparatory steps to the culminating moment of immersion into water. One was the understanding of symbolic meaning associated with each ritual action, and the other was the sincere acceptance of the core tenets of born-again faith. They strongly discouraged participation for participation's sake and warned the youth that pleasing one's parents could not be the underlying motive. By the day of water baptism, participation was ideally an *expression* of preexisting sincere commitment to the relationship with God, not a *means* to achieve or strengthen social ties with significant others.

One reason why converts insisted on the self-aware understanding of meanings in signs and acts is that without it, their rituals would resemble those of Catholics. That was something they wanted to avoid. During the study session for prospective converts, for instance, one woman stood up and asked if she could be baptized again when she had already been baptized in the Catholic Church at birth. Pastor Cid responded that to born-again Christians, infant baptism was not authentic because it was not based on the participant's intentional decision with a clear understanding of the act. He then went on to recollect his mother's experience of water baptism, which took place in a small town in São Paulo when he was a child. When she stepped out of the small indoor pool where her Pentecostal church was holding the ceremony, the first thing she told him was that it was "a good bath" (*bom banho*). He chastised his mother, saying that it was not a mere bath but a moment of death to the old self and rebirth in the life-giving blood of Jesus Christ. "Without this deep reflection on the meaning of the act, you'll be just taking a nice bath during water baptism, just like my mother," the pastor added. "And she reverted to her old ways soon after the baptism." He himself underwent water baptism several years afterward and remained active as a church leader to this day, which presumably means his baptism was not a "good bath."

The leaders at Missão Apoio thus placed the efficacy of ritual action in the inner sincerity of the participant rather than the ritual of water baptism itself. A set of implicit views on language, meaning, and belief supported this official stance. First, they designed the ritual process in ways that encouraged interiority, individuality, and intentionality. At every step, each participant was urged to reflect on one's inner intention to ascertain that oneself—and no one else—was the author of one's own decision. The leaders also placed strong emphasis on the learning of each action's symbolic meaning because they thought that decision unfounded on articulate comprehension was ultimately void (e.g., infant baptism). Sincere intention required conscious understanding of meanings invested in objects and gestures. Many congregants thought that without such a mental state, there would be little difference between Pentecostal water baptism and Catholic infant baptism.

The church leaders also privileged the referential aspect of language, that is, a view that words represent preexisting entities and states. In such a way of thinking, each word or action has symbolic meaning, standing for something else other than the utterance or act itself. Immersion into water *represents* death and rebirth; bread and grape juice *symbolize* the body and blood of Jesus; saying "yes" right before immersing into water *stands for* one's inner sincerity. This referential framework shapes the "gestalt" of Protestant language practices: "Viewed as a gestalt, then, the Christian language 'ideologue' . . . could be identified by a rather small though recurrent constellation of features, chief of which are a marked predilection for sincerity, interiority, intimacy, intentionality, and immediacy as an ethics of speech, and a privileging of the referential aspects of language."[8] With its emphasis on sincerity, interiority, and intentionality as an "ethics of speech," water baptism constructs faith as sincere belief, or intentional assent to articulable meanings. Seconds before the immersion into water, initiates are asked one last time to verbally confirm their assent to the three core propositions on which Pentecostal faith rests: spontaneous free will, belief in Jesus Christ as the savior, and commitment to the relationship with Him. All the previous preparatory steps ascertain that each convert truly *means* what he or she says in this crucial moment.

But does this official account of water baptism by the leaders actually reflect the experiences of the initiates? To probe possible divergences between the public narrative and personal sentiments, I now turn to the story of one woman whom I will call Leticia.

Burn Me with My Ancestors: Leticia's Story

Fifty-three-year-old Leticia Kikuchi had been living in Japan for roughly twenty years—thirteen years of which were in Homi Danchi—when I became acquainted with her during fieldwork. Having lost her husband to cancer in

2009, she was living with two of her four children, twenty-five-year-old Kenji and sixteen-year-old Sakura. Sakura was born in Japan and schooled only in Japanese schools. Whenever Leticia talked to her in Portuguese, she would respond in Japanese. Kenji, in contrast, was six when he was brought to Japan and spent four years of his adolescence with his uncle in Brazil. Although he could speak both Japanese and Portuguese, he often described his language skills as *chūto hampa* (half-baked). Since the education he received in each country was intermittent, he felt that his vocabulary and reading skills of each language were incomplete. Due to his fluency in spoken Japanese and Portuguese, however, he frequently received requests for translation from his Brazilian friends. He found some of them difficult, especially when they involved reading and writing Japanese. It was Kenji whom I first became close to because he occasionally asked me to assist him with the translation of Japanese texts.

Since I did not find Leticia and Kenji alike in appearance, I did not realize that they were related for several weeks. One Sunday, the presbyter asked if there were any volunteers who wanted to testify on their experiences at the church event called Veredas Antigas (see Chapter 6). Kenji raised his hand and walked up to the front. Slowly, he related how the conversation with God during the retreat made him realize that he still held unresolved bitter feelings toward his parents for painful childhood memories. "But God told me that, you see, everyone is human. We have to forgive just as Jesus forgives us and loves us." His eyes were teary and his voice was trailing off.

The presbyter then asked Kenji's mother to step forward for a moment of reconciliation. Leticia—who had also participated in the retreat—walked up to embrace her son affectionately. "I love you, son."

"I love you, too, mother."

Since Leticia always spoke passionately of God, I assumed she was also a convert like Kenji and Shinji, her two sons who attended Missão Apoio Toyota. One spring afternoon in 2014, I visited her apartment for an interview. Like most of my interviewees from Missão Apoio, one of her first questions was about my religious identity: "So, when did you convert?" Some assumed I had to be a rare Japanese born-again Christian to decide to study a place like their church.

I responded that I was not a Christian but instead a "non-practicing Buddhist" (*budista não praticante*).

"Oh, so you are not *crente* [born-again Christian]?"

"No."

"Me either." I was rather taken aback. She added, "My sons are, but I am not . . . not yet, at least."

Leticia was born in 1961 in a neighborhood in the city of São Paulo with a sizable Okinawan community. In Brazil, Nikkeis of Okinawan descent—those who have ties to the present-day Okinawa Prefecture in Japan—have developed an ethnic identity distinct from the rest of Nikkeis. When I asked Leticia about her family, for instance, she immediately responded, "My father is from the Higa family and my mother from Shimabuku. You know, they were both *Okinawa-jin* [Okinawan]!" Aside from the distinctly Okinawan surnames, her parents also maintained the Okinawan vernacular in their household, especially when Leticia's grandparents were still alive. As a third-generation Nikkei, she herself grew up speaking mostly Portuguese. When she was eight, the family moved to Sorocaba, where they lived in a "mixed" neighborhood with non-Nikkei Brazilians. In the new city, the family was no longer embedded in a tight Okinawan network because the few Nikkeis they became acquainted with were *nihon-jin* (Japanese)—which, to Leticia, is quite different from *Okinawa-jin* (Okinawan).

Leticia's upbringing was shaped by Roman Catholicism as well as Okinawan rites of ancestral commemoration. She was raised in the Catholic Church because her mother was active in the local parish. When it came to her kin, however, she stressed that "we are Shintoist because Okinawan is Shintoist— Okinawan is not Buddhist."[9] Although she spoke of Catholicism as a fact of public life in Brazil, Shinto was a distinct marker of Okinawan identity to Leticia since she associated Buddhism with non-Okinawan Nikkeis and Japanese people (*japoneses*). When I asked her what Shinto was for her, she answered that it primarily consisted in taking care of the family altar in gratitude toward one's ancestors. "There, have a look," Leticia said as she slid open the door to the next room. On a wooden dresser, at eye level, was a small black house-shaped altar with a triangle roof and double doors. "That's the altar."

"Many Okinawans have one?" I asked.

"Yes, but this one is from Seichō-no-Ie, because that's where I learned how to take care of my ancestors." To my puzzled look, Leticia continued her story.

When she was twenty-three years old, her mother passed away. The death sensitized her to the question of how to venerate the spirits of the dead according to the traditional ways of Okinawan culture, which her mother had firmly embraced throughout her life. It was a critical issue that troubled Leticia for several years after her mother's death but, to her frustration, her six siblings did not seem to share her concern. In fact, all of them married *brasileiros* (Brazilians, by which she meant non-Nikkeis) one after another during this period. It seemed to Leticia that the eldest son, who was supposed to continue the veneration of ancestral spirits by looking after the altar he inherited, was not doing much to keep the tradition going. Not being the eldest male of the household, she did not own a family altar. "It was this desire to learn how to properly look after the family altar that drew me to Seichō-no-Ie, because I wanted to take care of my mother's spirit." Three years after her mother's death, Leticia joined the local chapter of the organization. Seichō-no-Ie does not have any historical ties to Okinawa, as it was founded by a Japanese man named Masaharu Taniguchi in the Japanese mainland in 1930. What attracted her was the primal emphasis Seichō-no-Ie places on the veneration of the ancestral spirits. The founder, for example, wrote a whole book on the spiritual necessity of commemorating the dead, titled *Commemoration of Ancestors Determines Our Life* (*Jinsei wo Shihaisuru Senzo Kuyō*).[10] In his words, "The earth is God, the root is ancestors, the trunk is parents, and I am the branch; for the branch to grow flowers of prosperity, one must first look after the ancestors who reside at the root."[11] Seichō-no-Ie officially encourages everyone—including those who are neither male nor the eldest—to engage in the practices to venerate the dead. To her joy, Leticia also found out that Seichō-no-Ie upholds the principle of *bankyō ki'itsu* (All Teachings Return to One), a view that all religions are one and the same at the root. There were no rigid rules as to which style of family altar members must acquire. It could be Shinto-style (*kamidana*), Buddhist (*butsudan*), or something else. She obtained a small altar for herself. Seichō-no-Ie provided her with philosophies, practices, and communities with which to strengthen the perceived ties with the ancestors in ways that did not conflict with her desire to maintain Okinawan heritage.

Soon after she joined Seichō-no-Ie, she met another Nikkei member who served as a lecturer at the center she frequented. He was a *naichi* (inland), which means non-Okinawan Nikkei Brazilian in this context. They married within a year and had three sons in the first five years of their marriage. In 1995, the family migrated to Japan due to financial hardship in Brazil. Like many Nikkei migrants at the time, they intended to stay in Japan for "a year or two, save money, and go home." Leticia and her husband were so sure about their plan of immediate return to Brazil that for the first year, they did not send their sons to school. After a year, the municipal education committee of Seto City showed up at their doorstep because the neighbors had notified the city that several school-aged children were at home without receiving education. The children started going to Japanese elementary school, Leticia became pregnant with another child, and Sakura was born. A year turned into two, then five, and then a decade. When her husband passed away in Japan in 2009, she realized that "there was no way" they could go back to Brazil and start a decent life there.

Since there were no branches of Seichō-no-Ie that she knew of in either Seto or Toyota, the two cities in which the family had lived since their migration, they could not maintain active participation in Japan. It took them roughly two hours by bus and train to reach the closest center in Kariya City from Homi Danchi. Soon after her husband's death, around 2010, her two younger sons— Kenji and Shinji—started frequenting Missão Apoio Toyota. "At first, I found it wonderful, you know, that they were searching the path of God [*caminho de Deus*]," Leticia reminisced. "But as soon as they started messing with me, we had a conflict." What troubled her was the Pentecostal emphasis on purified religious boundary. Because she was someone who had never found fault with multiple identities and moved seamlessly between Catholicism, Okinawan ancestral worship, and Seichō-no-Ie, her sons' "lack of tolerance" toward other religions felt like an "attack" to her sense of self. As her sons learned the Pentecostal ideal of immaterial faith, they also started interpreting her relationship with the family altar as "idolatry." That is when her inner turmoil reached its peak. "Eles abominam, eles não querem, não aceitam" (They just abominate it, do not want it, do not accept it), Leticia said, using some of the strongest words to describe her sons' distaste toward the altar. "Now what? What's going to happen? Who will take care of the altar when I die? What will happen to our ancestors, and my mother?" Although her eldest son was not converted, he had been living in Tokyo for years to make his career in Japan and was simply indifferent to such matters. There was "no peace" in her mind.

I was speechless. Having interacted with her only in the context of church, I could never have imagined the extent of her inner distress until then. Remembering the scene of reconciliation that I had witnessed at church several months earlier, I asked if the conflict still continued. Leticia responded no. "What sensitized me," she explained, "was prayers of my sons. When they told me, with tears in their eyes, that they were praying for me with all their might, I finally stopped to think. It was the biggest gift in my life, because that's what I wanted—someone praying for me. I had been praying for others all my life, you know." She gradually opened up to her sons and began to participate in church activities. At the same time, she visited the Seichō-no-Ie center in Kariya to "ask for permission." She explained to the leaders there that she did not want the "disharmony in the family" to continue because of the conflicts she had with her sons. She was reassured to hear the leaders affirm that "God is one and the only, including Jesus Christ. Walk with your friends and relatives, because family cannot walk on two separate paths for there to be harmony."

In addition to the religious leaders, she also sought permission from God in Seichō-no-Ie: "And God, as time went by, made things clearer for me, showing for me, you see. 'Yes, my child, you know the truth. The truth is one. Take the path with your sons because I will be with you. Independent of others, what you have already learnt will continue within.' Here in my mind, in my heart. 'So, do not worry,' God told me." As Leticia prayed, not only God but also her ancestors came to understand her decision. Instead of the scriptures of Seichō-no-Ie, she started reciting some passages from the Bible to the altar, and she thought she sensed their approval. "My ancestors, too, understand, because what matters is family—family is important," Leticia said. By the time of my fieldwork, Leticia had been participating in the church activities just like any other member, if not more actively. Every Sunday, she attended a service at Missão Apoio Toyota with her three children. Her Bible was covered by sticky notes, with passages marked with highlighters and the margin full of handwritten notes.

However, there was one thing Leticia had not conceded to her sons. She insisted that the family altar would stay until her death. To her sons, who thought that "there was a way" to discard it, Leticia explained that an altar could not be thrown away "just anywhere, in whatever way" (*em qualquer lugar, de qualquer jeito*). She elaborated, "I already asked for permission, so there is no connection. But, . . . 'I want you [her sons] to place it in my coffin.' If I die here in Japan, I want that, um, to be cremated together with them [ancestors]. They will be cremated together with me. Because I asked for the permission that way." She sighed. "As long as they can do this, my soul will rest in peace [*minha alma vai ficar tranquila*]."

Leticia then asked me if my family commemorated the spirits of ancestors. I told her that I had actually traveled to my mother's natal city several months earlier to attend a Buddhist ritual for the first anniversary of my uncle's death. "I have to go visit my family's graves again soon, you know, because *obon* is in August," I added.

"That's wonderful," Leticia said as she nodded with approval. "You are blessed. Continue respecting your parents, because the ancestors of the parents are the ancestors of God [*Continua reverenciando e respeitando seus pais, porque avós dos pais é avós de Deus*]. Do you understand?" I nodded and answered yes. I realized that all the rituals of ancestral veneration that I took for granted, and even found bothersome as a child, were something Leticia had fought hard to maintain as a way to make sense of her diasporic identity and cultural belonging. I thought of Kenji, with whom I had had many lengthy conversations as we worked together on translation. I had never heard the word *okinawano* from his mouth. What was more, he would likely have been troubled by what his mother had just said about the "ancestors of God" because he, like other converts, upheld that God was utterly transcendent from human kinship.

Leticia did convert that year, together with her daughter Sakura. Leticia was one of the last initiates to step into the river water and did so with a big bright smile. Her sons were behind her, happily capturing the moment with their iPhones. Leticia gave a firm and loud yes to all the three questions, and then she was under water. "Eitcha Glória [Glory to God]!" She exclaimed as she walked back to the bank all soaked, with her arms up to the sky. Her sons helped her get out of the river and hugged her while the entire congregation surrounded them with warm smiles and congratulations. Several weeks later, I visited Leticia's apartment in Homi Danchi again to help her read some documents Sakura brought back from her Japanese school. At one point, Leticia opened the sliding door to ask Sakura, who was taking a nap in the next room, when the forms were due with the parent's signature. The altar was still there, quietly sitting on the black dresser.[12]

Between Ancestral Personhood and Sincere Self

Leticia's experience diverges from the church's official view on faith in a number of ways. For example, how she envisioned God differs from the dominant narrative in Pentecostal culture, which emphasizes the transcendental character of God and the radical break between the human and the divine.[13] To Leticia, who creatively combined a number of approaches accumulated through her past affiliations, what characterized the space between humans and deities was not a radical rupture but gradual continuity. This is the most obvious in how she related to the ancestral spirits, including her own deceased mother. In her view, living humans eventually transitioned into ancestral spirits, making the continuous character of human-divine relationship tangible. This human-divine continuity across generations was essential to Leticia's sense of cultural identity, which was Okinawan. She cherished the family altar as a material medium that crystallized her continuing ties with the ancestors, spirits, and homelands. Additionally, the altar was a tangible nexus of what Jacob Hickman called "ancestral personhood," or "a particular view of the life course as eternally embedded in kinship-based relationships and hierarchies that are enacted through ritual and discourse."[14]

Initially, she was deeply hurt by her children's insistence on immaterial faith and purified religious boundary, which undergirded the accusation that she was practicing idolatry.[15] Although she eventually opened up to her sons and started participating in church activities, her narrative still resists the radical break from the past that often accompanies Pentecostal conversion. Indeed, she asked for permission to convert from the Seichō-no-Ie leaders as well as the ancestral spirits, which shows her effort for peaceful transition rather than sudden rupture. She also rejected her sons' request to discard the family altar. Although she "severed the tie" with the object, she insisted that the ancestral spirits gave her permission to do so only on the condition that they would be cremated with her upon her death. Furthermore, her motive for conversion also defies the model of individual sincere belief that church leaders upheld. To Leticia, "what matters is family—family is important." Her participation in Pentecostal activities was in large part driven by her desire to restore "harmony" in the family, which runs counter to the primary emphasis the church leaders placed on the individual relationship with God.

Faith as Relational Commitment

Does all this mean that her conversion was inauthentic? Or, to put it more bluntly, did she *lie* when she answered "yes" to all the three questions seconds before immersing into water? Although no one except Leticia can ever know what was going through her mind during water baptism, many of her fellow congregants would likely perceive her action as inauthentic should they discover the altar at her home. As far as the official views of the church are concerned, maintaining an ancestral altar contradicts the tenet expressed in one of the questions—to "serve and love Him every day of your life"—because doing so is to allow the presence of other spirits to linger on. Leticia's desire for familial harmony, along with the principal role it played in her decision to convert, may also go against the church's interpretation of "being baptized out of your free and spontaneous will." Although the firmness of her will is hardly contestable, she seemed to draw her strength from her connectedness—with her children, family, and ancestors—rather than from her individuality. Conversion driven by the sense of commitment to family was something that the church typically frowned on, since it was ideally the personal relationship with God that should move one to such a decision.

Of course, that the church had to repeatedly stress the individuality of conversion experience indicates that there were always some who failed to meet this ideal. A handful of congregants at Missão Apoio Toyota indeed told me that they had initially undergone water baptism out of the sense of obligation to their converted family members. Beatriz, for instance, told me matter-of-factly that she underwent baptism "following everyone's lead [nori-de]" at the age of fifteen. "Everyone was getting baptized, so I thought it was only natural for me to do the same thing." Not surprisingly, such an admission often came from "second-generation crentes," or the younger generation who grew up in the church. Typically, it was their parents who migrated from Brazil and converted to Pentecostalism in Japan. The church leaders were aware of this generational shift, along with the moral threat it posed to what they viewed as authentic conversion experience.

After the reading of biblical passages during water baptism, Pastor Cid called two prospective converts to his side. He wanted them to speak about their experiences with God before the immersion into water. The first man, seemingly in his forties, spoke about his difficult life as a migrant laborer in Japan, indulgence in sinful ways of life to fill the emptiness he felt within, and eventual encounter with Jesus Christ as the savior. Before he passed the microphone to the next person, a teenage girl with a shy smile, the pastor inserted his view on "the new generation of crentes." "Since she grew up in a godly home, she never experienced the world [aproveitou o mundo]. Sometimes this makes it more difficult to understand how precious the encounter with God is, but here she is—she wants to have an individual relationship with God for the rest of her life!" Her parents—a third-generation Nikkei mother and a non-Nikkei father who had converted together in Japan right before her birth—were smiling with pride in front of her. The pastor's remark ironically suggested that a sizable number of converts—particularly the younger ones raised in Pentecostal homes—went through water baptism in ways that did not live up to the ideal of individual sincere belief. And many church leaders were aware of such a phenomenon—conversion as familial obligation and social conformity.

And this is where I would like to highlight *relational commitment* as an integral part of faith in this ethnographic context. Most of my informants, of course, would disagree with me. To them, those who converted primarily to commit to their families and friends were being inauthentic. As an ethnographer, however, my concern encompasses both the exemplary and the pragmatic, that is, both envisioned ideals as well as actual practices. When a sizable number of my informants consistently diverge from the ideal scenario, I must entertain the possibility that they are not a group of outliers but rather a legitimate constituency that shapes shared cultural reality. Moreover, I am not the first to point out that Christians—even charismatic Christians—are not quite the believers that they claim or appear to be. Granted, Protestant branches of Christianity have been interpreted first and foremost as cultures of sincere belief.[16] However, an increasing number of ethnographers have been reevaluating the equation of belief with individualized propositional assent. Thomas Kirsch, for example, advocated replacing *belief*, defined as an achieved interior state, with *believing* defined instead as a condition that is constantly sought after and always in the process of being internalized.[17] Similarly, in an article entitled "Faith Beyond Belief" based on a study of American evangelical churches, Omri Elisha asked: "Is it possible that evangelical Protestants are not quite the believers that they appear to be?"[18] He then suggested that the analytical vocabulary of anthropologists should attend to *faith*, which shapes "the practice of performative rituals and religious disciplines."[19] Along a similar line, Brian Howell argued that the cross-cultural study of Christianity would benefit from recasting *belief* as *commitment*.[20] The Filipino Baptists of his ethnography were less concerned with whether everyone affirmed the same doctrines than with whether everyone was equally invested in everyday ritual life. James Bielo also observed that the "emerging evangelicals" in the contemporary United States "have shifted the organizing logic of their religious selves from doctrinal belief to the cultivation of community relationships."[21] In fact, such Christians "seek a faith where human-human relationships are a precondition for human-divine relations to flourish."[22] Taking cues from these scholars, I suggest that faith as a cultural reality at Missão Apoio is more than just an individual cognitive belief; it is also a relational commitment to social and spiritual others. Seen in this light, Leticia—or anyone else who converted to foster human-human relationships, for that matter— was not necessarily being inauthentic during water baptism. Characterizing her conversion as insincere is to privilege the referential aspect of language and action. Words, however, do not merely *represent* but also *act, achieve*, and *perform*.[23]

If "yes" in water baptism was a speech act rather than a descriptive statement, what did it achieve? The most obvious answer in the case of Leticia is that it performed faith as relational commitment. By uttering "yes" to a circle of audience members who were there to bear witness, she publicly declared and, to some degree, achieved her commitment to social others. If the personal relationship between oneself and God were truly the only dimension of faith, water baptism would not require the presence of witnesses—social others who watch, listen, embrace, and applaud new converts. Yet it very much does. Water baptism was a collective and celebratory occasion at Missão Apoio, as it is at innumerable other churches around the world.

Communion: The Ontological Unity of the Social and the Religious

In fact, the ceremony of water baptism itself was only a small part of the day's gathering. By the time the new converts—still in soaked clothes—were partaking in their first Lord's Supper on the riverbank, we could already smell burning charcoal in the air. As soon as the "official" part ended in the early afternoon, the roughly one hundred attendants quickly gathered around a dozen barbecue grills that they had set up and started a festive *churrasco* (barbecue party). They ate thick meat chunks, drank *guaraná* soft drinks, grilled banana for dessert (something Japanese people seldom do), played soccer when they became full, and listened to Brazilian gospel music pouring out of the large speakers someone had brought on a truck. The party went on after dark as well with the help of portable camp lights. Surrounding one such light, my home group members sat in a circle and sang worship songs to the tune of the guitar Presbyter Bruno played. After a whole day by the river, everyone looked relaxed and content.

"Crentes gostam muito de comunhão, né?" [Born-agains love communion, right?], Presbyter Bruno said as he put down his guitar on the ground. "Actually, that's the first impression people have about us. We are always getting together. Church, Bible study, prayer group, fundraising party, and *churrasco*. It's true, it's like having a second job to be a *crente*." Everyone giggled. "But we do this for God, to praise the name of Jesus, to offer our fellowship to the glory of His Kingdom." He paused and then added, "The biggest error we men can make, the most serious error, is to think that 'I can do it alone.' We can't. We need God for everything. Let's not forget that we are completely dependent on Him. It's very important to have an intimate and constant communion with God [*É importantíssimo ter uma comunhão íntima e constante com Deus*], okay?" Note the multiple connotations of *comunhão*, which shares the same Latin root with such words as *comum* (common), *comunicar* (communicate), and *comunidade* (community). On the one hand, *comunhão* refers to the close companionship of those who self-identify as Christians, or what they call "brothers and sisters in faith." Presbyter Bruno half-jokingly characterized the dense human relationships facilitated by the church as a "second job." To him, this was among the main features of Pentecostal life that outsiders took notice of at first glance. On the other hand, *comunhão* also means the intimate and personal relationship that each convert ideally cultivates with God. Presbyter Bruno emphasized that the "intimate and constant communion with God" was integral to the moral subjectivity that he described as "complete dependence on God." At churches like Missão Apoio, prayer was key to this latter kind of comunhão. In fact, some converts compared prayer to water; prayer was to comunhão as water was to life. They would also add that comunhão was in fact life itself, because human life depended on divine grace.

The layered import of *comunhão* becomes even more apparent in light of yet another meaning of the word: the Eucharist, or the Holy Communion based on Jesus Christ's last meal. Although this usage of the term is commonplace in the Portuguese language, the congregants at Missão Apoio Toyota referred to their Pentecostal Eucharist as *santa ceia* (the "holy supper" or the Lord's Supper) and never identified it as a comunhão. They used *comunhão* to refer to the Catholic Eucharist, as Catholic Brazilians themselves did consistently. At first glance, this is a straightforward linguistic tactic to construct a desired theological boundary: *comunhão* for Catholics and *santa ceia* for Pentecostals. But the fact that Pentecostal converts reserved the word *comunhão* for relationality, both human-human and human-divine, points to something more profound. This rhetorical choice is, first, a refusal to contain the connotation of communion within a bounded ritual setting and, second, an attempt to permeate human sociality with divine presence. Ideally, even a *churrasco* party is just as much of a communion as the formal Lord's Supper to the extent that the upheld purpose is to "praise the name of Jesus." The multivocal character of comunhão as a concept points to the inseparability of social fellowship and charismatic faith. How the day of water baptism unfolded also supports this observation. The water baptism and the first Lord's Supper were followed by a festive barbecue party, which congregants considered as an equally effective occasion for fostering comunhão. From the very outset of one's life as a *crente*, then, the human-human relationality is an integral part of, and even the very condition for, the cultivation of human-divine relationality.

There is something ontologically significant about the collapsing of the distinction between "the social" and "the religious" that the Pentecostal concept of comunhão seems to strive for. This is so because it defies the conventional line that generations of social scientists have reified by discussing various "social" motives and benefits surrounding religion. Religion is about "social support," "social network," "social solidarity," "social strategy," and "social capital," just to name a few.[24] To the extent that such interpretations resonate well with the view of religion as collective effervescence, they attest to the enduring influence of Durkheimian legacy in the study of religion.[25] Such an analytical prioritization of the social, however, implicitly reinforces the conceptual split between the secular and the religious as well as the public and the private. Not all cultural realities adopt these dichotomous categories, which are modern discursive configurations first articulated in the West.[26] Pentecostalism is a case in point. As David Smilde observed in his study of evangelical Christianity in Venezuela, "There is no natural distinction between religious and nonreligious goals; this common distinction always depends on the religious meanings used to conceptualize it."[27] Depending on the aim, process, and intent, the same act can be "holy and Christian" or "unholy and of the world." Scholars must take seriously the fact that Christian converts, like any other cultural group, are creating, reaffirming, and sometimes contesting their own concepts and theories about the world. The Pentecostal notion of comunhão shows that there is no given or fixed distinction between "social network" and "religious faith" in this ethnographic context. By welding together the human-human relationality and human-divine relationality, converts defied the ontological separation between the social and the religious and instead upheld another epistemological category that they called the *espiritual*.

This is why I argue that relational commitment is not a by-product but an indispensable element of faith. At first glance, converts like Leticia appear to directly contest the dominant narrative of charismatic faith. Seen in the analytical light of comunhão, however, they are not necessarily inauthentic pretenders but instead genuine practitioners of faith.

Part Five

RETURNS

9

ACCOMPANIED SELF

Sincere Nonsense?

After a church service one Sunday, I carpooled with a dozen young congregants to a nearby restaurant for *kaiten zushi* (rotating sushi). I shared a table with Leonardo, Shunsuke, and Shunsuke's girlfriend. Being young men in their early twenties, Leonardo and Shunsuke picked up plates of sushi that "rotated" on the conveyor belt rather quickly, one after another. Although Shunsuke's girlfriend and I could eat only five plates of sushi, they devoured at least a dozen each. Rotating sushi was a popular choice of restaurant among my informants, partly because they did not need to speak Japanese to order or to pay. One only needs to take whatever looks appealing from the conveyor belt and let an employee count the number of empty plates on the table to calculate the bill. As we sipped green tea and chatted after the meal, Shunsuke—Leonardo's younger brother—asked me where I had been the previous Sunday. "I didn't see you at church. Were you sick?" With some hesitation, I told him that I had to travel to my mother's natal city to attend a Buddhist commemoration ceremony called *isshūki* for my deceased uncle.

"Oh," he responded, "You mean, like, a ceremony where a monk does chants [*faz rezas*] for ancestral spirits?" I confirmed that chants were indeed part of the ceremony.

"I'm sorry for your loss, Suma," Leonardo, the older brother, interrupted with a concerned look. "But look, God doesn't hear those meaningless chants very well. He wants His children to speak to Him in simple, honest words, like you are talking to your best friend."

"Yeah, um, I see," I mumbled, scratching my head.

Although I had heard similar comments about Buddhism (and Catholicism) many times, this particular exchange with Shunsuke and Leonardo stood out for one reason. Earlier in the evening, I had heard them speak in tongues during the special prayer session led by a visiting pastor from Brazil. After a vigorous sermon, he invited the congregation to step forward to receive blessings. They quickly moved all the chairs to the sides to make more space and moved closer to the pulpit, from where the visiting pastor started praying fervently. Some congregants remained on foot while others knelt down. Almost everyone prayed with eyes firmly shut, arms up in the air, and palms open to the ceiling. Many were sobbing. Several minutes into this collective prayer, a handful of attendants started speaking in tongues. Shunsuke and Leonardo were among them. Leonardo then started shaking and fell down to the floor while being assisted by the people around him who noticed his erratic movements. The Resting in the Spirit, a form of charismatic bodily expression that involves falling onto the floor, was a relatively rare occurrence at Missão Apoio Toyota.[1] That two people did by the end shows the fervor of this particular prayer session. I happened to be standing next to Shunsuke and saw tears streaming down his cheek as he uttered nonsensical syllables. The wave of collective voices gradually toned down after five minutes or so, as if there were a shared sense of rhythm that they all could feel with their skin.

Speaking in tongues, or glossolalia, is a free-flowing vocalization of speech-like syllables that lack any readily comprehensible meaning. Although the speaker does not understand the words coming out of his or her mouth, converts say, God certainly does. Charismatic Christians thus consider tongues to be the divine language of heaven, due in part to its radical departure from daily language whose meaning is accessible to the speaker. Put otherwise, the shared appreciation of tongues as a gift from the Spirit hinges on the transcendence of its meaning beyond human comprehension. Authentic tongues must, at least on the semantic level, be "nonsense."

Given that both Shunsuke and Leonardo prayed in nonsensical utterances just hours earlier, I decided to probe why they were so confident in characterizing Buddhist chants as "meaningless." It was true that many Buddhist chants lacked transparent referential meaning to the majority of lay Japanese practitioners today. "But," I thought, "so does tongues in Pentecostalism."

"Look," I started hesitantly, "it's true that most Japanese people probably don't understand what chants mean. But when you speak in tongues, you also don't understand what you are saying, right?"

They looked at me with a blank expression and my heartbeat quickened slightly. Leonardo spoke after a few seconds. "But speaking in tongues edifies the faith and edifies oneself [*edifica a fé, e edifica a si mesmo*].[2] It's not the same thing. It's the language from the heaven; it's for reinvestment of power." His tone indicated that he was not being defensive but simply surprised at such an inquiry. His response mostly reiterated the common biblical phrases regarding speaking in tongues, and his view on the relationship between language, faith, and the self seemed unshaken.

Christianity, Religion, and the Self: An Uneasy Alliance

If speaking in tongues indeed "edifies the faith and the self," then what kinds of faith and self would they be? Put otherwise, what constitutes Pentecostal personhood in this ethnographic context? According to Shunsuke and Leonardo, how one speaks shapes how one believes, which in turn changes who one is. The exchange also indicates that their understanding of language, faith, and personhood is layered in distinctive ways. Effective prayer can encompass both ordinary speech ("honest words like you are talking to your best friend") and radical nonsense ("the language from the heaven"). Although the former appears to correspond with the sincere belief discussed in Chapter 8, the latter seems to go beyond the realm of self-reflective thought. It is therefore worthwhile to ask what kind of moral self emerges in nonsensical utterances, the kind of language practice that their official ideal of sincere speech does not necessarily encompass. The triangulation of language, faith, and the self thus seems to be a promising point of departure to interrogate the elements of Pentecostal personhood. To Leonardo and Shunsuke, this personhood is quite different from the kind of self implied in Japanese Buddhist practices—the moral subjectivity that manifests in "meaningless chants" instead of "honest words." As it turns out, Christian personhood and Japanese selfhood have occupied quite different, even opposite, places in the anthropological study of culture and self.

The notion of the individual—the hallmark of "Western" personhood in much of anthropological literature—has loomed large in the study of the Christian subject.[3] For example, Joel Robbins has described how charismatic converts among the Urapmin in Papua New Guinea struggle to become individuals-in-Christ, the sole unit of salvation in Pentecostal eschatology.[4] Such a Pentecostal vision of individuality, however, often generates social tension in contexts where traditional relational values persist. Urapmin converts thus find it challenging to fully embrace Pentecostal emphasis on the individual mind's moral autonomy, which leads to the prevalent self-perception as "sinners." The presumption that Christian individualism is a static accomplished state can thus be misleading and perhaps inaccurate. Indeed, many scholars are quite attentive to the ambiguities, nuances, and limits of Christian individuality. For example, Girish Daswani suggested that Christian identity among Pentecostals in Ghana can be understood as "a living tension between states of individuality and dividuality."[5]

The study of the Christian subject has thus revolved around the theme of individuality, while the image of "relational selves" has dominated the literature on Japanese culture. Generations of scholars have variably characterized Japanese personhood as "dependent," "interdependent," "sociocentric," "interactional," "situational," "contextual," "contingent," and "flexible," among others.[6] Although these authors do not necessarily agree with each other, they echo one another in one general observation: that individualist logics of the self are seldom socially endorsed in Japan. "Individual" and "relational" can therefore serve as two analytical themes that are "good to think with," just as the conceptual juxtaposition of "individual" and "dividual" has stimulated a lively discussion among ethnographers of Africa and the Pacific.[7] This chapter explores the ramifications of Christian individualism in transnational Japan while asking if the individual and the relational are really as opposed as they appear to be at first glance.

"Beyond Religiosity": Sincere Self Among Pentecostal Converts

Sara was a third-generation Nikkei in her mid-twenties who converted to Pentecostalism in Japan in 2008, several years after her arrival. Like most of the migrant converts whom I met, she was from a Catholic background. Her *japonês* (Japanese Brazilian) father was baptized as an infant at the Catholic Church, but he was more invested in Buddhist rituals by the time Sara was a teenager.[8] Unlike her "non-practicing Catholic" (*católico não praticante*) father, her *brasileira* (non-Nikkei Brazilian) mother was more active and took Sara and her sister to a nearby Catholic church every Sunday when they were little. As she recounted her conversion in Japan, she constantly contrasted her current Pentecostal identity with her childhood religion. "God is your best friend [o melhor amigo], you see," she said, repeating the phrase Pentecostal churchgoers often used to stress the personal relationship converts aspire to cultivate with God. "When I prayed with my own words for the first time, as if I were talking to my best friend, it felt so good!" She then continued:

> SARA. In Brazil, at the Catholic church, I didn't understand anything, you know. It was all ceremony [cerimônia]. People did what they did because of religiosity [religiosidade].
> SUMA. For example?
> SARA. Well, the rosary. "Ave Maria, Cheia de Graça, O Senhor é convosco . . ." I didn't understand what it meant! And no one understands—maybe fathers, yes, but no one cares about the meaning because no one explains. You are just told to repeat the same thing again and again. I didn't feel anything because I didn't understand, but I still did it as a child because I thought I had to. . . .
> SUMA. So, what is prayer for you?
> SARA. Prayer is conversation with God [Oração é conversar com Deus]. You pray with sincere heart and simple words [coração sincera e palavras simples]. Just like we are talking here. He is your friend. Sincerity always [sempre sinceridade], you see, because we can say one thing and feel another but God always knows our heart.

Sara contrasted the "sincere simplicity" of Pentecostal prayer with the "ceremonious religiosity" of Catholic practices such as the rosary. According to her, the former consists of "one's own words" and is therefore more transparent, spontaneous, and sincere, but the latter is centered on repeating fixed phrases, whose meaning is not readily available to lay practitioners.

We can see how Sara's sense of sincere self is firmly connected to the ideal of sincere and transparent speech—a prominent feature of Protestantism. According to Webb Keane, Protestant semiotic ideology upholds the ideal of sincerity by requiring speaking subjects to closely monitor the alignment between their inner intentions and their outward speech. They must mean what they say to cultivate the moral self, since doing otherwise is to undermine human agency entrusted to the individual's interiority. Indeed, Calvinists insisted, "words are merely the external expressions of inner thoughts."[9] Although Calvinism and Pentecostalism are two distinct forms of Christianity, the Protestant semiotic ideology that Keane articulated often shapes Pentecostal subjectivities as well.[10] His insights can therefore help illuminate the background assumptions behind Sara's remarks. Her characterization of Catholicism—that is, dependence on formulaic expressions, "ceremonious" ritual practices, and inattentiveness to words' semantic meanings—points to the semiotic ideology of sincerity at work. For her born-again sensibility, Catholic practices appear less sincere because they do not reflect an "authentic inner self." Pentecostals, Sara thinks, pray in words that are semantically accessible as well as reflective of the speaker's sincere inner intention.

Sara appealed to the word *religiosidade* (religiosity) to point out what she identified as compromised sincerity. It is well known that Pentecostalism in Latin America typically expanded as a movement posed against the institutional hegemony of the Catholic Church. In this context, Pentecostals have often associated the term *religion* with Catholicism and other traditions that have historically coexisted with the Church by accepting its dominance.[11] In other words, they tend to invoke "religion" as an institutionalized "traditional" way of faith that they may have culturally inherited (through infant baptism, First Holy Communion, and so on) but later deliberately chose to leave behind by converting to Pentecostalism. My Pentecostal informants who grew up in Catholic families, for instance, often described their preconversion past as "trapped in religiosity" (*preso na religiosidade*) while stressing the authenticity of their current faith with phrases such as "free in Jesus" (*livre em Jesus*). In such rhetoric, "religion" is something that converts must ideally "free" themselves from through sincere conversion. For this reason, my informants generally resisted characterizing their born-again faith as a "religion" and instead considered it as a newfound "truth" that helped them transcend the old ways of "traditional religiosity." As such, *religion (religião)*—along with other terms such as *religiosity (religiosidade)* and *tradition (tradição)*—broadly signified to them uncritical adherence to inherited "external forms" such as conventional rules and customs. Consequently, most converts distanced themselves from the ways of life meant to be represented in these terms because conversion ideally allows them to "make a complete break with the past" to embrace sincere selfhood.[12]

When migrant converts such as Sara contrast the "sincerity" of Pentecostal personhood with the "religiosity" of their past affiliations, they seem to be invoking what Webb Keane called the "moral narrative of modernity": "the cultivation of and high value given to individual agency and inwardness, the goal of individual self-creation, and, paralleling these in the domain of the social, the devaluation of tradition in the name of historical progress."[13] The moral weight Sara attaches to "sincere heart" and prayers "in one's own words" suggests that she locates prayer's efficacy in "individual inwardness." As she related later in the same interview, she felt such a style of prayer was "better than religious prayers" because it originates "in your own heart and not in tradition." The semiotic ideology of sincerity and the moral narrative of modernity thus jointly shape Pentecostal discourse of "trans-religion."

To the extent that, as Keane argued, the cultivation of the sincere self is a modern project, converts like Sara are embodying modernity through conversion. In such a project of self-transformation, converts ideally experience something like a moment of awakening from "tradition" and "religion" in which they come to realize that their old ways did not allow for deep interiority, sincere intention, and independence from social relations. The Pentecostal emphasis on the inner self's autonomy from "tradition" and "religion" points to an aspect of individualism at play in the remaking of the moral self among migrant converts.

"Nonreligion" and Disciplined Selves Among the Japanese Majority

Emiko-san, a Japanese housewife in her forties, was an active volunteer who frequented the nongovernmental organizations for foreign residents in Homi Danchi. One day, I visited her home for an interview. When I explained to her that I was a researcher studying the role of religion among Brazilian migrants in the area, she responded, "Oh, you mean, like that building down the road with the green roof?" Since she was referring to one of the Brazilian Pentecostal churches in the neighborhood, I answered that I indeed studied such groups. She told me that she guessed it was a church but was never sure. I asked if she had heard of Pentecostal Christianity (*pentekosute-ha*). With a quick laugh, she responded, "No, I have no clue. I don't know much about religion." Then she added rather firmly, "Because I am nonreligious [*watashi mushūkyō desukara*]."

When I asked her a few follow-up questions later in our conversation, however, it became clear that she engaged in a number of Shinto and Buddhist practices on a regular basis. Before the construction of their house, for example, she and her husband invited a Shinto priest to hold *jichinsai*, a ceremony to calm the spirit of the land and ask for permission to build on it. The *ohuda* (rectangle-shaped paper amulet) from this ceremony years earlier was still on the wall of her living room. When I challenged her jokingly that some may find *jichinsai* "religious," she tilted her head with a doubtful look and paused for a moment. Then she countered:

> But I don't think these things have absolute meaning. Well—how can I say this—it's all up to how you hold your heart [*ki no mochi yō*]. Just the fact that you visited a shrine and did something about what worries you already makes you feel a little lighter [*ki ga hareru*]. This paper amulet [points at the *ohuda* from the ceremony], I don't really believe in it. I mean, it doesn't have any real supernatural power—everyone knows that, right? But it's soothing [*ki ga shizumaru*] to see it and feel that you are protected. It also feels more fulfilling to pray [*te wo awaseru*] to *ohuda* than toward somewhere in the sky—supposing there is some god up there—without any focus.

To Emiko-san, religion primarily consists in "believing" and "finding absolute meaning in" ritual actions and objects. Since she does not, she thinks it is only appropriate to characterize herself as "nonreligious." Such a belief-centered understanding of religion is widespread in contemporary Japan. For example, in the survey conducted by the Institute of Statistical Mathematics, only 28 percent of the 1,591 respondents had religious faith (*shinkō*) or devotion (*shinjin*), while 72 percent answered that they "do not have faith or devotion, do not believe, or are not interested in such matters."[14] While the majority of Japanese do not "believe in" religion, a different picture emerges when we shift our attention to religious practice. According to a public opinion poll, the majority of the 1,837 respondents answered that they engaged in the following practices: "frequently pray [*te wo awaseru*] to Buddhist or Shinto altar at home" (56.7 percent), "pay visit to family's grave on the Buddhist holidays for commemoration of ancestral spirits [*bon* and *higan*]" (78.3 percent), and "visit local shrine or temple for New Year's Day" (73.1 percent).[15] Furthermore, 94 percent answered that they "have a feeling of deep respect for ancestors," which reflects the close historical tie between Buddhism and veneration of ancestors in Japan.

As Ian Reader and George Tanabe succinctly put it, religion in Japan is "less a matter of belief than it is of activity, ritual, and custom. The vast majority may not assert religious belief but . . . that same majority participates in religious activities and rituals."[16] This focus on practice, coupled with the popular understanding of "religion" as a product of self-conscious belief, sustains the dominant "nonreligious" self-image among the Japanese majority. The discourse of "nonreligion" also fuels a widespread perception that "religion" is for the foreign Other who "believes." Like Emiko-san, many Japanese associate the term with institutionalized monotheism, most commonly Christianity.

The underlying cultural logic behind the claim of "nonreligion" among the Japanese majority, then, clearly diverges from the semiotic ideology of sincerity invoked by Brazilian Pentecostal migrants. For Emiko-san, what Pentecostals typically perceive as insincere and thus immoral—that is, a "gap" between inner intention and outward act—is not necessarily immoral or even insincere. Take, for example, how she spoke about the act of prayer. Both Emiko-san and the Public Opinion Poll used the phrase *te wo awaseru*, the literal translation of which would be "to put one's palms together." Although there are other Japanese words such as *inoru* that refer to a certain state of mind and thus better approximate the connotation of "to pray," *te wo awaseru* is in itself a purely descriptive phrase that focuses on the outwardly visible form of prayer. Such a focus on form is closely tied to the theory of *ki*, which can be loosely translated as "energy field." Ki, a central concept in many East Asian medicines, continues to shape the thoughts and experiences of many contemporary Japanese. It is an "organizing force-field" that unites seemingly disparate domains of life such as nature, the self, mind, body, and well-being.[17] To Emiko-san, the efficacy of religious practice does not lie in meaning, belief, or intrinsic power of objects but rather in "how one maintains one's own energy field" (*ki no mochiyō*). In this framework, material objects such as amulets help her "quiet the energy field" (*ki ga shizumaru*), and formal actions such as visits to shrines similarly "clear the energy field" (*ki ga hareru*). In other words, what matters to Emiko-san is not whether "genuine" inner intentions preceded and gave rise to "spontaneous" actions but instead how form-centered ritual behavior can facilitate the alignment of the self through bodily practices and material mediations.

Following Dorinne Kondo, here I refer to such a cultural vision as "disciplined selves." Her insights highlighted the cultural emphasis placed on the interdependence between form, social relationship, and self-cultivation in Japan: "Yet the moral weight is placed not on some sense of the 'self' as inviolable essence, separate from 'society,' but on the construction of disciplined selves through relationship with others and through forms we might find coercive.... But it is by first keeping the rules which define the form, even if one's understanding is incomplete or one disagrees with them, that a sincere attitude is eventually born."[18] Sincerity in the cultural framework of discipline, then, is not so much the individual's transcendence from social and material contexts inasmuch as it is a well-trained alignment between social roles, other persons, and the self. Kondo added, "Sincerity, *magokoro*, becomes sensitivity to social context and to the demands of social roles—not dogged adherence to an 'authentic,' inner self to which one must be true, regardless of the situation or the consequences for others."[19]

Although both Brazilian Pentecostal converts and the Japanese majority frequently engage in the discourse of "nonreligion," the underlying cultural logics for such a claim vary between the two. Migrant converts invoke "religion" (*religião*) as an unreflective adherence to inherited ritual forms. They detach themselves from it because the cultivation of modern sincere selfhood hinges on transcendence from material and social entanglements. Many Japanese, in contrast, understand "religion" (*shūkyō*) as a self-conscious articulation of consistent internal belief. They distance themselves from it, since the cultural framework of discipline places greater emphasis on the interdependence between the self, material forms, and social others. The diverging ways in which the category of religion is invoked reflect how multiple logics govern the cultivation of moral self in transnational Japan.

Encounters: Insincere Japanese?

Given the divergences between the logics of sincerity and discipline, what does it entail to be born-again Christian in a country where Buddhism, Shinto, and the vision of relational selves predominate? It is important to first note that the cultural logic of discipline often extends beyond explicitly "religious" contexts and informs many activities in people's day-to-day lives in Japan. Cleaning, for example, is at once a part of Zen ascetic life as a training of mind-body unification as well as a regular activity at Japanese schools and companies aimed at furthering general ethics.[20] This means that the contexts in which migrant converts encounter the logic of discipline are not limited to "religious" settings but also include their daily interactions with Japanese society. Some, for instance, complain about *chōrei* (morning ceremony), a customary practice at many Japanese companies that consists of daily briefing, collective recitation of fixed phrases such as company slogans, and sometimes brief warm-up exercises. At the factory where Takashi worked, employees collectively vocalized a set of greeting phrases such as *yoroshiku onegai shimasu* (please) and *arigatō gozaimasu* (thank you) during *chōrei*. Takashi expressed his distaste in a mixture of Portuguese and Japanese: "It doesn't make sense [Não faz sentido]. I don't need to shout these phrases every day to remember them. When we don't say them loud enough, *hanchō* [team leader] is like, 'Gen ki nai' [You don't have energy]. And in my head [I'm thinking], 'Gen ki aru. Shitakunai' [I am well, I just don't want to]. [Laughs.] I just don't like it; you sound like a robot, repeating the same thing mechanically every day." He then shook his head and added, "I really like Japanese people, but I just don't like the meaningless tradition—so rigid. No human warmth [*nenhum calor humano*]."

Takashi himself was a longtime Pentecostal who converted in Japan, but a similar perception about the rigidity of Japanese society and people is widely shared among Brazilian migrants at large. Like the interlocutors of Daniel Linger, who conducted fieldwork in Homi Danchi almost two decades before me, my Brazilian informants also insinuated to me repeatedly that "Brazilians are warm; Japanese are cold."[21] Brazilians are expressive, playful, and open; Japanese are rigid, serious, and closed. As stereotypical as they are, such contrastive images persist in part because they reflect a certain experiential truth from the migrants' perspective. In Brazil, "spontaneity in interaction is of the utmost importance. . . . Interactional selves should be more than status constellations; inner selves should show through."[22] Coming from a society in which interpersonal improvisation is highly valued, most Brazilian migrants perceive the Japanese emphasis on context and social role as lacking in intimacy. Collective ritualized vocalization thus gives out a strong impression of inauthenticity to Brazilian migrants because it focuses on adherence to fixed form rather than spontaneous "showing through" of "inner selves."

For Pentecostal converts like Takashi, such practices also go against the semiotic ideology of sincerity cultivated through their church activities. In its formulaic character, vocalization practice in the Japanese workplace resembles styles of prayer that do not reflect the Pentecostal ideal of sincerity, such as the Catholic rosary and Buddhist sutra. In fact, my informants used two separate verbs to distinguish "sincere" kinds of prayer from "insincere" ones: *orar* (to pray) for what they considered as spontaneous prayer with one's own words and *rezar* (to pray) for form-centered prayer based on fixed phrases. This latter form of prayer, *rezar*, is what Pentecostals often call "vain repetitions" (*vãs repetições*), invoking the term from Matthew 6:7. Sara used *rezar* to refer to fixed prayers in other traditions and *orar* to describe "spontaneous" prayers in born-again Christianity. The majority of congregants at Missão Apoio Toyota did the same. In Pentecostal framework of thought, then, *rezar* holds a similar function to other terms such as *religião* and *tradição*. It linguistically constructs and marks off the insincere premodern subject, which the sincere modern person must transcend through a set of techniques such as speech reflective of "inner self."

Catholics would not agree with such views, since their rich techniques for self-cultivation are grounded on a different set of logics centered on materiality, embodiment, and "saintliness."[23] Nor do the Japanese. The rationale behind the disciplinary pedagogy is still widely accepted in Japanese society, namely, *katachi kara hairu* (enter through the form). "The process of true learning begins with a model, a form, repeated until perfectly executed. Without this form, there can be no transformation of the *kokoro* [mind-heart]."[24] *Kata*— standardized postures, movements, and compositions—forms the foundation of training in many Japanese arts and ascetic traditions, ranging from flower arrangement to martial arts. *Kata* training aims "to fuse the individual to the form so that the individual becomes the form and the form becomes the individual."[25] Granted, very few would reach such an advanced level in aesthetic or ascetic training. Yet the fundamental premise of the philosophy of *kata* is still reflected in the emphasis placed on proper form in many social contexts in contemporary Japan.[26] To Takashi and many other Pentecostal Brazilians, however, the pedagogy of *kata* that underlies practices such as collective vocalization gave out an impression of insincere, superficial conformity. Indeed, Japanese preoccupation with form often invited the opinion that Japanese people seemed *falso*—"fake."

Contrary to my Brazilian informants' perception, however, many Japanese do find the pedagogy of *kata* coercive. Although Takashi attributed his frustration to the lack of "meaning" in the "tradition" of "Japanese people," not all Japanese workers supported such activities. When I worked at an auto parts factory in Toyota, I heard virtually all the other Japanese contingent laborers openly complain about these practices as *mendōkusai* (troublesome, tiresome). In contrast, full-time employees who enjoyed more job security and therefore saw themselves firmly belonging to the workplace seldom, if ever, expressed similar feelings in public. There was, in fact, a sense of resentment among part-time workers about the fact that they were being forced to "discipline" themselves for social others—including their superiors—who could dismiss them on a day's notice, anytime. As the Japanese labor system becomes increasingly neoliberal, flexible, and unequal, more and more marginalized Japanese workers today share the same frustration that Takashi expressed. Some foreign migrant laborers, however, at times conflate the ongoing class issues with essential cultural differences, thereby reifying the perceived boundary between "Japanese" and "Brazilian."

I must therefore stress that the points I have made thus far are not about a "clash" between two inherently different religious and cultural entities. Rather, they are about diverging *logics* that govern the grammar for self-cultivation, which people often use as a scaffold to make sense of—and sometimes reify—their identities. That being said, I would summarize that the logic of sincerity places emphasis on ethical cultivation "from within," and disciplinary pedagogy foregrounds embodiment "from without."

Accompanied Self: Is Pentecostal Selfhood "Individual"?

Is the ideal self in Pentecostal culture an individual? The logic of sincerity indeed places great emphasis on individualist visions such as agency reserved to inner self, transcendence from material mediations, and abstraction of the self from social embeddedness. It appears individualistic especially against the backdrop of disciplined selves in Japan, which seek to train the alignment between the self, context, and social others. Given such apparent divergences, it is indeed tempting to conclude with a contrastive picture between Christian individuality and Japanese relationality, as some have in the past.[27]

The individual, however, remains a contentious concept among the Brazilian Pentecostals whom I studied. That is, the cultural emphasis on sincerity and interiority does not necessarily equal the idealization of the bounded autonomous subject who exerts free will. In fact, efforts to control one's own self by sheer conscious will are devalued among my informants as "depending on oneself" (*depender de si próprio*), the antithesis of the ultimate virtue, which is to rely on God (*depender de Deus*). Congregants certainly used the word *individual* to stress the inviolability of person-in-Christ as the sole eschatological unit (e.g., "Everyone should have an individual relationship with God; no one, not even your parents, can tell you to convert"). At the same time, they also invoked the concept of individual in a negative light, especially in remarks critical of what they perceived as liberal morality in a "relativistic world." On rare occasions when they brought up contentious issues such as abortion, the word *individualista* was used as a virtual synonym for "lacking fear of God." Pentecostal personhood, then, is multifaceted, and divergent from the bounded subject with autonomous free will on two interrelated points.

First, the Pentecostal person is not a bounded subject. As culturally significant as the self's interiority may be as the locus of sincerity, such inner self is not closed but open to the divine Other—God and God's associates such as Jesus and the Holy Spirit. Lara, for instance, explained the ideal of utter transparency and openness toward the Other with a metaphor of the self as a house. Many people, she observed, "hide dirty things about oneself in the rooms on the second floor" while welcoming Jesus to "the clean living room on the first floor." One day, a demon breaks into the house and starts destroying the second floor, but Jesus remains on the first floor and does not do anything about it. When the host blames Jesus that He could easily expel the demon with His power, He answers that He could only enter the rooms the host lets him in. "If you open up only half of yourself to Jesus, then Jesus can work in only half of your life. If you let Him into all the rooms of your heart, then His power permeates all of your self," Lara concluded.

What is significant about Pentecostal Christianity is that its sensory and immersive practices seek to transform such a story from a mere metaphorical allegory to experiential reality. As Pastor Cid once put it, "God is not an abstract idea but someone [alguém]" who is there for dedicated congregants. Absorption in immersive prayer with rich sensory components can, for example, make God feel real: "People train absorption by focusing on sensory detail. They practice seeing, hearing, smelling, and touching in their mind's eye. They give these imagined experiences the sensory vividness associated with the memories of real events. What they are able to imagine becomes more real to them, and God must be imagined, because God is immaterial."[28] Training to interpret affective and mental movements in one's mind as the experience of an external presence teaches people "to blur the distinction between inner and outer, self and other" when it comes to God.[29] Inner self is ideally neither bounded nor private in such forms of Christianity. The conventional boundary between "inner" and "outer" becomes porous. Although interiority continues to be identified as the locus of sincerity, it must also be trained as an interactive realm open to the perceived presence of alterity.

Since the notion of sincerity does not fully capture the centrality of the Other in the construction of Pentecostal personhood, here I will refer to it as "accompanied self." In much of Pentecostal Christianity, the ideal person is not self-sufficient but instead susceptible to and reliant on the Other, whose presence people seek to make real by training to reinterpret the boundary of the self. The training of accompanied self consists in (1) the emphasis on inner sincere self, (2) the blurring of the line between "inner" and "outer" when it comes to the culturally consecrated Other, and (3) the eventual enmeshment of the sense of self in the perceived presence of alterity. As such, the accompanied self does not replace the sincere self but instead builds and expands on it. Common phrases such as "I am filled with the Holy Spirit" and "Jesus Christ lives in me" reflect the moral weight placed on the vision of accompanied self.

Second, Pentecostal personhood is not autonomous, at least not with respect to the relationship with God. The blurring of the line between inner self and outer Other leads to a shift in locus of agency from conscious mind to the realm of perceived Other. Accompanied selfhood places moral emphasis on enhancing the self's susceptibility to the agency attributed to the divine Other, thus delimiting the monopoly of will by individual consciousness. Lucas's testimony can serve as an example here. Lucas, a twenty-five-year-old Nikkei who served as an interpreter at Missão Apoio Toyota, was first brought to Japan at the age of three. Although he started his education initially at a local Japanese public school, his parents were forced to transfer him to a Brazilian private school after several months due to severe bullying. Since all classes were taught in Portuguese, he could not speak good Japanese despite the fact that he virtually grew up in Japan. In fact, he detested the language. Some years after his conversion in late adolescence, a Japanese man walked into the church one Sunday. Since Lucas happened to be the only one present who could speak some Japanese, he had to translate the whole procession for the man, including a sermon with biblical quotes. The result, Lucas felt, was disastrous: "Cabou! [It's over!] This man will never come to our church again!" To Lucas's great surprise, the man kept on coming back every week, and Lucas continued to interpret for him despite his reluctance to do so.

> So I started praying to God. "Lord, what should I do? I can't speak Japanese well—you know that!" Then, He answered my prayer: "You are the interpreter of my Word. You will be used by me." But I was still resistant to God, because back then, my favorite subject was mathematics! I hated languages—Japanese, especially. But then, God talked to my heart: "Lucas, who made your tongue? I did. Do you think you'll be speaking with *your* tongue? No. I made it, so why do you think that you cannot do something with the tongue I made?" I said,

"All right, God." And I started studying like a crazy person that day. I would come home from [Brazilian] school, then I would sit down and just write *kanji, kanji, kanji* (Japanese alphabet) . . . God was working in me; God was using me.

Here, the agency of his own conscious thoughts and emotions is overridden and deemed "incorrect" by that of alterity. The sense of the Other inhibits the monopoly of will on the part of individual consciousness.

Lucas's testimony adds an important layer to how the self is understood and cultivated in Pentecostal culture. Not only is the self open and susceptible to the presence of the Other, but it is ideally also yielding to the Other's agency. That is, alterity—that which is perceived to arise from the margins of consciousness—can exert just as much, if not more, agency as one's own conscious mind. In fact, any markers of the autonomous self—self-will, self-control, and self-reliance—must be surrendered to the agency of the Other to cultivate the ideal accompanied self in this cultural context. Many of my informants referred to this ultimate virtue as "obedience to God."

The Baptism in the Holy Spirit

Few Pentecostal practices are more reflective of the vision of accompanied self than the baptism in the Holy Spirit, an occasion that hinges on the agency of the Other. At Missão Apoio Toyota, members distinguished between two different kinds of baptism. The first was water baptism (see Chapter 8), and the other was the baptism in the Holy Spirit (*batismo no Espírito Santo*). Unlike the former, Spirit baptism was not a planned event on a set date. According to my informants, it is a spontaneous phenomenon that takes place whenever and wherever the Holy Spirit manifests to baptize a person. As such, the church leaders could not organize Spirit baptism as they did water baptism. The total spontaneity that churchgoers accorded to Spirit baptism was clear in their unwillingness to view it as a ritual. Although many would concede that water baptism was a ritual (*rito*) or ceremony (*cerimônia*), they would never use such terms to characterize the other baptism. This is because, as one congregant put it, "the baptism in the waters is done by men, but the baptism in the Spirit is done by Jesus." Since the latter cannot be achieved by human will alone but instead is dependent on the divine agency, it is beyond what converts saw as the realm of ritual—that is, the means to facilitate human efforts to reach God.

Given that the Holy Spirit is immaterial, how can congregants know that they have been baptized by it? Although there are several signs to confirm this, many regarded speaking in tongues as the chief evidence of Spirit baptism. Church members acknowledged that the two were not exactly the same, but they often referred to glossolalia and Spirit baptism interchangeably; when you speak in tongues, the Holy Spirit is baptizing you. Despite its apparent spiritual importance, however, glossolalia received significantly less attention as a subject of explicit teaching. For example, the weekly Bible study usually dedicated one or two full weeks to give clear instructions on sincere prayer—with themes such as "How to Pray" and "How to Speak to God." Such lessons emphasized the importance of simple and transparent speech as the basis of effective prayer. Compared with the abundance of clear guidelines on sincere prayer, the scarcity of the same kind of information about how to speak in tongues stood out. Whenever I inquired, experienced members of the church were eloquent about their own experiences of tongues but offered noticeably less on how to speak in tongues.

Although both were considered as "baptism," there were significant differences in how people viewed and experienced water baptism and Spirit baptism. Samuel, for instance, had the following to say when I asked him why there were two baptisms: "I think that many are baptized in the Holy Spirit after the baptism in the waters. Why? Well, the first baptism is much easier. The water baptism, you just need to understand what you are about to do, what it all means, and accept it. You don't need to do much, in my opinion. But the baptism in the Holy Spirit is way beyond what you can understand with your head [*cabeça*]." Although a handful of long-term members at the church agreed with Samuel that people tended to experience Spirit baptism after water baptism, the attributed reasons were not always the same. Another person, Gaby, speculated that it was probably because the water baptism is an occasion for converts to dissociate from worldly sins (such as drinking), thus "readying the body" (*preparar o corpo*) for the reception of the Holy Spirit. In her opinion, keeping the body—the vessel of the Spirit—clean and holy is crucial for any chance of Spirit baptism. The perspectives of Samuel and Gaby converge on one point: the Spirit baptism shifts the locus of agency away from the intentional human subject. Samuel thinks it cannot be understood or willed by one's "head." Gaby believes one has to "prepare the body" to receive the Spirit. Such remarks suggest that the experience of Spirit baptism hinges on certain embodied pathways that go beyond the control exerted by conscious mind.

This does not mean that church members saw speaking in tongues as an automatic process that simply took over the speaker's consciousness. Instead, many who had experienced glossolalia reported a heightened sense of focus in the moment. Joana, for instance, told me:

> Praying to God as if you were talking to a friend is a natural form of prayer. Praying in tongues is a spiritual form.... [Speaking in tongues feels as if] warm water is gushing out of my heart, body, and soul ... like a river of gratitude that never ends. What is leaving your mouth is not under your control, but God never takes away your consciousness. People think *crentes* are crazy because we look possessed, but we are actually very aware, super aware. God is a gentleman, and He never possesses you against your will. You can stop speaking if you wish. It is demons that take away your consciousness.

The remark can be read as an effort to distance Pentecostalism from other religions that some converts view as "demonic," especially Afro-Brazilian religions such as Umbanda. The word *possession* reminds many Brazilians of such traditions known for spirit mediumship.[30]

At the same time, Joana is also hinting at a significant theory about the relationship between language, body, and the self. Speaking in tongues is a "spiritual" form of prayer that involves "heart, body, and soul." Although utterances are not formed through purposeful articulation ("not under your control"), glossolalia also makes the speaker "very aware, super aware." In fact, she claims she can stop speaking if she wishes. Joana stresses this point by contrasting Spirit baptism with demonic possession, which takes away one's sense of agency against one's will. Taken together, her comment suggests a state of energized focus in the present accompanied by a temporary suspension of reflective self-consciousness—what some call "flow" or "zone."[31]

Just like Shunsuke and Leonardo in the opening scene, many tongues speakers regarded such a flow-like absorption in verbal utterances as a way to "build" (*edificar*) one's faith and self. Tomomi, who spoke in tongues regularly, told me: "Speaking in tongues strengthens oneself [*se edifica*]. You don't understand what you are saying but God understands. He knows what you need, even if you don't know it yet yourself.... The baptism in the Holy Spirit is not something of the mind [*da mente*]. It is something by faith [*pela fé*]. You feel it in your heart [*coração*]." Like Samuel, who thought Spirit baptism was beyond "what you can understand with your head," Tomomi also stressed that it is "not something of the mind." Instead, it is in "your heart" and "by faith." The faith that Spirit baptism cultivates, then, is not coterminous with the model of faith reinforced during the ceremony of water baptism. Water baptism encourages articulable belief affirmed by the conscious mind. Spirit baptism, however, shifts the locus of faith to the embodied mind.[32] And it is in this embodied realm that the experience of accompanied self becomes the most vivid. It is no longer you who is doing the speaking; it is the Holy Spirit. It is no longer you who determines the meaning of words; God decides and understands it on your behalf. But your self is not hijacked. You can stop if you wish. Glossolalia is the accompanied self in action par excellence.

Faith as Embodied Disposition

In *Metaphors We Live By*, George Lakoff and Mark Johnson wrote about "the myth of objectivism" that is influential in Western views on language and meaning. The myth of objectivism dictates that the world is made up of objects of innate properties, and words express fixed meanings that fit preexisting things, concepts, and categories. In such a view, "expressions . . . can be said to have objective meaning only if that meaning is independent of anything human beings do, either in speaking or in acting. That is, meaning must be disembodied."[33] Speaking in tongues reveals the limits of objectivism by collapsing the distinction between words and things, signs and meanings, and the signifier and the signified. As it consists in semantic nonmeaning, or "nonsensical" utterances, glossolalic speech cannot stand for preexisting objects separate in existence. Instead, its meaning comes from the act of speaking itself and therefore is episodic. The conventional separation between the signifier and the signified is no longer tenable here because meaning cannot be separate from the speaker, the place, and the time from which utterances are born—in other words, the speaker's embodied existence as part of the world.[34] As Thomas Csordas put it: "The stripping away of the semantic dimension in glossolalia is not an absence, but rather the drawing back of a discursive curtain to reveal the grounding of language in natural life, as a bodily act. Glossolalia reveals language as incarnate, and this existential fact is homologous with the religious significance of the Word made Flesh, the unity of human and divine."[35] Speaking in tongues is thus a pathway through which the speaker can experience embodied meaning, meaning that is founded not on semantic representation but on sensory intelligibility.

This does not mean, however, that each speaker of tongues can invent any kind of meaning that he or she wishes to experience. That would be to make a subjectivist error. "The myth of subjectivism" is an influential counterdiscourse to the objectivist perspective that upholds the primal importance of feelings, intuitions, and sensibilities.[36] In the subjectivist view, meaning is purely personal and private. Put otherwise, meaning is unstructured and free-forming, and therefore resistant to be shared between different persons. However, subjectivism ignores the existence of socially informed body, or habitus, which provides a foundation for embodied meaning.[37] As I mentioned earlier, very few—virtually no—congregants start speaking in tongues on the first day of their born-again life. Although many eventually experience Spirit baptism, the church does not offer articulate instructions on how to make this happen. These facts indicate that glossolalia is a learned skill that is acquired on a tacit bodily level.

Larissa, for instance, recounted the following story. In 2007, she participated in the Encounter with God, a three-day prayer camp that the church organizes annually. Although she had never spoken in tongues, her desire to do so was very strong. She had heard other church members say that glossolalia enables Christians to "have the boldness to pray better, and better understand the Bible" (*tem ousadia para orar melhor, entender melhor a Bíblia*). She was curious to find out what it meant. At the end of the camp, leaders held a special prayer session in which all the participants were encouraged to pray together for the manifestation of the Spirit. Fervent prayers filled the room. Soon, some participants—who were considered spiritually mature—started speaking in tongues. Those who wished to experience Spirit baptism were told to just keep on praying with earnest passion. Despite her enthusiasm, Larissa did not seem to be able to speak in tongues. Sensing her frustration, several people came over and prayed with her, but she still could not. Just as she was about to give up and stop praying, someone Larissa looked up to as "a very spiritual person"— her home group leader—walked over to her. She told Larissa that words were "boiling in her belly," trying to get out. "But I see a knot in your throat. That's in the way, preventing the boiling words to come out. Now I will pray to make that knot disappear, so you pray aloud with me with all your might while I do it, OK?" The home group leader started praying, and soon her words turned into tongues.

Larissa also prayed, feeling the touch of the leader's palm on her throat. Then, at last, she started speaking in tongues. "It was, shall we say, like baby's tongues [*akachan no igen*]," Larissa told me. "Because I had just started speaking. It sounded different from the leader's tongues, you know, like a baby. But it was still speaking in tongues. I was not thinking to speak. It felt amazing."

Larissa's recounting of her first experience of glossolalia demonstrates that the learning process is more mimetic and tacit than instructional and explicit. The only verbal direction given during the prayer session is to pray aloud with as much ardor as one can muster. Implicit cues, in contrast, are abundant. The participants in the camp were encouraged to pray with more experienced practitioners of prayer, many of whom started speaking in tongues right in front of their eyes. When newer members seemed to be having difficulty, other congregants—typically those with leading roles in the church—would come over to speak in tongues in closer proximity. When even this did not work, Larissa's home group leader placed her palm on her throat to "bring out the boiling words" from her belly. With this tactile encouragement and demonstration of glossolalia from someone she personally looked up to, Larissa could finally speak in tongues, but in its rudimentary form. Larissa's acknowledgment that it was only "baby's tongues" reveals her view on glossolalia as a skill that one learns, develops, and masters over time. Thus, speaking in tongues involves a mimetic training of the body through intense social moments shared with others.

If speaking in tongues "edifies the faith," then, this faith must be grounded in embodiment—an inchoate process of the self that is socially informed and experientially tangible. Faith in this sense is no longer a semantic articulation but an embodied disposition. It is this dimension of faith that can give converts a renewed sense of unity across ethnic, national, and linguistic boundaries. During my fieldwork, guest pastors visited Missão Apoio Toyota from around the world—Indonesia, Kenya, the United States, and South Korea, to name a few. Naturally, the congregants relied on the interpreters to understand their sermons and regular prayers. Whenever a guest pastor started speaking in tongues, however, the translation into Portuguese immediately stopped. Glossolalia cannot be translated in the conventional sense, and for this very reason, everyone understood it as a gestural and embodied act, without semantic translation. This does not necessarily mean that all the participants shared one single transnational and transhuman language when they spoke in tongues. Linguists have shown that even the most senseless and cacophonic utterances of glossolalia seem to have a minimal pattern that is determined by the range of sounds available in the languages familiar to the speaker.[38] In other words, Portuguese glossolalia and Japanese glossolalia will always sound a little different. Both are, however, equally "nonsense," and congregants equated this shared absence of semantic meaning with the universal presence of divine significance.[39] It is in this sense that speaking in tongues could perhaps help charismatic Christians experience "Pre-Babel lucidity," if only ever so fleetingly.[40]

Ephemeral Returns

What constitutes Pentecostal personhood? A case study of Brazilian Pentecostals in transnational Japan yields a twofold response to this question. First, some individualist logics do inform Pentecostal visions of moral selfhood, as seen in the ideals of sincere speech, agency of human interiority, and abstraction of the self from material and social interdependence. Such an ethical emphasis stands out especially in the Japanese context, where relational selves and disciplinary pedagogy—which do not necessarily value the "inner self"—predominate.

The ethnographic picture, however, is more complex than the relational/individual, Japanese/Christian dichotomy, which brings me to my second point. The ideal self in Pentecostal culture is "accompanied" by the Other, that is, neither bounded nor autonomous. In fact, its primary focus is on the direct relationship with the divine Other, to whom the self must be open and transparent. Ideally, the dependence on the conscious "I" eventually yields to the obedience to the transcendent "Him," whose agency practitioners seek to render tangible through a set of sensory and bodily practices including glossolalia.[41] Thus, although Pentecostal personhood may be characterized as individualistic, it is also founded on the relational interdependence with the culturally legitimized Other such as God, Jesus, and the Holy Spirit. In fact, in that they both place great emphasis on self/Other relationships, accompanied self and disciplined selves are not completely opposed to each other. The accompanied self in Pentecostal vision of moral personhood, then, can be considered as a kind of relational individuality—the "space between persons" that makes ethical experience possible.[42]

But this relational individuality is not a static state because personhood is constantly in the becoming. The accompanied self is a cultural ideal, vision, and process, and it is never a permanent attainment. Many of my informants, who strived to make real the enmeshment of one's sense of being and the agency of the Other, knew this fact well: You stumble, fall, and sin in your journey toward the envisioned moral personhood. They would admit that it was extremely difficult to completely depend on God. They would concede that it was next to impossible for humans to be ego-free. And they were surprisingly frank about their own "failures" because to err is human; perfection belongs only to God. It is perhaps fitting that the vivid experience of accompanied self, such as the one fostered through glossolalia, seemed rather sporadic and ephemeral. The second you feel that you are in that space where the self meshes with the Other, the place where the thinking "I" dissolves and the encounter with "Him" starts, the moment is quickly over. Many migrant converts then yearn to return to this powerful zone, a kind of mind-space that you cannot locate on a map but can only reach through trained absorption in the moment. They still speak about their planned return to Brazil, but they have also learned another way to return, albeit ephemeral and fleeting, which is an embodied return to the present with no nations.

10

JESUS LOVES JAPAN

Moses Walks in Toyota

I did not embark on the research that yielded this book intending to study Pentecostalism or even religion in general. Instead, I initially envisioned it as a project on transnational migration and mental health, and looked for phenomena that spoke to the link between the two during my first visits to Toyota. It did not take long before I found the Pentecostal churches that were thriving in the migrant communities there. At first I was unsure about whether I wanted to focus on them. Hesitant, I decided to formally visit one such church, which turned out to be Missão Apoio Toyota. It was the summer of 2012, and I was captivated at my very first visit.

Pastor Cid's sermon that day happened to address the incident back in 1999 that continued to define the public image of Homi Danchi—the "clash" between a group of Japanese right-wing nationalists and some Brazilian youth in the neighborhood (see Chapter 4). I had already heard some residents in Toyota, both Japanese and Brazilian, speak about the memories of the event. Some framed it as a proof of Brazilian volatility and criminality; others brought it up as yet another example of Japanese oppression against foreign minorities. In such typical narratives, the Brazilian migrants in Homi were either troubled delinquents or victims of marginalization. Pastor Cid told a new story from the pulpit that day, which did not conform to either rhetorical pattern. It did not even start with Homi, Toyota, Japan, or Brazil. It instead started with Moses in the Egyptian desert, the Exodus of Jews from slavery:

Do you think God said, "Moses, don't worry, nothing will harm you, everything will be okay. Now, be assured and go into the desert"? No! Moses was a man of faith, and he told the terrified Israelites, "Do not be afraid. Stand firm and you will see the deliverance of the Lord," and went into the desert without any doubt in the power of God. And as he led his people, without looking back, the cloud of the angel followed and protected them from behind. Do you understand, brothers and sisters? You don't do what you do because God guaranteed something; you go forward with faith, praising His name, and you shall be blessed.[1] . . .

I still remember. Back in 1999, there was this rising tension between Japanese nationalists and young Brazilian delinquents in Homi Danchi. . . . The Japanese would come in their black vans, circle around Homi over and over again, shouting that Brazilians and foreigners should leave. Some Brazilian youth were becoming agitated, and they could have acted in a wrong way at any moment. Back then, we were having a prayer walk [*caminhada de oração*] for seven weeks in a row, and our seventh and last prayer walk around Homi coincided with the day when Japanese nationalists were circling Homi Danchi in their vans. . . .

Many were afraid, and I was concerned as well. But I prayed to God, and started walking, without looking back. We walked around Homi Danchi, as the loud black van passed by us many times. We prayed aloud. Brothers and sisters, soon there were people behind us. Some were Brazilian youngsters who were troubled delinquents; they wanted to know what we were doing there, the work we were doing for God. . . . So we walked and walked, many times, around Homi, praying with all our heart that God may bless Homi and the people there, Brazilian and Japanese. . . . "Jesus ama o Japão!" (Jesus loves Japan!) We'd pray aloud as these black vans passed by us—they were not harming us. "Jesus ama o Japão!"

"There is something going on here," I thought to myself as I stood there, being washed by the waves of amens and hallelujahs from the congregants. The ethnographer in myself was murmuring excitedly in my head. In the sermon, Homi Danchi was the Egyptian desert, the Japanese nationalist vans were the pharaoh's army, the pastor was Moses, and those who followed him were God's chosen people. They were, of course, not literally these biblical things, persons, and places, but I sensed that the comparisons were not just a bunch of clever metaphors either. Pastor Cid and his listeners were making a new time and space by blurring the conventional boundary between the ancient and the contemporary, between the faraway and the right here. It was what some scholars call mimesis that I was witnessing, by which people redefine what is real by deep imitation, a performance in which pretending can lead to becoming.[2] Obviously, Moses did not walk in Toyota—but he did, in a sense, for those to whom the Bible is not a dead text. The ancient was still alive and animate, and the present was not a mere postscript to the grand dramas of mythic times. I also noted that this creative work converts put into their conception of time and space in turn affected their relationship with Japan, where they were at once distant kin and alien foreigners. "Jesus loves Japan!"

With this realization, I decided to forgo the initial research question that I was planning to pursue: Does religion enhance mental health? This is no doubt a legitimate question for many projects, but it was no longer so for mine. The ethnographic cues I was starting to amass in the field pointed to another direction, or rather, another analytic plane. To begin with, I was not necessarily witnessing "religion" as an entity. Instead, what I was observing pertained to the realms of narrative, ritual, myth, time, space, identity, self, citizenship, and belonging, just to name a few. Sure, what migrant converts did in regard to such constructs may well be therapeutic and therefore protective of "mental health" through some cause-and-effect pathways. But I felt the need to ask a more— for lack of a better word—fundamental question: How are they remaking their worlds and realities with these vivid enactments of new time, space, and belonging? What is happening to their experience of transnational mobility and multiple national origins, when Moses can walk in Toyota?

Morality of Mobility

This book provided some answers, which I have elaborated in four steps. First, I illuminated the predominant sense of "suspended life" that plagues Nikkei Brazilians upon their migration to Japan. Like many other migrants, they experience their movements in temporal terms and see their initial decision to move for work as a means to build a "better future." The twist is that their right to mobility in this case hinges on their past ancestral ties to the nation. As such, Nikkei migrants grapple with the images of the past, the present, and the future in complex ways. In Japan, they realize that the new social environment of unskilled manual labor robs them of the "modern Asian minority" status from Brazil and transforms them into a "backward Latino minority" amid the Japanese majority. Their movements between multiple regimes of race, citizenship, and national identity render the rhetoric of "neither here nor there" increasingly potent for the psyches of Nikkei migrants. Furthermore, the aspirational temporality of labor migration exacerbates the common sentiment that they cannot enjoy the present; the discomfort and humiliation of the current state as foreign laborers must be endured for the procurement of material goods, economic wealth, and education for the offspring. In other words, the present must be sacrificed for the future—the future that no one can guarantee for them. Suffocated by their own aspiration and uncertainty, many Nikkei migrants come to feel that they have "stopped living" in Japan.

This cultural reality of suspended life prepares the stage for Pentecostal conversion in Japan. One powerful characteristic of born-again subjectivity is an emphasis on the "right now, right here"—the immediacy of spiritual renewal. No charismatic Christian in her right mind is supposed to say "I will start working on my relationship with God next week." As one pastor jokingly told me once, faith is no diet. Rather, it is imperative that each convert regards it morally urgent to renew one's self by accepting Jesus in that moment. The charismatic temporality of "right now, right here" touches Nikkei migrants who have "stopped living" like a fresh breeze of air. Unlike the aspirational temporality of "a better future one day," the new Pentecostal time firmly situates the locus of living in the present. Life—and new life with Jesus at that—must start right now, right here, in Japan. Thus, instead of returning to the future in Brazil as labor migrants with savings, Nikkeis find a way to return to the present in Japan as "new creatures in God." Once converted, migrant converts also start speaking about their citizenship in "the Kingdom of God." In such rhetoric of transnational transcendence, they are now members of "the culture of love," which ostensibly overcomes narrow ethnonational affiliations. A number of church initiatives, such as Married for Life and Ancient Paths, spring up to teach converts how to love. These collective endeavors for "family restoration" through the affective labor of love alleviate the common anxiety that family is crumbling down under the pressure of labor migration. Nikkeis do not necessarily regain their lost "culture of discipline" associated with Japanese ethnicity in Brazil, but they reclaim a new modern identity by fostering "the culture of love."

The Pentecostal insistence on the transcendence of their Christian fellowship from ethnonational boundaries, however, does not go unchallenged. Part 4 detailed how the converts' ideal vision of universal culture and spiritual kinship becomes contested both from without and from within. Powerful as the blood of Jesus may be as the medium of charismatic kinship that unites "brothers and sisters in faith," the fact remains that Nikkeis are granted the right of sojourn in the nation by virtue of their "Japanese blood" and proximity to the national kinship. Although the symbolic kinship through Jesus's blood emphasizes the importance of continuous conversion in the charismatic present, the material kinship of "the Japanese blood" locates the source of migrants' moral entitlement to national belonging in their Japanese ancestral past. The ethical friction between the two diverging logics of kin-making does not easily disappear, especially in the context of Japan. The nation crafted a kind of religious nationalism founded on State Shinto in its modern history, which fostered distinct understandings of religion, secularity, and citizenship. Nikkei migrant converts are thus of two bloods. Meanwhile, there are also those who contest the dominant narrative of sincere belief and authentic conversion from within the Pentecostal communities. Leticia, who converted while maintaining an ancestral altar at home, is one of them. Her creative understanding of conversion, as a means to achieve relational commitment to her family, demonstrates that "Pentecostals" do not constitute a monolith. While the church leaders uphold the ideal of sincere individual belief, experiential diversity continues to proliferate, thus reshaping the cultural reality of "faith" in practice.

As their life in Japan is suspended, renewed, and then contested again, the lines between "Japanese," "Brazilian," and "Christian" continue to shift but never entirely disappear. Oftentimes, Pentecostal conversion that is supposed to transcend existing ethnonational boundaries ends up forming new fault lines in the migrant converts' ethical landscape. The tension between the rhetoric of "Christian individual" and "Japanese relational selves" is one of them. The Nikkei converts who embrace the ideal of transparent speech and internal sincerity often perceive the logic of discipline common in Japanese society as "fake." The ethical mode of discipline locates sincerity in the well-trained alignment between the self, other persons, and social context, not necessarily in the strict adherence to inner essence within the individual. This often appears, to converts, as a superficial and inauthentic conformity to external forms. However, it is not the case that the Pentecostal ethics of the self are devoid of moral emphasis on the relationality between the self and the Other—the culturally legitimated Other such as God, Jesus, and the Holy Spirit. On the contrary, converts invest a tremendous amount of energy in making the Other real through immersive prayer. The Pentecostal individual, then, is not an autonomous person bounded off from the influences of the Other. Rather, he or she should ideally be open to the Other, hopefully to the extent that the self is continuously accompanied by the thc Other's presence. This ethical vision of "the accompanied self" is the most apparent in the charismatic practice of speaking in tongues. Converts argue that, in an episode of glossolalia or "the baptism in the Holy Spirit," they no longer understand what is flowing out of their mouths but God certainly does. In such moments, they may experience a fleeting and yet powerful return to the "pre-Babel lucidity," where discursive labels such as "Japanese," "Brazilian," and "Christian" temporarily recede into the cognitive background as speakers actively immerse themselves into nonsensical utterances. In this last sense, glossolalia may mediate an ephemeral return to the embodied present, an all-too-brief refuge from the structure of normal language that reifies their multiple identities.

I have thus told a story of suspension, renewal, contestation, and ephemeral return by tracing the journey of Nikkei Brazilian Pentecostal migrants in Japan. What their experiences make clear is that, far from being solely spatial, diasporic mobility is at once temporal, affective, and ethical. When migratory movement fails to fulfill the aspirations of migrants, religious movement often steps in, but in this process, their subjectivities undergo a decisive change. Thus, when the mentality of "Go forward and get ahead in life" does not easily deliver the initial economic reward of migration, the Pentecostal rhetoric of "conversion to modernity" may in turn appeal to their future-oriented drive for life. When Nikkei migrants feel that they have "put aside living" in Japan, in the temporal limbo of precarious migrant labor, the Pentecostal emphasis on the "right now, right here" brings them back to life. When they feel that they are "neither here nor there," the Christian "culture of love" springs up to propose the third transnational culture to migrant converts. When the negotiation between their "Japanese," "Brazilian," and "Christian" identities is constant and endless, speaking in tongues challenges the very linguistic foundation of such identifying categories by immersing speakers into the embodied nonsensical utterances. All of these ethnographic expositions show that migratory and religious movements do not constitute two separate phenomena to migrant converts. On the contrary, they form one unified process of subject formation and ethical transformation. By morality of mobility, I mean the inseparability of diasporic mobility and religious sensibility in the reformation of ethical self.

Jesus Loves Japan

Pastor Cid's sermon reaffirms the ethnographic significance of moral mobility. His prayerful walk in the story mimics the threatening move of Japanese nationalist vans; both go around Homi Danchi in a circular movement, but with different purposes. The black vans circle around the housing complex to intimidate and expunge its foreign segments, at least in the narrative of Pastor Cid and many other long-term residents there. The migrant converts, in contrast, circle around their living space to "bless" the people in it, both Japanese and Brazilian, by walking "without looking back." To the former, the place represents a breach in the borders of pure Japanese nationhood. To the latter, it provides a spiritual battleground where their faith is tested. Converts walk not because anything about their future is guaranteed, or because they are chased by the horror of the past. They walk because, in the right state of mind, the walk in itself can make an ethical difference, just like it did to Moses in the ancient desert. "You don't do what you do because God guaranteed something; you go forward with faith, praising His name, and you shall be blessed." The walk enacts their ethical freedom.[3] The tensions arising from transnational mobility and contested citizenship are thus mapped onto the spiritual struggles for freedom in their moral landscape. And their determination to exercise their ethics of mobility comes out in this cry: "Jesus loves Japan."

Through morality of mobility, then, they are rewriting and reliving their origin stories. When Moses can walk in twenty-first-century Toyota, it is clear that origin is not something of the essence stored in the inaccessible past. Their origins, instead, are in the present, the kind of present that can change both the past and the future. "Jesus loves Japan" is an ethical call to reclaim their citizenship with their Christian origin, which in turn interacts with their Brazilian and Japanese identities in generative ways. Their diaspora with three origins goes on.

EPILOGUE

En Route to Impossible Homes

I left Toyota in the summer of 2014. At the last Sunday service I attended, Pastor Cid announced that I was leaving and invited me to speak briefly in front of the congregation. I stood by the pulpit, slightly nervous, and asked everyone to open the Bible. "Friends [*Amigos*]," I started. It was my last day but I still could not bring myself to say "brothers and sisters" (*irmãos e irmãs*). "First I want to share the words that spoke to my heart this week." And then I read the passage from James 4:13 that I had come across a few days earlier while reading the Bible in my spare time: "Now listen, you who say, 'Today or tomorrow we will go to this or that city, spend a year there, carry on business and make money.' Why, you do not even know what will happen tomorrow. What is your life? You are a mist that appears for a little while and then vanishes. Instead, you ought to say, 'If it is the Lord's will, we will live and do this or that.'" Closing my Bible, I then thanked everyone for hospitality, kindness, and friendship. "Now, I really want to say I'll come back next year," I continued, "But let me just say that, if it is the Lord's will, we will meet again in the future." I could see many familiar faces smiling at me as I stood there listening to the congregation clap—Luana, Takeshi, Marcelo, Leticia, Guilherme, Beatriz, Kenji, Shunsuke, Shinji, and many more.

To some of their disappointment, there I was, leaving without being saved. "It's such a waste [*mottainai yo*]," Shinji had told me weeks earlier when I was dropping him off after vigil late at night. "If you understand that much about forgiveness, it's just one more step to salvation." He was referring to the testimony I offered during the Japanese service of that week. I spoke about how the passages from John 8 resonated with my personal struggle at the time. "You are starting to see what God's grace means," Shinji said. "Why don't you accept Jesus?"

I unwittingly confused some people on several occasions during the last months of my fieldwork. At the "talent show" of one fundraising party at church, I told the story of Jesus with sand art, by drawing with fine sand on a glass table lit from below. I had actually planned to be an observer, not a participant, but then the organizer of the event asked me to fill an empty slot. My ten-minute visual story of Christ from his birth to crucifixion won me the first prize. As I later found out, a pastor from Indonesia who happened to be visiting that day found my performance moving and suggested to Pastor Cid that maybe he could invite me to his church. "And I had to tell him," Pastor Cid later told me with a warm smile, "that you aren't really here for that reason. You are here for a different reason. So I said, maybe in the future, when the Holy Spirit has spoken to her heart." Although "the Holy Spirit had not spoken to my heart," my sand art was Christian enough, whatever it means, to compel the Indonesian pastor to invite me all the way to his country. The performance spoke, visually as it may, in a language he recognized, in an idiom he knew as Christian. So maybe this was the source of confusion: I was starting to speak like a Christian. And to some, speaking like a Christian was a sign of becoming a Christian, a manifestation of transformation, a dawn of born-again life. If, as Susan Harding once wrote, "speaking is believing," then perhaps I was starting to believe. But I went only halfway, stood at the crossroads, and left the field.

There are other crossroads as well. "So, you'll become an American?" Beatriz asked me. We were having another late night conversation over a cup of coffee in her apartment in Building 127 in Homi Danchi. My partner, who arrived in Japan as a boyfriend two weeks prior for a short visit, had just left as a fiancé. I shrugged my shoulders and looked down at the ring on my left hand. I could not quite look ahead to the future when I was not even used to seeing it there.

I decided to answer with another question. "So, do you think your children with José will be Japanese?" I was not the only one wearing a new ring. A young man from the church had proposed to her several months earlier. She initially said no ("He is two years younger than me!"). But the second time was the charm. Since both were the leaders of the youth ministry, everyone knew about their courtship. Her fiancé had made it clear that he was ready to start a family once they were wed the following year. Beatriz tilted her head with a thoughtful expression and, eventually, shrugged her shoulders as well. We both laughed.

"Mirai no koto wa wakannai ne" (We don't know about the future), she said. Since both Beatriz and José were already yonsei (fourth-generation Nikkei), their offspring would not qualify for the Nikkei-jin visa. They would most likely grow up in Japan as dependents of permanent residents and then as permanent residents themselves, unless they decide to naturalize one day. "I can't say if my children will be Brazilian or Japanese. I mean, some people say that even I'm not Brazilian enough. . . . I just know that they'll be with God." She played with the rim of her coffee mug. "And really, what more can we hope for?"

I visited Toyota again two years later in the summer of 2016. When I stepped into the church, I saw Beatriz and José in the back of the room with a blue stroller between them. As they rocked their bodies in prayer with one hand up in the air, they placed the other hand—Beatriz her right hand and José his left hand—on the stroller and gently rocked it as well. Their six-month-old baby girl was beautiful like a pearl. Following the custom, the new parents had given her two names, one Brazilian and the other Japanese: Cristina Midori. As I later learned, Midori was the name of Beatriz's maternal grandmother, who was born decades earlier in Maringá, Brazil. The old Midori lived as a daughter of Japanese immigrants in mid-twentieth-century Brazil, during which many Nikkeis gave up the dream of returning to Japan and accepted their new homeland. The new Midori will grow up as a daughter of Nikkei Brazilian migrants in early twenty-first-century Japan, where many Nikkeis still yearn to return home to Brazil. Unlike her great-grandmother, little Cristina Midori did not receive the citizenship of the country where she was born as a birthright. Nor could she obtain the Nikkei-jin, or Japanese descendant, visa, since her fifth-generation "Japanese blood" was legally too thin and too distant from the "origin." Yet there she was, breathing quietly but steadily, surrounded by her fellow migrants who continued to travel the borderlands of nations, identities, and belongings. She had just joined this diasporic journey of one century, two nations, five generations, and countless identities, en route to impossible, but ever so real, home.

Ursula Le Guin once wrote that true journey is return. This book, then, is about a group of people who have been undertaking a true journey, with gods, ancestors, spirits, and most recently, God. And if God is the name of what will always be with you, what feels the sweetest in its simultaneous presence and absence, perhaps their return is through God.

"And really, what more can we hope for?"

NOTES

CHAPTER 1

1. All the names of informants are pseudonyms except Pastor Cid Carneiro, the lead pastor of Missão Apoio Toyota. How I interacted with each person during fieldwork determines the way in which he or she is addressed in the book. As I was on a first-name basis with my Brazilian informants, they will appear under their first names. Since I addressed most of my Japanese subjects with -san following the linguistic convention, the book refers to them in such a way as well. I decided to use the actual name of the denomination—Missão Apoio—because I cite a number of existing publications that already made public its real name. See Shoji, "Making of 'Brazilian Japanese' Pentecostalism." A note on foreign words is also in order. The fieldwork took place in multicultural and multilinguistic settings. I collected roughly 70 percent of my ethnographic data in Portuguese and 30 percent in Japanese. Some informants, especially the bilingual youth, freely switched back and forth between the two languages even within a single utterance. All non-English words—either Portuguese or Japanese—will be uniformly italicized in this book to follow the stylistic convention, but I would like to remind the reader of this porous quality of linguistic and cultural boundaries.

2. The Missão Apoio churches did not encourage the members to use one single version of the Bible. Although many owned paper copies of King James Atualizada or João F. Almeida, others simply used free Bible apps on their smartphones without much regard to which translated version they were reading. Presbyter Bruno happened to be using the João F. Almeida version of the Portuguese Bible in this scene: "andai em temor durante o tempo da vossa peregrinação."

3. Clifford, "Diasporas," 322, original italic. For a discussion of nostalgia and homeland in diaspora studies, see Quayson and Daswani, "Introduction."

4. Although some anthropologists differentiate between morality and ethics, others do not necessarily find such a strict distinction analytically productive. Both sides offer some compelling arguments on the issue, but in this book I use morality and ethics interchangeably and focus on ethnographic illustrations. See Laidlaw, *Subject of Virtue*; Zigon, "Within a Range of Possibilities."

5. Engelke, *Problem of Presence*, 9.

rews, *Blacks and Whites*; Warren and Sue, "Comparative Racisms." ling, *Book of Jerry Falwell*, ch. 9.

rgument is not that return migration in Asia started in the past several decades but instead that it is a converging trend of an increasing number of nations in the region, gaining momentum since the 1990s.

9. Ong, *Flexible Citizenship*.

10. Xiang, Yeoh, and Toyota, *Return*; Freeman, *Making and Faking Kinship*; Jo, *Homing*.

11. Adachi, *Japanese and Nikkei*; Hirabayashi, Hirabayashi, and Kikumura, *New Worlds*; Lesser, *Searching for Home Abroad*.

12. Roth, *Brokered Homeland*; Tsuda, *Strangers in the Ethnic Homeland*.

13. Freston, "Transnationalisation of Brazilian Pentecostalism."

14. For case studies from India, see Roberts, *To Be Cared For*; Viswanath, "Emergence of Authenticity Talk."

15. The study of return migration has matured significantly compared with a decade ago, when a mere mention of the literature's scarcity sufficed to justify the scholarly value of the topic. The growing body of work includes Christou, *Narratives of Place*; Conway and Potter, *Return Migration*; Markowitz and Stefansson, *Homecomings*; Olsson and King, "Introduction"; Potter, Conway, and Phillips, *Experience of Return*; Tsuda, *Diasporic Homecomings*. Few of them, however, focus on the religious dimension of return. For exceptions, see Capone, *Searching for Africa*; Seeman, *One People, One Blood*; Napolitano, *Migrant Hearts*.

16. For the discussion of the ethnic lens, see Glick-Schiller, Çaglar, and Gulbrandsen, "Beyond the Ethnic Lens." For an overview of the anthropology of Christianity, see Cannell, *Anthropology of Christianity*; Jenkins, "Anthropology of Christianity"; Robbins, "Anthropology of Christianity."

CHAPTER 2

1. Glick-Schiller and Salazar, "Regimes of Mobility," 186.

2. Instituto Brasileiro de Geografia e Estatística (IBGE), "Anuário Estatístico."

3. J. Amândio Sobral, "Os Japoneses em São Paulo," *Correio Paulistano*, June 25, 1908, cited in Lesser, *Immigration, Ethnicity, and National Identity*, 154.

4. Skidmore, *Black into White*, 199.

5. Skidmore, "Racial Ideas," 9.

6. Adachi, "Japonês."

7. Sasaki, "Between Emigration and Immigration," 55.

8. Maeyama, "Ancestor, Emperor, and Immigrant," 162.

9. *Burajiru Jihō* cited in Maeyama, "Ancestor, Emperor, and Immigrant."

10. Rocha, "Zen Buddhism," 31.

11. For a historical overview, see Josephson, *Invention of Religion*.

12. Maeyama, "Ancestor, Emperor, and Immigrant," 170–71.

13. Maeyama, "Ethnicity, Secret Societies, and Associations."

14. Lesser, *Discontented Diaspora*, 8.

15. Lesser, "Japanese, Brazilians, Nikkei," 5.

16. Shoji, "Failed Prophecy."

17. For example, many Okinawan Nikkeis started to travel to Okinawa in the 1950s to bring their mortuary tablets of ancestors and ritual tablets for Fire God (*hinukan*) back to Brazil. Mori, "Burajiru Okinawakeijin"; Mori, "Identity Transformations."

18. Maeyama, "Ancestor, Emperor, and Immigrant," 177.

19. In the Brazilian census, the category of "yellow" (*amarelo*) is designated to Asian immigrants and their descendants.

20. IBGE, "Censo Demográfico 2010 Características Gerais," 149 (see Table 1.4.6).

21. Pew Research Center, "Brazil's Changing Religious Landscape."

22. Freston, "Latin America," 585. For additional context, see Freston, "Pentecostalism in Brazil." For the "explosive" growth of Pentecostalism, see Martin, *Tongues of Fire*.

23. Chesnut, *Born Again in Brazil*.

24. Pew Research Center, "Christian Movements." For more details on Pentecostalism in the Global South, see Engelke and Tomlinson, *Limits of Meaning*; Corten and Marshall-Fratani, *Between Babel and Pentecost*. There is as yet no scholarly consensus on just where to draw Pentecostalism's borders. Since this book's focus is not on the theoretical determination of theological boundaries, I choose to approach *Pentecostalism* in inclusive terms and define it loosely as the following. Pentecostalism's experiential characteristics are, first, "an emphasis on the achievement of a personalized and self-transforming relationship with Jesus Christ"; second, "ritual performance that highlights the ever-present power of the Holy Spirit"; and, third, "religious enthusiasm centered on the experience of charismata," including prophecy, exorcism, healing, and glossolalia. See Hefner, "Unexpected Modern," 2.

25. Rocha and Vásquez, *Diaspora of Brazilian Religions*.

26. For Mozambique, see van de Kamp, *Violent Conversion*; Premawardhana, *Faith in Flux*. For Portugal, see Mafra et al., "Igreja Universal." For the United States, see Margolis, *Good Bye, Brazil*. For Japan, Quero and Shoji, *Transnational Faiths*.

27. Margolis, *Invisible Minority*.

28. Higuchi, "Keizai Kiki," 51.

29. Kawamura, *Para Onde Vão Os Brasileiros?*

30. Tsuda, "Acting Brazilian."

31. Tsuda, for instance, wrote: "The nikkeijin, as descendants of those who initially fled to Brazil because they could not survive in Japan, have now returned to Japan because they could not survive economically in Brazil either." Tsuda, *Strangers in the Ethnic Homeland*, 111. For a relevant discussion of return migration, see Sasaki, "To Return or Not to Return."

32. Higuchi, "Keizai Kiki," 52–53.

33. Ministry of Justice, "The Current Number of Foreigners." Brazilians are more numerous than all the other Latin Americans combined—roughly 48,000 Peruvians, 5,600 Bolivians, 2,700 Argentinians, and 2,400 Mexicans, to name a few. See Ministry of Justice, "Zairyū Gaikokujin." The majority of Peruvians and Bolivians in Japan are

also Nikkei, but Brazilians are ranked higher than the other Latin American Nikkeis in the perceived ethnic hierarchy for a number of reasons. First, Brazil is considered to have a higher status because of its higher GDP, larger population, and greater political influence. Second, Nikkei Brazilians in general have more Japanese cultural and phenotypic features akin to the Japanese majority in Japan compared with Nikkei Peruvians (the ratio of *mestiços* is greater among Nikkei Peruvians). Lastly, migrants from Peru included more non-Nikkei Peruvians, generally from poorer background, some of whom entered Japan using fraudulent documents. Thus, "unlike Japanese Brazilians who asserted their Brazilianness, Japanese Peruvians, particularly of those of racially unmixed and middle-class backgrounds, tried to distance themselves from 'pure Peruvians,' or non-Japanese Peruvians, emphasizing instead their status as *nikkei* Japanese descendants." Takenaka, "Ethnic Hierarchy," 262–63.

34. Ministry of Justice, "On the Acceptance of Fourth-Generation."

35. Ministry of Justice, "Zairyū Gaikokujin." This holds true on a more regional scale. In 2014, 3,276 (63 percent) of the 5,120 registered Brazilians in Toyota City were on permanent resident visas, but only 1,328 (26 percent) lived as long-term residents. Toyota City, "Toyotashi Gaikokujin."

36. Indeed, foreign migrants constitute one of the main groups that are diversifying and transforming Japanese society today. Kelly and White, "Students, Slackers, Singles."

37. Japanese New Religions that have thrived in postwar Brazil have returned to Japan with the migrants—most notably, Seichō-no-Ie, Tenri-kyō, Perfect Liberty, and Sekai-kyūsei-kyō. See Clarke, *Japanese New Religions*; Matsuoka, *Japanese Prayer*; Shimazono, "Expansion of Japan's New Religions." Espiritismo is a mediumship religion that focuses on communication with spirits and reincarnations. Umbanda is an Afro-Brazilian religion that blends African traditions, Roman Catholicism, Espiritismo, and indigenous spirituality.

38. Shoji, "Making of 'Brazilian Japanese' Pentecostalism," 37–39.

39. Despite the Pentecostal insistence on exclusive affiliation, I occasionally spotted a handful of active members from the local Pentecostal churches at the Catholic church in Toyota. Multiple and flexible religious identities seemed to be more common than many Pentecostal converts were willing to admit in public.

40. A number of other researchers have found that Pentecostalism has flourished among Brazilian migrant communities in Japan. Yamada, "Bestowing the Light"; Hoshino, "Potentiality."

41. In terms of the places of worship (and not the number of members, which is more elusive), Missão Apoio is the second-largest Brazil-derived Protestant denomination in Japan after Assembleias de Deus (Assemblies of God, 23 percent) and on par with Igreja Universal do Reino de Deus (The Universal Church of the Kingdom of God, 10 percent). Shoji, "Making of 'Brazilian Japanese' Pentecostalism," 40.

42. Yamada, "Bestowing the Light."

43. Jesuit missionaries first brought Roman Catholicism to Japan in 1549. Since Catholicism arrived concomitantly with the colonial expansion of the Spanish and Por-

tuguese in Asia, Japanese authorities soon came to regard it as a serious threat to the country's internal stability. In 1614, the Tokugawa Shogunate ordered a nationwide order to prohibit Christianity and expelled foreign missionaries. Those who refused to abandon their faith faced torture, exile, or execution. Even when the central government finally lifted the ban more than two centuries later in 1873, and Protestant missionaries started to arrive primarily from the United States, the prejudices against Christians did not easily disappear. Today, the great majority—roughly 94 percent of the population, according to some reports—participate in Buddhist and Shinto activities, but that same majority consider themselves "non-religious" (*mushūkyō*) when polled. See Agency for Cultural Affairs, "Shūkyō Kanren Tōkei"; Watanabe, "Nihon no Shūkyō Jinkō"; Miyazaki, "Roman Catholic Mission"; Mullins, *Christianity Made in Japan*.

44. Tokyo Christian University, *JMR Study Report*.

45. Aichi Prefectural Government, "Current Number of Foreign Residents."

46. Roth, *Brokered Homeland*; Tsuda, *Strangers in the Ethnic Homeland*.

47. For another ethnography conducted in Homi Danchi, see Linger, *No One Home*. For a more recent study on Brazilian migrants that was also conducted in the Aichi Prefecture in Japan, see von Baeyer, "National Worlds."

48. Toyota City, "Toyotashi Gaikokujin." The contexts in which I conducted participant observation in Homi Danchi were diverse, ranging from the local Brazilian supermarket to the annual summer festival in the neighborhood. For example, I taught a weekly Japanese course as a volunteer at a nongovernmental organization called Torcida for three months during my fieldwork. Torcida provided free Japanese language classes to the children from migrant families in and around Homi Danchi. The majority of my students at Torcida were Brazilian.

49. Of Missão Apoio Toyota's five hundred members, roughly fifty were Nikkei Peruvians who attended their own Spanish service scheduled in Sunday morning. In early afternoon, the church subsequently held a Japanese service, which was attended mostly by Brazilian youth who were fluent in Japanese. At the time of my fieldwork, Missão Apoio Toyota had only one Japanese convert. After the Japanese service, the church would become much more crowded with Brazilian attendants of Portuguese service. Since the church space could not accommodate all the Portuguese-speaking congregants at once, there were two Portuguese services on Sunday, one at 4 P.M. and the other at 7 P.M.

50. Glick-Schiller and Fouron make an insightful observation in this regard: "Even the naming of immigrants' children as a 'second generation' reflected and contributed to the notion of the incorporation of immigrants as a steplike irreversible process and one in which immigrants' children were socialized solely by forces within the land of their birth." Glick-Schiller and Fouron, "Generation of Identity," 175.

51. Anderson, *Imagined Communities*; Barth, "Introduction."

52. Eckstein, "On Deconstructing," 215. As most of my informants' extended kin were in other parts of Japan or in Brazil, I could not carry out a genealogical work to determine their migrant generations. The generational identities in this book are

therefore based on their voluntary self-identifications, which they reported primarily in relation to their Nikkei-jin visas. A handful, for example, had two Nikkei parents, one issei (first-generation) and the other nisei (second-generation). Such migrants typically acquired the visa through the issei parent since their offspring, in turn, would then count as sansei (third-generation) and still legally qualify to be Nikkei-jin. Only a minority of my informants grew up in tight-knit Nikkei communities in Brazil (*colônias*) and were already used to identifying with Japanese immigrant generation prior to Nikkei-jin visa application. To many like Sergio, migrant generational identity was more about one aspect of their genealogy and less about their ethnic subjectivity. Since generation thus figured as a flexible construct in my fieldwork, I cannot provide a concise and factual definition of the term here; the best I can do is to emphasize that it is an evolving sociohistorical concept.

53. Linger, "Do Japanese Brazilians Exist?," 212. For a relevant discussion of Japanese Brazilian identity in diaspora, see Nishida, *Diaspora and Identity*.

54. Harding, *Book of Jerry Falwell*, xi–xii.

CHAPTER 3

1. It was 10.7 percent, or 20 out of 186 valid responses.

2. Lesser, *Discontented Diaspora*, xxvi.

3. See Adachi, "Japonês."

4. Seventeen out of 160 respondents who answered this item on my survey said they received some higher education. According to the 2010 Brazil Census, 11.3 percent of Brazilians had college degrees. See IBGE, "Censo Demográfico 2010 Educação e Deslocamento," 61–62.

5. Datafolha, "Centenário da Imigração Japonesa." The same source adds that this high number makes Nikkeis the group with "the most educated profile in the city of São Paulo, where 15 percent have obtained college-level education."

6. Many Brazilian migrants paid staffing agencies for arranging their visa and trip to Japan, the cost of which they were obligated to pay back.

7. Ezaki, "Quero Ajudar," 20. "The Japanese" (*os japoneses*) refers to both Japanese nationals in Japan and Japanese descendants in Brazil in colloquial Portuguese; the two are often considered interchangeable. See Lesser, *Discontented Diaspora*, 45.

8. Brettel, *Anthropology and Migration*, 71.

9. Borges, *Chains of Gold*, 113.

10. Schneider, *Futures Lost*, ch. 2.

11. Beltrão and Sugahara, *Ciclo e a Tangente*.

12. Vertovec, "Migrant Transnationalism," 153. For another discussion of bifocality, see Besnier, *On the Edge*, 12.

13. *Vitrine*, "Naturalização," 14.

14. Befu, *Hegemony of Homogeneity*; Befu, "Nationalism and *Nihonjinron*."

15. Ryang, *Japan and National Anthropology*; Ryang and Lie, *Diaspora Without Homeland*; Weiner, *Japan's Minorities*.

16. Dávila, *Hotel Trópico*. For an example of the "mythic" value attached to racial mixture, see Freyre, *Masters and the Slaves*.

17. Burgess, "Japan's 'No Immigration.'"

18. James and Mills, "Introduction," 2.

19. Gell, *Anthropology of Time*.

20. For a study of neoliberal Japan, see Allison, *Precarious Japan*.

21. Pine, "Migration as Hope," 100. For a relevant discussion of temporality in migration studies, see Gabaccia, "Time and Temporality."

CHAPTER 4

1. *Chūnichi Shimbun*, "Conflict Between Foreigners and Nationalist," 27.

2. *Yomiuri Shimbun*, "Tension Between Brazilians and Right-Wing," 31.

3. Matsumiya and Yogo, "Masu Media," 65.

4. Levitt and Glick-Shiller, "Conceptualizing Simultaneity," 186.

5. *Pensão por Morte*, or Pension by Death, is a type of benefit in social welfare that the legal dependents of the deceased can receive, given that they meet certain conditions.

6. Beltrão and Sugahara, *Ciclo e a Tangente*, 29.

7. IBGE, "Censo Demográfico 2010 Família e Domicílio," 66.

8. *O Estado de S. Paulo*, "Dekasseguis Abandonam."

9. *O Estado de S. Paulo*, "Dekasseguis Abandonam."

10. Marra, "Leia Depoimentos"; Matsuki, "Abandonados por Dekasseguis."

11. The struggle to maintain family ties in the face of physical and psychological distances is something that Nikkei Brazilians share in common with numerous migrant groups around the globe. See Boehm, *Intimate Migrations*; Coe et al., *Everyday Ruptures*; Cole, *Affective Circuits*; Leinaweaver, "Outsourcing Care"; Yarris, *Care Across Generations*.

12. Yamamoto, "Gender Roles."

13. Portes and Hao, "Price of Uniformity"; Portes and Rumbaut, *Legacies*.

14. For an exemplary study on the relationship between transnational migration and idiom of distress, see Yarris, "Pensando Mucho."

15. Berg and Ramos-Zayas, "Racializing Affect," 656. Following the authors, I understand affect as "endemic to social practices that are decidedly historical, rational, and, in some instances, intentional while also being sustained through embodied practices that are phenomenological, reflective (and self-reflexive), and visceral" (Berg and Ramos-Zayas, "Racializing Affect," 655). For a relevant discussion on the politics of emotion, see Abu-Lughod and Lutz, *Language and the Politics of Emotion*; Lutz, "Emotion, Thought, and Estrangement." Following these scholars, I do not draw a strict theoretical line between "affect" and "emotion" and regard them as mutually inclusive in many contexts. For other works that support this stance, see Lutz, "What Matters"; Yang, "Politics of Affect"; Mazzarella, "Affect." For an alternative approach that theoretically distinguishes between the two, see Massumi, *Parables for the*

Virtual; Stewart, *Ordinary Affects*. For an overview of this conceptual debate, see White, "Affect: An Introduction."

16. Ischida, "Experiência Nikkei," 175. For a relevant discussion on the Nikkei families in Brazil, see Cardoso and Ninomiya, *Estrutura Familiar*.

17. To learn more about the "culture" of Japanese schooling, see Benjamin, *Japanese Lessons*; Hendry, *Becoming Japanese*.

18. Allison, "Japanese Mothers," 203.

19. White, *Perfectly Japanese*, 134.

20. *Omuraisu* is a Japanese rendition of omelet, which comes with fried rice inside. Pikachū is a popular character in Pokémon, a media franchise that ranges from video games to TV shows.

21. Besse, *Restructuring Patriarchy*; Mayblin, *Gender, Catholicism, and Morality*; Samara, "Família no Brasil"; Souza and Botelho, "Modelos Nacionais."

22. Ashikari, "Urban Middle-Class"; Kelsky, *Women on the Verge*; Lebra, *Japanese Women*.

23. For racism and nationalism in Japan, see Creighton, "Soto Others"; Kaneko, "Constructing Japanese Nationalism"; Murphy-Shigematsu, "Multiethnic Japan"; Willis and Murphy-Shigematsu, *Transcultural Japan*. For specific discussions of the mixed-race people, see Burkhardt, "Institutional Barriers"; Carter, "Mixed Race Okinawans"; Fish, "'Mixed-Blood' Japanese"; Rivas, "Mistura for the Fans"; Watarai, "Can a Mestiça Be a Haafu?"

24. For the politics of affect, see Muehlebach, "On Affective Labor"; Stoler, "Affective States"; Richard and Rudnyckyj, "Economies of Affect."

CHAPTER 5

1. Fajans, *Brazilian Food*; Ohnuki-Tierney, *Rice as Self*.

2. Mariz, *Coping with Poverty*.

3. For time and Christianity, see Bielo, "Creationist History-Making"; Daswani, *Looking Back*; Robbins, "Continuity Thinking."

4. For Ghanaians and Jamaicans in England, see Fumanti, "Virtuous Citizenship"; Toulis, *Believing Identity*. For Latin Americans in the United States, see Williams, Steigenga, and Vásquez, *Place to Be*. For Haitians in French West Indies, see Brodwin, "Pentecostalism in Translation."

5. For a discussion of tension between conversion and "culture," see Seeman, "Coffee and the Moral Order."

6. van der Veer, *Conversion to Modernities*. For an overview, see Robbins, "Anthropology of Christianity."

7. Meyer, *Translating the Devil*, 215.

8. Modern sensibility can be characterized as "a sense that the passage of time should expectably be marked by progress and improvement vis-à-vis the past," which appears "so ubiquitous today." Knauft, *Critically Modern*, 7. For modernity and temporality in Global Christianity, see Klaver and van de Kamp, "Embodied Temporalities"; McGov-

ern, "Turning the Clock"; Meyer, "Make a Complete Break"; Scherz, "Let Us Make God."

9. Coleman, "Right Now!"

10. Coleman, "Right Now!," 443.

11. Munn, "Cultural Anthropology of Time," 94.

12. Luhrmann, *When God Talks Back*, 200.

13. Thompson, "Time, Work-Discipline."

14. Luhrmann, "Hyperreal God."

15. Munn, "Cultural Anthropology of Time," 116.

16. For the psychological views on absorption, see Csikszentmihalyi, *Flow*.

17. van Dijk, "Time and Transcultural Technologies," 228.

18. Coleman, *Globalisation of Charismatic Christianity*, 224.

CHAPTER 6

1. Luhrmann, *When God Talks Back*, ch. 4. For another ethnographic study of The Vineyard, see Bialecki, *Diagram for Fire*.

2. Zigon, "On Love"; for more detailed discussion, see Zigon, *"HIV Is God's Blessing."*

3. Burdick, *Color of Sound*; Burdick, *Blessed Anastacia*.

4. van Klinken, "Queer Love."

5. For diverse case studies from around the world, see Hirsch and Wardlow, *Modern Loves*; Padilla et al., *Love and Globalization*. For an extended study from Nepal, see Ahearn, *Invitations to Love*.

6. Associação MMI Brasil in Atibaia, São Paulo, distributed the Portuguese materials of Married for Life.

7. Adogame and Shankar, *Religion on the Move*; Levitt, "Religion on the Move"; van de Kamp and van Dijk, "Pentecostals Moving South-South."

8. van de Kamp, "Love Therapy."

9. Phillipps and Phillipps, *Casados Para Sempre*, 35. I translated the Portuguese text into English myself.

10. Hirsch and Wardlow, *Modern Loves*; Padilla et al., *Love and Globalization*.

11. On "love" in Japan, see Ryang, *Love in Modern Japan*. For how foreign migrants enact the idiom of love, see Faier, "Filipina Migrants in Rural Japan."

12. Stromberg, *Language and Self-Transformation*.

13. In Brazil, working women's average income was 72.3 percent of men's in 2011. IBGE, "Mulher No Mercado," 16. In Japan, it was 72.2 percent in 2014. Ministry of Health, Labour and Welfare, "Heisei 26 nen," 4.

14. Phillipps and Phillipps, *Casados Para Sempre*, 51–57.

15. Austin-Broos, *Jamaica Genesis*; Eriksen, "Pastor and the Prophetess"; Eriksen, "Sarah's Sinfulness"; van Klinken, "Male Headship."

16. Brusco, "Colombian Evangelicalism."

17. Brusco, "Colombian Evangelicalism." For a discussion of machismo, see Gutmann and Vigoya, "Masculinities."

18. Brusco, *Reformation of Machismo*, 137.

19. For detailed discussions of Christian citizenship, see O'Neill, "But Our Citizenship Is in Heaven"; O'Neill, *City of God*.

20. For sexual culture in Brazil, see Parker, *Bodies, Pleasures, and Passions*.

21. Coe, "How Children Feel," 97.

CHAPTER 7

1. Blood is also an important element in Brazilian nationalist discourses, particularly for ideological concepts such as racial democracy, whitening, and *mestiçagem* (racial mixture). Since this chapter focuses on Japan, these issues will not be discussed here, but please see Chapter 2 for relevant discussions.

2. Carsten, *Cultures of Relatedness*; McKinnon, *Relative Values*; Peletz, "Kinship Studies"; Schneider, *American Kinship*.

3. For the significance of blood in Christianity, see Anidjar, *Blood*; Bynum, "Blood of Christ"; Bynum, *Wonderful Blood*. For a comparative discussion of spiritual kinship, see Thomas, Malik, and Wellman, *New Directions*.

4. For both Japanese and Christians, the idiom of blood provides a collective template for storytelling, which in turn constitutes a crucial "cultural model." Shore, *Culture in Mind*, 58.

5. Cannell, "Blood of Abraham"; Carsten, *After Kinship*; McKinnon and Cannell, *Vital Relations*; Stone, *New Directions*.

6. Weiner, "'Self' and 'Other,'" 1.

7. Wilson, "Family or State?" For broader context, see Wilson, *Nation and Nationalism*.

8. Robertson, "Hemato-Nationalism," 99.

9. Robertson, "Hemato-Nationalism," 99. For a relevant discussion of the ideological significance of blood in Japan, see Robertson, "Blood Talks."

10. Linger, *No One Home*, 277.

11. Roth, *Brokered Homeland*; Tsuda, "From Ethnic Affinity"; Tsuda, *Strangers in the Ethnic Homeland*; Tsuda, "When Identities Become Modern."

12. With the introduction of the "specific activities" visa in July 2018, which grants some fourth-generation Nikkei foreigners a right for sojourn up to five years, things may change in the next few years.

13. Keane, "Evidence of the Senses." Keane builds on Peirce's theory on signs, particularly the distinction between symbol, icon, and index. Although symbol is a type of sign in which the form of signification is arbitrary (e.g., the English word *dog* and a class of animals), the relationships between the signifier and the object are *not* arbitrary in icon and index; icon possesses formal resemblance to the thing signified (e.g., "phallic" ritual object), and index is part of or affected by the signified entity (e.g., dark clouds index rain, and hourglass indexes passage of time). See Hardwick, *Semiotics and Significs*.

14. Keane, "Semiotics," 417. Original italic.

15. Weiner, "'Self' and 'Other,'" 1.

16. Nelson, *Dancing with the Dead*.

17. Mori, "Identity Transformations," 60–61. Some Okinawan communities in Brazil make an active collective effort to preserve the language. Petrucci and Miyahira, "Language Preservation."

18. The idiom spoken in Okinawa is locally called Uchināguchi. Whether the group of vernacular idioms spoken in Okinawa constitutes a "language" or "dialect" is a question that is as political as it is academic due to the history of the islands. Matsumori, "Ryûkyuan."

19. For Koreans, see Ryang, *North Koreans*; for Okinawans, see Inoue, *Okinawa and the US*; for Buraku-min, see Hankins, *Working Skin*; for the Ainu, see Siddle, *Race, Resistance, and the Ainu*.

20. Ramos-Zayas, *National Performances*; Ramos-Zayas, *Street Therapists*.

21. Baran, "Girl, You Are Not Morena"; Telles, *Race in Another America*; French, *Legalizing Identity*.

22. For the tension between Pentecostal churches and kin networks, see van de Kamp, "Converting the Spirit Spouse"; van de Kamp, *Violent Conversion*.

23. See Matthew 12:46–50 and Mark 3:31–35 for relevant messages.

24. Ebaugh and Curry, "Fictive Kin." The concept of "fictive" kinship, however, has been criticized as reifying the assumption about what counts as "real" kinship. Carsten, *Cultures of Relatedness*.

25. Shoji, "Making of 'Brazilian Japanese' Pentecostalism," 42–43. The cellular system is not unique to Missão Apoio. A number of Pentecostal denominations in Latin America and beyond have employed it with great success. O'Neill, *City of God*, 26.

26. Keane, "Sincerity, 'Modernity,' and the Protestants."

27. Harding, *Book of Jerry Falwell*, ch. 7.

28. For the relationship between Catholicism, Protestantism, and other religions in Brazil, see Selka, "Morality in the Religious Marketplace"; Stoll, *Is Latin America Turning Protestant*.

29. Keane, "Semiotics," 419.

30. Bielo, *Emerging Evangelicals*; Keane, *Christian Moderns*; Taylor, *Sources of the Self*.

31. Josephson, *Invention of Religion*.

32. Hardacre, *Shintō and the State*, 123.

33. Hardacre, *Shintō and the State*, 123.

34. Miura, *Life and Thought*, 52.

35. Rowe, *Bonds of the Dead*.

CHAPTER 8

1. The media—both Japanese and foreign—often characterize the Hōnen Festival as a "rare" and "strange" tradition (*kisai* or *chinsai*) and cover it extensively. The event consequently attracts a large number of tourists from both inside and outside Japan.

2. Geertz, "Religion as a Cultural System," 74.

3. Geertz, "Religion as a Cultural System," 75.

4. Needham, *Belief, Language, and Experience*, 1–2.

5. Lopez Jr., "Belief," 22.

6. Asad, *Genealogies of Religion*, 198.

7. The Toyota calendar ("Toyota *karendā*" in Japanese) determines the workdays and holidays of all the employees working in factories affiliated with or under contract with the Toyota Motor Corporation. *Obon* is one of the only three occasions in a year when workers can take multiple days off outside the weekend.

8. Bialecki and del Pinal, "Introduction," 580.

9. In Portuguese, "Nós somos xintoísta porque okinawa-jin é xintoísta né . . . okinawa-jin não é budista." By "Shintoist," Leticia meant to refer to the set of Okinawan rites for local gods and ancestral spirits, not necessarily State Shinto or other mainland branches of Shinto. She also grouped all of the mainland Japanese as "Buddhist," which helped her draw a clear line between the Okinawan and the Japanese.

10. Taniguchi, *Jinsei wo Shihaisuru*.

11. Taniguchi, *Jinsei wo Shihaisuru*, 195.

12. Four years later, in 2018, I heard from a friend in Toyota that Leticia had chosen to burn the ancestral altar in a ritual she coconstructed in consultation with the church leaders. From what I was told, the concerns she expressed were still the same: although she knew that she was not supposed to keep the altar, she could not just throw it away like regular trash. The church personnel acknowledged Leticia's moral anxiety surrounding the object by devising a small ceremony for her to formally bid farewell. This new piece of information reached me too late to enter the body of the book manuscript. If anything, it testifies to the fact that the ethnographic picture is always incomplete, in the sense that it is necessarily a snapshot of never-ending human drama.

13. Robbins, "Is the Trans- in Transnationalism."

14. Hickman, "Ancestral Personhood," 323.

15. For the flexibility of the boundary between the material and the immaterial in Christianity, see Engelke, *Problem of Presence*.

16. Keane, "Sincerity, 'Modernity,' and the Protestants."

17. Kirsch, "Restaging the Will."

18. Elisha, "Faith Beyond Belief," 57.

19. Elisha, "Faith Beyond Belief," 57. For a more detailed ethnographic account of the topic, see Elisha, *Moral Ambition*.

20. Howell, "Repugnant Cultural Other."

21. Bielo, "Belief, Deconversion, and Authenticity," 274.

22. Bielo, "Belief, Deconversion, and Authenticity," 258.

23. Austin, *How to Do Things with Words*.

24. Ferraro and Koch, "Religion and Health"; Lim and Putnam, "Religion, Social Networks"; Smidt, *Religion as Social Capital*.

25. Durkheim, *Elementary Forms*.

26. Asad, *Formations of the Secular*.

27. Smilde, *Reason to Believe*, 14.

CHAPTER 9

1. For a detailed discussion of resting in the Spirit, see Csordas, *Sacred Self*.

2. Most of these phrases draw on the Bible, particularly 1 Corinthians 14.

3. See Geertz, "From the Native's Point of View."

4. Robbins, *Becoming Sinners*.

5. Daswani, "(In-)Dividual Pentecostals," 257. For other studies about the nuances of Christian individuality, see Coleman, "Materializing the Self"; Vilaça, "Culture and Self"; Vilaça, "Dividualism and Individualism"; Werbner, "Charismatic Dividual."

6. Doi, *Anatomy of Dependence*; Kelly, "Directions in the Anthropology," 398–403; Kitayama et al., "Individual and Collective"; Markus and Kitayama, "Culture and the Self"; Ozawa-de Silva, "Demystifying Japanese Therapy"; Plath, *Long Engagements*; Rosenberger, "Dialectic Balance"; Rosenberger, *Japanese Sense of Self*.

7. Bialecki and Daswani, "Introduction."

8. Although there was a *butsudan* (Buddhist altar) in Sara's natal home in Brazil, her Nikkei father did not really encourage her to learn such rituals. He instead approved his children's attendance at the Catholic Church, probably to maintain a good relationship with his non-Nikkei wife and her kin.

9. Keane, *Christian Moderns*, 15.

10. Robbins, "God Is Nothing but Talk."

11. Mariano, "Laicidade à Brasileira."

12. Meyer, "Make a Complete Break."

13. Keane, *Christian Moderns*, 201.

14. Institute of Statistical Mathematics, "Kokuminsei Chōsa."

15. *Yomiuri Shimbun*, "Nihonjin," 25.

16. Reader and Tanabe, *Practically Religious*, 7.

17. Ozawa–de Silva, "Beyond the Body/Mind?," 28.

18. Kondo, *Crafting Selves*, 107.

19. Kondo, *Crafting Selves*, 107–8.

20. Reader, "Cleaning Floors."

21. Linger, *No One Home*, 290.

22. Linger, *No One Home*, 299.

23. For example, see Corwin, "Changing God"; Lester, *Jesus in Our Wombs*; Mafra, "Saintliness and Sincerity."

24. Kondo, *Crafting Selves*, 106.

25. Yano, *Tears of Longing*, 26.

26. Bardsley and Miller, "Manners and Mischief."

27. Lebra, *Japanese Self*, 224–54.

28. Luhrmann, *When God Talks Back*, 221–22.

29. Luhrmann, *When God Talks Back*, 222.

30. Seligman, "Unmaking and Making of Self"; Selka, *Religion and the Politics*.

31. Flow is characterized by the following qualities: intense and focused concentration on what one is doing in the present moment, merging of action and awareness,

loss of reflective self-consciousness, a sense that one can control one's actions, distortion of temporal experience (typically, a sense that time has passed faster than normal), experience of the activity as intrinsically rewarding. Csikszentmihalyi, *Flow*; Nakamura and Csikszentmihalyi, "Concept of Flow."

32. Csordas, "Asymptote of the Ineffable."

33. Lakoff and Johnson, *Metaphors We Live By*, 199.

34. See Desjarlais, *Body and Emotion*.

35. Csordas, "Embodiment as a Paradigm, 25.

36. Lakoff and Johnson, *Metaphors We Live By*.

37. Bourdieu, *Logic of Practice*; Bourdieu, *Outline of a Theory of Practice*.

38. Harkness, "Glossolalia and Cacophony," 477. For a relevant study of glossolalia, see Samarin, *Tongues of Men*.

39. Tomlinson, "God Speaking to God."

40. Csordas, Embodiment as a Paradigm, 25.

41. Luhrmann and Morgain, "Prayer as Inner Sense Cultivation."

42. Parish, "Between Persons."

CHAPTER 10

1. This sermon was in reference to Exodus 14:10–20.

2. Potolsky, *Mimesis*.

3. For the current debates on ethics and morality in anthropology, see Faubion, *Anthropology of Ethics*; Heintz, *Anthropology of Moralities*; Keane, *Ethical Life*; Laidlaw, *Subject of Virtue*; Zigon, *Morality*. Such debates have called into question the equation of the moral with the social as the Durkheimian legacy. Morality in a Durkheimian sense tends to consist in conforming to social conventions, effectively eliminating the room for choice and freedom as elements in how people strive for good life. An important task for the current anthropology of morality and ethics is to forge a theoretical framework that can duly accommodate freedom—without replicating the autonomous agent with free will that generations of anthropologists have worked hard to deconstruct. This theoretical attention to ethical freedom has generated a growing focus on "moments of deliberate free choice rather than moments of social reproduction for actual moral action." Cassaniti and Hickman, "New Directions," 258. For relevant discussions on the tension between social reproduction and reflective freedom, see Robbins, "Between Reproduction and Freedom"; Zigon, "Moral Breakdown."

BIBLIOGRAPHY

Abu-Lughod, Lila, and Catherine Lutz. *Language and the Politics of Emotion.* Cambridge: Cambridge University Press, 1990.

Adachi, Nobuko, ed. *Japanese and Nikkei at Home and Abroad: Negotiating Identities in a Global World.* Amherst, NY: Cambria, 2010.

———. "Japonês: A Marker of Social Class or a Key Term in the Discourse of Race?" *Latin American Perspectives* 31, no. 3 (2004): 48–76.

Adogame, Afe, and Shobana Shankar, eds. *Religion on the Move! New Dynamics of Religious Expansion in a Globalizing World.* Leiden: Brill, 2012.

Agency for Cultural Affairs. "Shūkyō Kanren Tōkei ni Kansuru Shiryōshū" [Data for statistics on religious affairs]. Tokyo: 2015. Accessed May 21, 2018. http://www .bunka.go.jp/tokei_hakusho_shuppan/tokeichosa/shumu_kanrentokei/pdf/h26 _chosa.pdf.

Ahearn, Laura M. *Invitations to Love: Literacy, Love Letters and Social Change in Nepal.* Ann Arbor: University of Michigan Press, 2001.

Aichi Prefectural Government. "The Current Number of Foreign Residents in the Municipalities in the Aichi Prefecture." [In Japanese.] Nagoya, 2018. Accessed May 21, 2018. http://www.pref.aichi.jp/soshiki/tabunka/gaikokuzinjuminsu-h28-12.html.

Allison, Anne. "Japanese Mothers and Obentōs: The Lunch-Box as Ideological State Apparatus." *Anthropological Quarterly* 64, no. 4 (1991): 195–208.

———. *Precarious Japan.* Durham, NC: Duke University Press, 2013.

Anderson, Benedict. *Imagined Communities: Reflections on the Origin and Spread of Nationalism.* New York: Verso Books, 2006.

Andrews, George R. *Blacks and Whites in São Paulo, Brazil, 1888–1988.* Madison: University of Wisconsin Press, 1991.

Anidjar, Gil. *Blood: A Critique of Christianity.* New York: Columbia University Press, 2016.

Asad, Talal. *Formations of the Secular: Christianity, Islam, Modernity.* Stanford, CA: Stanford University Press, 2003.

———. *Genealogies of Religion: Discipline and Reasons of Power in Christianity and Islam*. Baltimore: Johns Hopkins University Press, 1993.

Ashikari, Mikiko. "Urban Middle-Class Japanese Women and Their White Faces: Gender, Ideology, and Representation." *Ethos* 31, no. 1 (2003): 3–37.

Austin, John L. *How to Do Things with Words*. Oxford: Clarendon Press. 1975.

Austin-Broos, Diane J. *Jamaica Genesis: Religion and the Politics of Moral Orders*. Chicago: Chicago University Press, 1997.

Baran, Michael D. "'Girl, You Are Not Morena. We Are Negras!': Questioning the Concept of 'Race' in Southern Bahia, Brazil." *Ethos* 35, no. 3 (2007): 383–409.

Bardsley, Jan, and Laura Miller. "Manners and Mischief: Introduction." In *Manners and Mischief: Gender, Power, and Etiquette in Japan*, edited by Jan Bardsley and Laura Miller, 1–28. Berkeley: University of California Press, 2011.

Barth, Fredrik. "Introduction." In *Ethnic Groups and Boundaries: The Social Organization of Culture Difference*, edited by Fredrik Barth, 9–38. Long Grove, IL: Waveland, (1969) 1998.

Befu, Harumi. *Hegemony of Homogeneity: An Anthropological Analysis of "Nihonjinron."* Melbourne: Trans Pacific Press, 2001.

———. "Nationalism and *Nihonjinron*." In *Cultural Nationalism in East Asia*, edited by Harumi Befu, 107–35. Berkeley: University of California Press, 1993.

Beltrão, Kaizô Iwakami, and Sonoe Sugahara. "O Ciclo e a Tangente: Dekasseguis Brasileiros no Japão" [Circle and tangent: Brazilian dekasegis in Japan]. Rio de Janeiro: IBGE, 2009. Accessed May 16, 2018. https://biblioteca.ibge.gov.br/visualizacao/livros/liv44723.pdf.

Benjamin, Gail R. *Japanese Lessons: A Year in a Japanese School Through the Eyes of an American Anthropologist and Her Children*. New York: NYU Press, 1998.

Berg, Ulla D., and Ana Y. Ramos-Zayas. "Racializing Affect: A Theoretical Proposition." *Current Anthropology* 56, no. 5 (2015): 654–77.

Besnier, Niko. *On the Edge of the Global: Modern Anxieties in a Pacific Island Nation*. Stanford, CA: Stanford University Press, 2011.

Besse, Susan E. *Restructuring Patriarchy: The Modernization of Gender Inequality in Brazil, 1914–1940*. Chapel Hill: University of North Carolina Press, 1996.

Bialecki, Jon. *A Diagram for Fire: Miracles and Variation in an American Charismatic Movement*. Berkeley: University of California Press, 2017.

Bialecki, Jon, and Girish Daswani. "Introduction: What Is an Individual? The View from Christianity." *HAU: Journal of Ethnographic Theory* 5, no. 1 (2015): 271–94.

Bialecki, Jon, and Eric Hoenes del Pinal. "Introduction: Beyond Logos: Extensions of the Language Ideology Paradigm in the Study of Global Christianity(-ies)." *Anthropological Quarterly* 84, no. 3 (2011): 575–93.

Bielo, James S. "Belief, Deconversion, and Authenticity Among U.S. Emerging Evangelicals." *Ethos* 40, no. 3 (2012): 258–76.

——. "Creationist History-Making: Producing a Heterodox Past." In *Lost City, Found Pyramid: Understanding Alternative Archaeologies and Pseudoscientific Practices*, edited by Jeb J. Card and David S. Anderson, 81–101. Tuscaloosa: University of Alabama Press, 2016.

——. *Emerging Evangelicals: Faith, Modernity, and the Desire for Authenticity*. New York: NYU Press, 2011.

Boehm, Deborah. *Intimate Migrations: Gender, Family, and Illegality Among Transnational Mexicans*. New York: NYU Press, 2013.

Borges, Marcelo J. *Chains of Gold: Portuguese Migration to Argentina in Transatlantic Perspective*. Leiden: Brill, 2009.

Bourdieu, Pierre. *The Logic of Practice*. Stanford, CA: Stanford University Press, 1990.

——. *Outline of a Theory of Practice*. Cambridge: Cambridge University Press, 1972.

Brettel, Caroline. *Anthropology and Migration: Essays on Transnationalism, Ethnicity, and Identity*. Walnut Creek, CA: Altamira, 2003.

Brodwin, Paul. "Pentecostalism in Translation: Religion and the Production of Community in the Haitian Diaspora." *American Ethnologist* 30 (2003): 85–101.

Brusco, Elizabeth. "Colombian Evangelicalism as a Strategic Form of Women's Collective Action." *Gender Issues* 6, no. 2 (1986): 3–13.

——. *The Reformation of Machismo: Evangelical Conversion and Gender in Colombia*. Austin: University of Texas Press, 1995.

Burdick, John. *Blessed Anastacia: Women, Race and Popular Christianity in Brazil*. London: Routledge, 1998.

——. *The Color of Sound: Race, Religion, and Music in Brazil*. New York: NYU Press, 2013.

Burgess, Chris. "Japan's 'No Immigration Principle' Looking as Solid as Ever." *Japan Times*, June 18, 2014.

Burkhardt, William R. "Institutional Barriers, Marginality, and Adaptation among the American-Japanese Mixed Bloods in Japan." *Journal of Asian Studies* 42, no. 3 (1983): 519–44.

Bynum, Caroline W. "The Blood of Christ in the Later Middle Ages." *Church History* 71, no. 4 (2002): 685–714.

——. *Wonderful Blood: Theology and Practice in Late Medieval Northern Germany and Beyond*. Philadelphia: University of Pennsylvania Press, 2007.

Cannell, Fanella, ed. *The Anthropology of Christianity*. Durham, NC: Duke University Press, 2006.

——. "The Blood of Abraham: Mormon Redemptive Physicality and American Idioms of Kinship." *Journal of the Royal Anthropological Institute* 19 (2013): S77–S94.

Capone, Stefania. *Searching for Africa in Brazil: Power and Tradition in Candomblé*. Durham, NC: Duke University Press, 2010.

Cardoso, Ruth, and Masato Ninomiya. *Estrutura Familiar e Mobilidade Social: Estudo dos Japoneses no Estado de São Paulo* [Family structure and social mobility: Study of Japanese in the state of São Paulo]. São Paulo: Primus Comunicação, 1995.

Carsten, Janet. *After Kinship*. Cambridge: Cambridge University Press, 2004.

———. *Cultures of Relatedness: New Approaches to the Study of Kinship*. Cambridge: Cambridge University Press, 2000.

Carter, Mitzi U. "Mixed Race Okinawans and Their Obscure In-Betweeness." *Journal of Intercultural Studies* 35, no. 6 (2014): 646–61.

Cassaniti, Julia L., and Jacob R. Hickman. "New Directions in the Anthropology of Morality." *Anthropological Theory* 14, no. 3 (2014): 251–62.

Chesnut, Andrew, R. *Born Again in Brazil: The Pentecostal Boom and the Pathogens of Poverty*. New Brunswick, NJ: Rutgers University Press, 1997.

Christou, Anastasia. *Narratives of Place, Culture and Identity: Second-Generation Greek-Americans Return "Home."* Amsterdam: Amsterdam University Press, 2010.

Chūnichi Shimbun. "Conflict Between Foreigners and Nationalist Right-Wing Group, Tension in the Air, the Aichi Prefectural Police on Watch, Toyota, Arson of Cars in the Neighborhood." [In Japanese.] June 8, 1999.

Clarke, Peter, ed. *Japanese New Religions in Global Perspective*. Richmond, UK: Curzon, 2000.

Clifford, James. "Diasporas." *Cultural Anthropology* 9, no. 3 (1994): 302–38.

Coe, Cati. "How Children Feel About Their Parents' Migration: A History of the Reciprocity of Care in Ghana." In *Everyday Ruptures: Children, Youth, and Migration in Global Perspective*, edited by Cati Coe, Rachel R. Reynolds, Deborah A. Boehm, Julia Meredith Hess, and Heather Rae-Espinoza, 97–114. Nashville, TN: Vanderbilt University Press, 2011.

Coe, Cati, Rachel R. Reynolds, Deborah A. Boehm, Julia Meredith Hess, and Heather Rae-Espinoza. *Everyday Ruptures: Children, Youth, and Migration in Global Perspective*. Nashville, TN: Vanderbilt University Press, 2011.

Cole, Jennifer, ed. *Affective Circuits: African Migration to Europe and the Pursuit of Social Regeneration*. Chicago: University of Chicago Press, 2016.

Coleman, Simon. *The Globalisation of Charismatic Christianity: Spreading the Gospel of Prosperity*. Cambridge: Cambridge University Press, 2000.

———. "Materializing the Self: Words and Gifts in the Construction of Charismatic Protestant Identity." In *The Anthropology of Christianity*, edited by Fanella Cannell, 163–84. Durham, NC: Duke University Press, 2006.

———. "'Right Now!': Historiopraxy and the Embodiment of Charismatic Temporalities." *Ethnos* 76, no. 4 (2011): 426–47.

Conway, Dennis, and Robert B. Potter, eds. *Return Migration of the Next Generations: 21st Century Transnational Mobility*. Farnham, UK: Ashgate Publishing, 2009.

Corten, André, and Ruth R. Marshall-Fratani, eds. *Between Babel and Pentecost: Transnational Pentecostalism in Africa and Latin America*. Bloomington: Indiana University Press, 2001.

Corwin, Anna I. "Changing God, Changing Bodies: The Impact of New Prayer Practices on Elderly Catholic Nuns' Embodied Experience." *Ethos* 40, no. 4 (2012): 390–410.

Creighton, Millie. "Soto Others and Uchi Others: Imagining Racial Diversity, Imagining Homogeneous Japan." In *Japan's Minorities: The Illusion of Homogeneity*, edited by Michael Weiner, 211–38. London: Routledge, (1997) 2009.

Csikszentmihalyi, Mihaly. *Flow: The Psychology of Optimal Experience*. New York: Harper Perennial, 1991.

Csordas, Thomas J. "Asymptote of the Ineffable: Embodiment, Alterity, and the Theory of Religion." *Current Anthropology* 45, no. 2 (2004): 163–85.

———. "Embodiment as a Paradigm for Anthropology." *Ethos* 18, no. 1 (1990): 5–47.

———. *The Sacred Self: A Cultural Phenomenology of Charismatic Healing*. Berkeley: University of California Press, 1994.

Daswani, Girish. "(In-)Dividual Pentecostals in Ghana." *Journal of Religion in Africa* 41, no. 3 (2011): 256–79.

———. *Looking Back, Moving Forward: Transformation and Ethical Practice in the Ghanaian Church of Pentecost*. Toronto: University of Toronto Press, 2015.

Datafolha. "Centenário da Imigração Japonesa" [Centenary of Japanese Immigration]. October 12, 2008. http://datafolha.folha.uol.com.br/opiniaopublica/2008/12/1223831-centenario-da-imigracao-japonesa.shtml.

Dávila, Jerry. *Hotel Trópico: Brazil and the Challenge of African Decolonization, 1950–1980*. Durham, NC: Duke University Press, 2010.

Desjarlais, Robert. 1992. *Body and Emotion: The Aesthetics of Illness and Healing in the Nepal Himalayas*. Philadelphia: University of Pennsylvania Press.

Doi, Takeo. *The Anatomy of Dependence*. New York: Kodansha America, 1981.

Durkheim, Émile. *The Elementary Forms of Religious Life*, translated by Carol Cosman. Oxford: Oxford University Press, (1912) 2001.

Ebaugh, Helen Rose, and Mary Curry. "Fictive Kin as Social Capital in New Immigrant Communities." *Sociological Perspectives* 43, no. 2 (2000): 189–209.

Eckstein, Susan. "On Deconstructing and Reconstructing the Meaning of Immigrant Generations." In *The Changing Face of Home: The Transnational Lives of the Second Generation*, edited by Peggy Levitt and Mary C. Waters, 211–15. New York: Russell Sage Foundation, 2002.

Elisha, Omri. "Faith Beyond Belief: Evangelical Protestant Conceptions of Faith and the Resonance of Anti-Humanism." *Social Analysis* 52, no. 1 (2008): 56–78.

———. *Moral Ambition: Mobilization and Social Outreach in Evangelical Megachurches*. Berkeley: University of California Press, 2011.

Engelke, Matthew. *A Problem of Presence: Beyond Scripture in an African Church.* Berkeley: University of California Press, 2007.

Engelke, Matthew, and Matt Tomlinson, eds. *The Limits of Meaning: Case Studies in the Anthropology of Christianity.* Oxford: Berghahn, 2006.

Eriksen, Annelin. "The Pastor and the Prophetess: An Analysis of Gender and Christianity in Vanuatu." *Journal of the Royal Anthropological Institute* 18, no. 1 (2012): 103–22.

———. "Sarah's Sinfulness: Egalitarianism, Denied Difference, and Gender in Pentecostal Christianity." *Current Anthropology* 55, no. S10 (2014): 262–70.

Ezaki, Alexandre. "Quero Ajudar o Brasileiro a Ter uma Vida Decente" [I want to help Brazilians have decent life]. *Alternativa Nishi,* March 6, 2014.

Faier, Lieba. "Filipina Migrants in Rural Japan and Their Professions of Love." *American Ethnologist* 34, no. 1 (2007): 148–62.

Fajans, Jane. *Brazilian Food: Race, Class and Identity in Regional Cuisines.* London: Bloomsbury Academic, 2013.

Faubion, James D. *An Anthropology of Ethics.* Cambridge: Cambridge University Press, 2011.

Ferraro, Kenneth F., and Jerome R. Koch. "Religion and Health Among Black and White Adults: Examining Social Support and Consolation." *Journal for the Scientific Study of Religion* 33, no. 4 (1994): 362–75.

Fish, Robert A. "'Mixed-Blood' Japanese: A Reconsideration of Race and Purity in Japan." In *Japan's Minorities: The Illusion of Homogeneity,* edited by Michael Weiner, 40–58. London: Routledge, (1997) 2009.

Freeman, Caren. *Making and Faking Kinship: Marriage and Labor Migration Between China and South Korea.* Ithaca, NY: Cornell University Press, 2011.

French, Jan H. *Legalizing Identity: Becoming Black or Indian in Brazil's Northeast.* Chapel Hill: University of North Carolina Press, 2009.

Freston, Paul. "Latin America: The 'Other Christendom,' Pluralism and Globalization." In *Religion, Globalization, and Culture,* edited by Peter Beyer and Lori Beaman, 571–94. Leiden: Brill, 2007.

———. "Pentecostalism in Brazil: The Limits to Growth." In *Global Pentecostalism in the 21st Century,* edited by Robert W. Hefner, 63–90. Bloomington: Indiana University Press, 2013.

———. "The Transnationalisation of Brazilian Pentecostalism: The Universal Church of the Kingdom of God." In *Between Babel and Pentecost: Transnational Pentecostalism in Africa and Latin America,* edited by André Corten and Ruth Marshall-Fratani, 196–213. Bloomington: Indiana University Press, 2001.

Freyre, Gilberto. *The Masters and the Slaves: A Study in the Development of Brazilian Civilization.* New York: Random House, (1933) 1964.

Fumanti, Mattia. "'Virtuous Citizenship': Ethnicity and Encapsulation among Akan-Speaking Ghanaian Methodists in London." *African Diaspora* 3, no. 1 (2010): 12–41.

Gabaccia, Donna R. "Time and Temporality in Migration Studies." In *Migration Theory: Talking Across Disciplines*, edited by Caroline Brettel and James Hollifield, 37–66. London: Routledge, 2015.

Geertz, Clifford. "'From the Native's Point of View': On the Nature of Anthropological Understanding." In *Culture Theory*, edited by Richard Shweder and Robert Levine, 123–36. Cambridge: Cambridge University Press, (1974) 1984.

———. "Religion as a Cultural System." In *A Reader in the Anthropology of Religion*, edited by Michael Lambek, 61–82. Malden, MA: Blackwell Publishing, (1966) 2002.

Gell, Alfred. *The Anthropology of Time: Cultural Constructions of Temporal Maps and Images*. Oxford: Berg, 1992.

Glick-Schiller, Nina, Ayse Çaglar, and Thaddeus C. Guldbrandsen. "Beyond the Ethnic Lens: Locality, Globality, and Born-Again Incorporation." *American Ethnologist* 33, no. 4 (2006): 612–33.

Glick-Schiller, Nina, and George E. Fouron. "The Generation of Identity: Redefining the Second Generation within a Transnational Social Field." In *The Changing Face of Home: The Transnational Lives of the Second Generation*, edited by Peggy Levitt and Mary C. Waters, 168–210. New York: Russell Sage Foundation, 2002.

Glick-Schiller, Nina, and Noel B. Salazar. "Regimes of Mobility Across the Globe." *Journal of Ethnic and Migration Studies* 39, no. 2 (2013): 183–200.

Gutmann, Matthew C., and Mara V. Vigoya. "Masculinities in Latin America." In *Handbook of Studies on Men and Masculinities*, edited by Michael S. Kimmel, Jeff Hearn, and Robert W. Connell, 114–28. Thousand Oaks, CA: Sage, 2005.

Hankins, Joseph D. *Working Skin: Making Leather, Making a Multicultural Japan*. Berkeley: University of California Press, 2014.

Hardacre, Helen. *Shintō and the State, 1868–1988*. Princeton, NJ: Princeton University Press, 1989.

Harding, Susan. *The Book of Jerry Falwell: Fundamentalist Language and Politics*. Princeton, NJ: Princeton University Press, 2000.

Hardwick, Charles, ed. *Semiotics and Significs*. Bloomington: Indiana University Press, 1977.

Harkness, Nicholas. "Glossolalia and Cacophony in South Korea: Cultural Semiotics at the Limits of Language." *American Ethnologist* 44, no. 3 (2017): 476–89.

Hefner, Robert W. "The Unexpected Modern: Gender, Piety, and Politics in the Global Pentecostal Surge." In *Global Pentecostalism in the 21st Century*, edited by Robert W. Hefner, 1–36. Bloomington: Indiana University Press, 2013.

Heintz, Monica. *The Anthropology of Moralities*. New York: Berghahn Books, 2009.

Hendry, Joy. *Becoming Japanese: The World of the Pre-School Child*. Honolulu: University of Hawaii Press, 1989.

Hickman, Jacob R. "Ancestral Personhood and Moral Justification." *Anthropological Theory* 14, no. 3 (2014): 317–35.

Higuchi, Naoto. "Keizai Kiki to Zainichi Burajirujin" [The economic crisis and the Brazilians in Japan]. *Journal of Ohara Research Center for Social Issues* 622 (2010): 50–66.

Hirabayashi, L. Ryo, James A. Hirabayashi, and Akemi Kikumura, eds. *New Worlds, New Lives: Globalization and People of Japanese Descent in the Americas and from Latin America to Japan.* Stanford, CA: Stanford University Press, 2002.

Hirsch, Jennifer S., and Holly Wardlow, eds. *Modern Loves: The Anthropology of Romantic Courtship and Companionate Marriage.* Ann Arbor: University of Michigan Press, 2006.

Hoshino, So. "The Potentiality of Brazilian Immigrants' Religious Communities as Social Capital: The Case of Christian Churches in Toyohashi under an Economic Depression." In *Transnational Faiths: Latin-American Immigrants and Their Religions in Japan*, edited by Hugo Córdova Quero and Rafael Shoji, 75–88. Farnham, UK: Ashgate, 2014.

Howell, Brian M. "The Repugnant Cultural Other Speaks Back: Christian Identity as Ethnographic 'Standpoint.'" *Anthropological Theory* 7, no. 4 (2007): 371–91.

Ikeuchi, Suma. "Accompanied Self: Debating Pentecostal Individual and Japanese Relational Selves in Transnational Japan." *Ethos* 45, no. 1, (2017): 3–23.

———. "Back to the Present: The 'Temporal Tandem' of Migration and Conversion Among Pentecostal Nikkei Brazilians in Japan." *Ethnos* 82, no. 4 (2017): 758–83.

———. "From Ethnic Religion to Generative Selves: Pentecostalism Among Nikkei Brazilian Migrants in Japan." *Contemporary Japan* 29, no. 2 (2017): 214–29.

Inoue, Masamichi S. *Okinawa and the US Military: Identity Making in the Age of Globalization.* New York: Columbia University Press, 2007.

Institute of Statistical Mathematics. "Kokuminsei Chōsa" [Survey on national character]. Tokyo: 2013. Accessed May 21, 2018. http://www.ism.ac.jp/kokuminsei/table/data/html/ss3/3_1/3_1_20132.htm.

Instituto Brasileiro de Geografia e Estatística (IBGE). "Anuário Estatístico do Brasil" [Annual statistics of Brazil]. Rio de Janeiro: Conselho Nacional de Estatística, 1954.

———. "Censo Demográfico 2010 Características Gerais da População, Religião, e Pessoas com Deficiência" [Demographic census 2010 general characteristics of the population, religion, and people with disability]. Rio de Janeiro: 2012. Accessed May 21, 2018. https://biblioteca.ibge.gov.br/visualizacao/periodicos/94/cd_2010_religiao_deficiencia.pdf.

———. "Censo Demográfico 2010 Educação e Deslocamento" [Demographic census 2010 education and displacement]. Rio de Janeiro: 2012. Accessed May 16, 2018. https://biblioteca.ibge.gov.br/visualizacao/periodicos/545/cd_2010_educacao_e_deslocamento.pdf.

———. "Censo Demográfico 2010 Família e Domicílio" [Demographic census 2010 family and household]. Rio de Janeiro: 2012. Accessed May 16, 2018. https://

biblioteca.ibge.gov.br/visualizacao/periodicos/97/cd_2010_familias_domicilios
_amostra.pdf.

———. "Mulher No Mercado de Trabalho: Perguntas e Respostas" [Women in the labor market: Questions and answers]. Rio de Janeiro: 2012. Accessed May 18, 2018. http://www.ibge.gov.br/home/estatistica/indicadores/trabalhoerendimento/pme _nova/Mulher_Mercado_Trabalho_Perg_Resp_2012.pdf.

Ischida, Camila Aya. "A Experiência Nikkei no Brasil: Uma Etnografia Sobre Imaginários e Identidades" [Nikkei experience in Brazil: An ethnography about imaginaries and identities]. Master's thesis, University of São Paulo, 2010.

James, Wendy, and David Mills. "Introduction: From Representation to Action in the Flow of Time." In *The Qualities of Time: Anthropological Approaches*, edited by Wendy James and David Mills, 1–26. London: Bloomsbury Academic, 2006.

Jenkins, Timothy. "The Anthropology of Christianity: Situation and Critique." *Ethnos* 77, no. 4 (2012): 459–76.

Jo, Ji-Yeon O. *Homing: An Affective Topography of Ethnic Korean Return Migration.* Honolulu: University of Hawaii Press, 2017.

Josephson, Jason A. *The Invention of Religion in Japan.* Chicago: University of Chicago Press, 2012.

Kaneko, Kenji. "Constructing Japanese Nationalism on Television: The Japanese Image of Multicultural Society." *New Cultural Frontiers* 1, no. 1 (2010): 101–16.

Kawamura, Lili. *Para Onde Vão Os Brasileiros? Imigrantes Brasileiros no Japão* [Where do the Brazilians go? Brazilian immigrants in Japan]. Campinas: Editora da Unicamp, 1999.

Keane, Webb. *Christian Moderns: Freedom and Fetish in the Mission Encounter.* Berkeley: University of California Press, 2007.

———. *Ethical Life: Its Natural and Social Histories.* Princeton, NJ: Princeton University Press, 2015.

———. "The Evidence of the Senses and the Materiality of Religion." *Journal of the Royal Anthropological Institute* 14, no. S1 (2008): S110–27.

———. "Semiotics and the Social Analysis of Material Things." *Language & Communication* 23, no. 3 (2003): 409–25.

———. "Sincerity, 'Modernity,' and the Protestants." *Cultural Anthropology* 17, no. 1 (2002): 65–92.

Kelly, William. "Directions in the Anthropology of Contemporary Japan." *Annual Review of Anthropology* 20, no. 1 (1991): 395–431.

Kelly, William, and Merry White. "Students, Slackers, Singles, Seniors, and Strangers: Transforming a Family-Nation." In *Beyond Japan: The Dynamics of East Asian Regionalism*, edited by Peter J. Katzenstein and Takashi Shiraishi, 63–84. Ithaca, NY: Cornell University Press, 2006.

Kelsky, Karen L. *Women on the Verge: Japanese Women, Western Dreams.* Durham, NC: Duke University Press, 2001.

Kirsch, Thomas G. "Restaging the Will to Believe: Religious Pluralism, Anti-Syncretism, and the Problem of Belief." *American Anthropologist* 106, no. 4 (2004): 699–709.

Kitayama, Shinobu, Hazel Rose Markus, Hisaya Matsumoto, and Vinai Norasakkunkit. "Individual and Collective Processes in the Construction of the Self: Self-Enhancement in the United States and Self-Criticism in Japan." *Journal of Personality and Social Psychology* 72, no. 6 (1997): 1245–67.

Klaver, Miranda, and Linda van de Kamp. "Embodied Temporalities in Global Pentecostal Conversion." *Ethnos* 76, no. 4 (2011): 421–25.

Knauft, Bruce M. *Critically Modern: Alternatives, Alterities, and Anthropologies.* Bloomington: Indiana University Press, 2002.

Kondo, Dorinne K. *Crafting Selves: Power, Gender, and Discourses of Identity in a Japanese Workplace.* Chicago: University of Chicago Press, 1990.

Laidlaw, James. *The Subject of Virtue: An Anthropology of Ethics and Freedom.* Cambridge: Cambridge University Press, 2014.

Lakoff, George, and Mark Johnson. *Metaphors We Live By.* Chicago: University of Chicago Press, (1980) 2003.

Lebra, Takie S. *The Japanese Self in Cultural Logic.* Honolulu: University of Hawaii Press, 2004.

———. *Japanese Women: Constraint and Fulfillment.* Honolulu: University of Hawaii Press, 1985.

Leinaweaver, Jessaca B. "Outsourcing Care: How Peruvian Migrants Meet Transnational Family Obligations." *Latin American Perspectives* 37, no. 5 (2010): 67–87.

Lesser, Jeffrey. *A Discontented Diaspora: Japanese Brazilians and the Meanings of Ethnic Militancy, 1960–1980.* Durham, NC: Duke University Press, 2007.

———. *Immigration, Ethnicity, and National Identity in Brazil, 1808 to the Present.* Cambridge: Cambridge University Press, 2013.

———. "Japanese, Brazilians, Nikkei: A Short History of Identity Building and Homemaking." In *Searching for Home Abroad: Japanese Brazilians and Transnationalism,* edited by Jeffrey Lesser, 5–20. Durham, NC: Duke University Press, 2003.

———, ed. *Searching for Home Abroad: Japanese Brazilians and Transnationalism.* Durham, NC: Duke University Press, 2003.

Lester, Rebecca J. *Jesus in Our Wombs: Embodying Modernity in a Mexican Convent.* Berkeley: University of California Press, 2005.

Levitt, Peggy. "Religion on the Move: Mapping Global Cultural Production and Consumption." In *Religion on the Edge: De-Centering the Sociology of Religion,* edited by Courtney Bender, Wendy Cadge, Peggy Levitt, and David Smilde, 159–78. Cambridge: Oxford University Press, 2013.

Levitt, Peggy, and Nina Glick-Schiller. "Conceptualizing Simultaneity: A Transnational Social Field Perspective on Society." In *Rethinking Migration: New Theoretical and Empirical Perspectives*, edited by Alejandro Portes and Josh DeWind, 181–218. New York: Berghahn Books, 2007.

Lim, Chaeyoon, and Robert D. Putnam. "Religion, Social Networks, and Life Satisfaction." *American Sociological Review* 75, no. 6 (2010): 914–33.

Linger, Daniel T. "Do Japanese Brazilians Exist?" In *Searching for Home Abroad: Japanese Brazilians and Transnationalism*, edited by Jeffrey Lesser, 201–14. Durham, NC: Duke University Press, 2003.

———. *No One Home: Brazilian Selves Remade in Japan*. Stanford, CA: Stanford University Press, 2001.

Lopez, Donald S., Jr. "Belief." In *Critical Terms for Religious Studies*, edited by Mark C. Taylor, 21–35. Chicago: University of Chicago Press, 1998.

Luhrmann, Tanya M. "A Hyperreal God and Modern Belief: Toward an Anthropological Theory of Mind." *Current Anthropology* 53, no. 4 (2012): 371–95.

———. *When God Talks Back: Understanding the American Evangelical Relationship with God*. New York: Knopf, 2012.

Luhrmann, Tanya M, and Rachel Morgain. "Prayer as Inner Sense Cultivation: An Attentional Learning Theory of Spiritual Experience." *Ethos* 40, no. 4 (2012): 359–89.

Lutz, Catherine. "Emotion, Thought, and Estrangement: Emotion as a Cultural Category." *Cultural Anthropology* 1, no. 3 (1986): 287–309.

———. "What Matters." *Cultural Anthropology* 32, no. 2 (2017): 181–91.

Maeyama, Takashi. "Ancestor, Emperor, and Immigrant: Religion and Group Identification of the Japanese in Rural Brazil (1908–1950)." *Journal of Interamerican Studies and World Affairs* 14, no. 2 (1972): 151–82.

———. "Ethnicity, Secret Societies, and Associations: The Japanese in Brazil." *Comparative Studies in Society and History* 21, no. 4 (1979): 589–610.

Mafra, Clara C. J. "Saintliness and Sincerity in the Formation of the Christian Person." *Ethnos* 76, no. 4 (2011): 448–68.

Mafra, Clara C. J., Ari Pedro Oro, André Corten, and Jean-Pierre Dozon. "A Igreja Universal em Portugal" [The Universal Church in Portugal]. In *Igreja Universal do Reino de Deus: Os Novos Conquistadores da Fé* [The Universal Church of the Kingdom of God: The new conquerors of Faith], 165–76. São Paulo: Paulinas, 2003.

Margolis, Maxine L. *Good Bye, Brazil: Émigrés from the Land of Soccer and Samba*. Madison: University of Wisconsin Press, 2013.

———. *An Invisible Minority: Brazilians in New York City*. Gainesville: University Press of Florida, 2009.

Mariano, Ricardo. "Laicidade à Brasileira: Católicos, Pentecostais e Laicos em Disputa na Esfera Pública" [Brazilian secularism: Catholics, Pentecostals and Seculars in dispute in the public sphere]. *Civitas-Revista de Ciências Sociais* 11, no. 2 (2011): 238–58.

Mariz, Cecília. *Coping with Poverty: Pentecostals and Christian Base Communities in Brazil.* Philadelphia: Temple University Press, 1994.

Markowitz, Fran II., and Anders H. Stefansson, eds. *Homecomings: Unsettling Paths of Return.* Lanham, MD: Lexington Books, 2004.

Markus, Hazel R., and Shinobu Kitayama. "Culture and the Self: Implications for Cognition, Emotion, and Motivation." *Psychological Review* 98, no. 2 (1991): 224–53.

Marra, Lívia. "Leia Depoimentos de Quem Se Diz Abandonado por Dekasseguis" [Read reports of those who claim to be abandoned by dekasegis]. *Folha de São Paulo*, October 20, 2002.

Martin, David. *Tongues of Fire: The Explosion of Protestantism in Latin America.* Cambridge, MA: Basil Blackwell, 1991.

Massumi, Brian. *Parables for the Virtual: Movement, Affect, Sensation.* Durham, NC: Duke University Press, 2002.

Matsuki, Edgard. "Abandonados por Dekasseguis e pela Falta de Legislação entre Brasil e Japão" [Abandoned by dekasegis and the lack of legislation between Brazil and Japan]. *Nippo Brasil.* June 8, 2010. Accessed on May 20, 2018. http://www.nippo brasil.com.br/dekassegui/554a.shtml.

Matsumiya, Ashita, and Kento Yogo. 2009. "Masu Media ni okeru 'Burajirujin Gensetsu' no Henyō (Jō)" [The shift in the discourse on Brazilians in the mass media, one]. *Aichi Kenritsu Daigaku Kyōiku Hukushi Gakubu Ronshū* 58 (2009): 61–66.

Matsumori, Akiko. "Ryûkyuan: Past, Present, and Future." *Journal of Multilingual and Multicultural Development* 16, no. 1–2 (1995): 19–44.

Matsuoka, Hideaki. *Japanese Prayer Below the Equator: How Brazilians Believe in the Church of World Messianity.* Lanham, MD: Lexington Books, 2007.

Mayblin, Maya. *Gender, Catholicism, and Morality in Brazil: Virtuous Husbands, Powerful Wives.* New York: Palgrave Macmillan, 2010.

Mazzarella, William. "Affect: What Is It Good For?" In *Enchantments of Modernity: Empire, Nation, Globalization*, edited by Saurabh Dube, 291–309. London: Routledge, 2009.

McGovern, Mike. "Turning the Clock Back or Breaking with the Past? Charismatic Temporality and Elite Politics in Côte d'Ivoire and the United States." *Cultural Anthropology* 27, no. 2 (2012): 239–60.

McKinnon, Susan. *Relative Values: Reconfiguring Kinship Studies.* Durham, NC: Duke University Press, 2001.

McKinnon, Susan, and Fenella Cannell. *Vital Relations: Modernity and the Persistent Life of Kinship.* Santa Fe, NM: School for Advanced Research Press, 2013.

Meyer, Birgit. "'Make a Complete Break with the Past': Memory and Post-Colonial Modernity in Ghanaian Pentecostalist Discourse." *Journal of Religion in Africa* 28, no. 3 (1998): 316–49.

———. *Translating the Devil: Religion and Modernity Among the Ewe in Ghana.* Trenton, NJ: Africa World Press, 1999.

Ministry of Health, Labour and Welfare. "Heisei 26 nen Chingin Kōzō Kihon Tōkei Chōsa no Gaikyō" [Overview of statistical survey on the basic wage structure year 2014]. Tokyo: 2015. Accessed May 18, 2018. http://www.mhlw.go.jp/toukei/itiran /roudou/chingin/kouzou/z2014/dl/14.pdf.

Ministry of Justice. "The Current Number of Foreigners in Japan: June 2018 (Preliminary Figures)." [In Japanese.] Tokyo: 2018. Accessed October 18, 2018. http://www .moj.go.jp/nyuukokukanri/kouhou/nyuukokukanri04_00076.html.

———. "On the Acceptance of Fourth-Generation Nikkeis." [In Japanese.] Tokyo: 2018. Accessed May 27, 2018. http://www.moj.go.jp/content/001255088.pdf.

———. "Zairyū Gaikokujin Tōkei" [Statistics on foreigners in Japan]. Tokyo: 2017. Accessed May 21, 2018. https://www.e-stat.go.jp/stat-search/files?page=1&layout =datalist&toukei=00250012&tstat=000001018034&cycle=1&year=20170&month =12040606&tclass1=000001060399.

Miura, Hiroshi. *The Life and Thought of Kanzo Uchimura 1861–1930.* Cambridge: William B. Eerdmans, 1996.

Miyazaki, Kentaro. "Roman Catholic Mission in Pre-Modern Japan." In *Handbook of Christianity in Japan,* edited by Mark R. Mullins, 1–18. Leiden: Brill, 2003.

Mori, Koichi. "Burajiru Okinawakeijin no Sosensūhai no Jissen: Karera to Burajiru, Okinawa, Nihon tono Kankei no Henka ni Chūmoku shite" [Ancestral worship among Okinawan Brazilians: With a focus on the shifting relationship between the people, Okinawa, and Japan]. *Ajia Yūgaku,* 76 (2005): 86–100. Tokyo: Benseisha.

———. "Identity Transformations among Okinawans and Their Descendants in Brazil." In *Searching for Home Abroad: Japanese Brazilians and Transnationalism,* edited by Jeffrey Lesser, 47–66. Durham, NC: Duke University Press, 2003.

Muehlebach, Andrea. "On Affective Labor in Post-Fordist Italy." *Cultural Anthropology* 26, no. 1 (2011): 59–82.

Mullins, Mark R. *Christianity Made in Japan: A Study of Indigenous Movements.* Honolulu: University of Hawaii Press, 1998.

Munn, Nancy D. "The Cultural Anthropology of Time: A Critical Essay." *Annual Review of Anthropology* 21 (1992): 93–123.

Murphy-Shigematsu, S. "Multiethnic Japan and the Monoethnic Myth." *Melus* 18, no. 4 (1993): 63–80.

Nakamura, Jeanne, and Mihaly Csikszentmihalyi. "The Concept of Flow." In *Flow and the Foundations of Positive Psychology,* edited by Mihaly Csikszentmihalyi, 89–105. Berlin: Springer, 2002.

Napolitano, Valentina. *Migrant Hearts and the Atlantic Return: Transnationalism and the Roman Catholic Church*. New York: Fordham University Press, 2016.

Needham, Rodney. *Belief, Language, and Experience*. Oxford: Basil Blackwell, 1972.

Nelson, Christopher T. *Dancing with the Dead: Memory, Performance, and Everyday Life in Postwar Okinawa*. Durham, NC: Duke University Press, 2008.

Nishida, Mieko. *Diaspora and Identity: Japanese Brazilians in Brazil and Japan*. Honolulu: University of Hawaii Press, 2017.

O Estado de S. Paulo. "Dekasseguis Abandonam ao Menos 300 Famílias no País" [Dekasegis abandon at least 300 families in the country]. April 15, 2010.

Ohnuki-Tierney, Emiko. *Rice as Self: Japanese Identities Through Time*. Princeton, NJ: Princeton University Press, 1994.

Olsson, Erik, and Russell King. "Introduction: Diasporic Return." *Diaspora: A Journal of Transnational Studies* 17, no. 3 (2008): 255–61.

O'Neill, Kevin L. 2009. "But Our Citizenship Is in Heaven: A Proposal for the Future Study of Christian Citizenship in the Global South." *Citizenship Studies* 13, no. 4 (2009): 333–48.

———. *City of God: Christian Citizenship in Postwar Guatemala*. Berkeley: University of California Press, 2010.

Ong, Aihwa. *Flexible Citizenship: The Cultural Logics of Transnationality*. Durham, NC: Duke University Press, 1999.

Ozawa–de Silva, Chikako. "Beyond the Body/Mind? Japanese Contemporary Thinkers on Alternative Sociologies of the Body." *Body & Society* 8, no. 2 (2002): 21–38.

———. "Demystifying Japanese Therapy: An Analysis of Naikan and the Ajase Complex Through Buddhist Thought." *Ethos* 35, no. 4 (2007): 411–46.

Padilla, Mark B., Jennifer S. Hirsch, Miguel Muñoz-Laboy, Richard G. Parker, and Robert Sember, eds. *Love and Globalization: Transformations of Intimacy in the Contemporary World*. Nashville, TN: Vanderbilt University Press, 2008.

Parish, Steven. "Between Persons: How Concepts of the Person Make Moral Experience Possible." *Ethos* 42, no. 1 (2014): 31–50.

Parker, Richard G. *Bodies, Pleasures, and Passions: Sexual Culture in Contemporary Brazil*. Nashville, TN: Vanderbilt University Press, 2009.

Peletz, Michael G. "Kinship Studies in Late Twentieth-Century Anthropology." *Annual Review of Anthropology* 24 (1995): 343–72.

Petrucci, Peter R., and Katsuyuki Miyahira. "Language Preservation in a Transnational Context: One Okinawan Community's Efforts to Maintain Uchinaguchi in São Paulo, Brazil." *Romanitas: Lenguas y Literaturas Romances* 4, no. 2 (2010). http://romanitas.uprrp.edu/vol_4_num_2/petrucci_miyahira.html.

Pew Research Center. "Brazil's Changing Religious Landscape." Washington, DC: 2013. Accessed May 21, 2018. http://www.pewforum.org/2013/07/18/brazils-changing-religious-landscape/.

———. "Christian Movements and Denominations." Washington, DC: 2011. Accessed May 21, 2018. http://www.pewforum.org/2011/12/19/global-christianity-movements -and-denominations/.

Phillipps, Mike, and Marilyn Phillipps. *Casados Para Sempre: Princípios Bíblicos Para o Casamento Manual do Casal* [Married for life: Biblical principles for marriage couple's manual]. Atibaia, São Paulo: Associação MMI Brasil, 1986.

Pine, Frances. "Migration as Hope." *Current Anthropology* 55, no. S9 (2014): 95–104.

Plath, David W. *Long Engagements: Maturity in Modern Japan.* Stanford, CA: Stanford University Press, 1980.

Portes, Alejandro, and Lingxin Hao. "The Price of Uniformity: Language, Family and Personality Adjustment in the Immigrant Second Generation." *Ethnic and Racial Studies* 25, no. 6 (2002): 889–912.

Portes, Alejandro, and Rubén G. Rumbaut. *Legacies: The Story of the Immigrant Second Generation.* Berkeley: University of California Press, 2001.

Potolsky, Matthew. *Mimesis.* London: Routledge, 2006.

Potter, Robert B., Dennis Conway, and Joan Phillips, eds. *The Experience of Return Migration: Caribbean Perspectives.* Aldershot, UK: Ashgate, 2005.

Premawardhana, Devaka. *Faith in Flux: Pentecostalism and Mobility in Rural Mozambique.* Philadelphia: University of Pennsylvania Press, 2018.

Quayson, Ato, and Girish Daswani. "Introduction—Diaspora and Transnationalism: Scapes, Scales, and Scopes." In *A Companion to Diaspora and Transnationalism*, edited by Ato Quayson and Girish Daswani, 1–26. Chichester, UK: John Wiley & Sons, 2013.

Quero, Hugo C., and Rafael Shoji, eds. *Transnational Faiths: Latin-American Immigrants and Their Religions in Japan.* Farnham, UK: Ashgate, 2014.

Ramos-Zayas, Ana Y. *National Performances: The Politics of Class, Race, and Space in Puerto Rican Chicago.* Chicago: University of Chicago Press, 2003.

———. *Street Therapists: Race, Affect, and Neoliberal Personhood in Latino Newark.* Chicago: University of Chicago Press, 2012.

Reader, Ian. "Cleaning Floors and Sweeping the Mind: Cleaning as a Ritual Process." In *Ceremony and Ritual in Japan: Religious Practices in an Industrialized Society*, edited by Jan van Bremen and D. P. Martinez, 227–45. London: Routledge, 1995.

Reader, Ian, and George J. Tanabe. *Practically Religious: Worldly Benefits and the Common Religion of Japan.* Honolulu: University of Hawaii Press, 1998.

Richard, Analiese, and Daromir Rudnyckyj. "Economies of Affect." *Journal of the Royal Anthropological Institute* 15, no. 1 (2009): 57–77.

Rivas, Zelideth María. "Mistura for the Fans: Performing Mixed-Race Japanese Brazilianness in Japan." *Journal of Intercultural Studies* 36, no. 6 (2015): 710–28.

Robbins, Joel. "The Anthropology of Christianity: Unity, Diversity, New Directions." *Current Anthropology* 55, no. S10 (2014): 157–71.

———. *Becoming Sinners: Christianity and Moral Torment in a Papua New Guinea Society*. Berkeley: University of California Press, 2004.

———. "Between Reproduction and Freedom: Morality, Value, and Radical Cultural Change." *Ethnos* 72, no. 3 (2007): 293–314.

———. "Continuity Thinking and the Problem of Christian Culture: Belief, Time, and the Anthropology of Christianity." *Current Anthropology* 48, no. 1 (2007): 5–38.

———. "God Is Nothing but Talk: Modernity, Language, and Prayer in a Papua New Guinea Society." *American Anthropologist* 103, no. 4 (2001): 901–12.

———. "Is the Trans- in Transnationalism the Trans- in Transcendent? On the Alterity and the Sacred in the Age of Globalization." In *Transnational Transcendence: Essays on Religion and Globalization*, edited by Thomas J. Csordas, 55–72. Berkeley: University of California Press, 2009.

Roberts, Nathaniel. *To Be Cared For: The Power of Conversion and Foreignness of Belonging in an Indian Slum*. Berkeley: University of California Press, 2016.

Robertson, Jennifer. "Blood Talks: Eugenic Modernity and the Creation of New Japanese." *History and Anthropology* 13, no. 3 (2002): 191–216.

———. "Hemato-Nationalism: The Past, Present, and Future of 'Japanese Blood.'" *Medical Anthropology* 31, no. 2 (2011): 93–112.

Rocha, Cristina, and Manuel A. Vásquez, eds. *The Diaspora of Brazilian Religions*. Leiden: Brill, 2013.

———. "Zen Buddhism in Brazil: Japanese or Brazilian?" *Journal of Global Buddhism* 1 (2000): 31–55.

Rosenberger, Nancy. "Dialectic Balance in the Polar Model of Self: The Japan Case." *Ethos* 17, no. 1 (1989): 88–113.

———, ed. *Japanese Sense of Self*. Cambridge: Cambridge University Press, 1992.

Roth, Joshua H. *Brokered Homeland: Japanese Brazilian Migrants in Japan*. Ithaca, NY: Cornell University Press, 2002.

Rowe, Mark M. *Bonds of the Dead: Temples, Burial, and the Transformation of Contemporary Japanese Buddhism*. Chicago: University of Chicago Press, 2011.

Ryang, Sonia. *Japan and National Anthropology: A Critique*. London: Routledge, 2004.

———. *Love in Modern Japan: Its Estrangement from Self, Sex and Society*. London: Routledge, 2006.

———. *North Koreans in Japan: Language, Ideology, and Identity*. Boulder, CO: Westview, 1997.

Ryang, Sonia, and John Lie, eds. *Diaspora Without Homeland: Being Korean in Japan*. Berkeley: University of California Press, 2009.

Samara, de Mesquita E. "A Família no Brasil: História e Historiografia" [The family in Brazil: History and historiography]. *História Revista* 2, no. 2 (1997): 7–21.

Samarin, William J. *Tongues of Men and Angels: The Religious Language of Pentecostalism*. New York: Macmillan, 1972.

Sasaki, Koji. "Between Emigration and Immigration: Japanese Emigrants to Brazil and Their Descendants in Japan." *Senri Ethnological Reports* 77 (2008): 53–66.

——. "To Return or Not to Return: The Changing Meaning of Mobility Among Japanese Brazilians." In *Return: Nationalizing Mobility in Asia*, edited by Biao Xiang, Breanda Yeoh, and Mika Toyota, 21–39. Durham, NC: Duke University Press, 2013.

Scherz, China. "Let Us Make God Our Banker: Ethics, Temporality, and Agency in a Ugandan Charity Home." *American Ethnologist* 40, no. 4 (2013): 624–36.

Schneider, Arnd. *Futures Lost: Nostalgia and Identity Among Italian Immigrants in Argentina*. Oxford: Peter Lang, 2000.

Schneider, David M. *American Kinship: A Cultural Account*. Chicago: University of Chicago Press, 1980.

Seeman, Don. "Coffee and the Moral Order: Ethiopian Jews and Pentecostals Against Culture." *American Ethnologist* 42, no. 4 (2015): 734–48.

——. *One People, One Blood: Ethiopian-Israelis and the Return to Judaism*. New Brunswick, NJ: Rutgers University Press, 2010.

Seligman, Rebecca. "The Unmaking and Making of Self: Embodied Suffering and Mind-Body Healing in Brazilian Candomblé." *Ethos* 38, no. 3 (2010): 297–320.

Selka, Stephen. "Morality in the Religious Marketplace: Evangelical Christianity, Candomblé, and the Struggle for Moral Distinction in Brazil." *American Ethnologist* 37, no. 2 (2010): 291–307.

——. *Religion and the Politics of Ethnic Identity in Bahia, Brazil*. Gainesville: University Press of Florida, 2007.

Shimazono, Susumu. "The Expansion of Japan's New Religions into Foreign Cultures." *Japanese Journal of Religious Studies* 18, no. 2/3 (1991): 105–32.

Shoji, Rafael. "The Failed Prophecy of Shinto Nationalism and the Rise of Japanese Brazilian Catholicism." *Japanese Journal of Religious Studies* 35, no. 1 (2008): 13–38.

——. "The Making of 'Brazilian Japanese' Pentecostalism: Immigration as a Main Factor for Religious Conversion." In *Transnational Faiths: Latin-American Immigrants and Their Religions in Japan*, edited by Hugo C. Quero and Rafael Shoji, 33–52. Farnham, UK: Ashgate Publishing, 2014.

Shore, Bradd. *Culture in Mind: Cognition, Culture, and the Problem of Meaning*. Oxford: Oxford University Press, 1996.

Siddle, Richard. *Race, Resistance and the Ainu of Japan*. London: Routledge, 1996.

Skidmore, Thomas E. *Black into White: Race and Nationality in Brazilian Thought*. Durham, NC: Duke University Press, 1997.

——. "Racial Ideas and Social Policy in Brazil, 1870–1940." In *The Idea of Race in Latin America, 1870–1940*, edited by Richard Graham, 7–36. Austin: University of Texas Press, 1990.

Smidt, Corwin E. *Religion as Social Capital: Producing the Common Good.* Waco, TX: Baylor University Press, 2003.

Smilde, David. *Reason to Believe: Cultural Agency in Latin American Evangelicalism.* Berkeley: University of California Press, 2007.

Souza, Candice Vidal E., and Tarcísio Rodrigues Botelho. "Modelos Nacionais e Regionais de Família no Pensamento Social Brasileiro" [National and regional models of family in Brazilian social thought]. *Estudos Feministas* 9, no. 2 (2001): 414–32.

Stewart, Kathleen. *Ordinary Affects.* Durham, NC: Duke University Press, 2007.

Stoler, Ann. "Affective States." In *A Companion to the Anthropology of Politics,* edited by David Nugent and Joan Vincent, 4–20. Oxford: Blackwell, 2005.

Stoll, David. *Is Latin America Turning Protestant? The Politics of Evangelical Growth.* Berkeley: University of California Press, 1990.

Stone, Linda. *New Directions in Anthropological Kinship.* Lanham, MD: Rowman & Littlefield, 2002.

Stromberg, Peter G. *Language and Self-Transformation: A Study of the Christian Conversion Narrative.* Cambridge: Cambridge University Press, 1993.

Takenaka, Ayumi. "Ethnic Hierarchy and Its Impact on Ethnic Identities: A Comparative Analysis of Peruvian and Brazilian Return Migrants in Japan." In *Diasporic Homecomings: Ethnic Return Migration in Comparative Perspective,* edited by Takeyuki Tsuda, 260–80. Stanford, CA: Stanford University Press, 2009.

Taniguchi, Masaharu. *Jinsei wo Shihaisuru Senzo Kuyō* [Commemoration of ancestors determines our life]. Tokyo: Nihon Kyōbunsha, (1974) 2004.

Taylor, Charles. *Sources of the Self: The Making of the Modern Identity.* Cambridge, MA: Harvard University Press, 1989.

Telles, Edward E. *Race in Another America: The Significance of Skin Color in Brazil.* Princeton, NJ: Princeton University Press, 2014.

Thomas, Todne, Asiya Malik, and Rose Wellman, eds. *New Directions in Spiritual Kinship: Sacred Ties Across the Abrahamic Religions.* New York: Palgrave Macmillan, 2017.

Thompson, Edward P. "Time, Work-Discipline, and Industrial Capitalism." *Past & Present* 38 (1967): 56–97.

Tokyo Christian University. *JMR Study Report 2016.* [In Japanese.] Tokyo: 2017. Accessed May 21, 2018. http://www.tci.ac.jp/wp-content/uploads/2017/05/JMR_report_2016.pdf.

Tomlison, Matt. "God Speaking to God: Translation and Unintelligibility at a Fijian Pentecostal Crusade." *Australian Journal of Anthropology* 23, no. 3 (2012): 274–89.

Toulis, Nicole Rodriguez. *Believing Identity: Pentecostalism and the Mediation of Jamaican Ethnicity and Gender in England.* Oxford: Berg, 1997.

Toyota City. "Toyotashi Gaikokujin Dēta shū" [Data sets for foreign residents of Toyota City]. Toyota: 2014. Accessed May 21, 2018. http://www.city.toyota.aichi.jp/_res /projects/default_project/_page_/001/004/767/10.pdf.

Tsuda, Takeyuki. "Acting Brazilian in Japan: Ethnic Resistance Among Return Migrants." *Ethnology* 39, no. 1 (2000): 55–71.

———, ed. *Diasporic Homecomings: Ethnic Return Migration in Comparative Perspective*. Stanford, CA: Stanford University Press, 2009.

———. "From Ethnic Affinity to Alienation in the Global Ecumene: The Encounter Between the Japanese and Japanese-Brazilian Return Migrants." *Diaspora* 10, no. 1 (2001): 53–91.

———. *Strangers in the Ethnic Homeland: Japanese Brazilian Return Migration in Transnational Perspective*. New York: Columbia University Press, 2003.

———. "When Identities Become Modern: Japanese Emigration to Brazil and the Global Contextualization of Identity." *Ethnic and Racial Studies* 24, no. 3 (2001): 412–32.

van de Kamp, Linda. "Converting the Spirit Spouse: The Violent Transformation of the Pentecostal Female Body in Maputo, Mozambique." *Ethnos* 76, no. 4 (2011): 510–33.

———. "Love Therapy: A Brazilian Pentecostal (Dis)Connection in Maputo." In *The Social Life of Connectivity in Africa*, edited by Rijk van Dijk and Mirjam de Brujin, 203–26. New York: Palgrave Macmillan, 2012.

———. *Violent Conversion: Brazilian Pentecostalism and Urban Women in Mozambique*. Oxford: James Curry, 2016.

van de Kamp, Linda, and Rijk van Dijk. "Pentecostals Moving South-South: Ghanaian and Brazilian Transnationalism in Southern Africa." In *Religion Crossing Boundaries: Transnational Dynamics in Africa and the New African Diasporic Religions*, edited by Afe Adogame and James Spickard, 123–42. Leiden: Brill, 2010.

van der Veer, Peter, ed. *Conversion to Modernities: The Globalization of Christianity*. London: Routledge, 1995.

van Dijk, Rijk. "Time and Transcultural Technologies of the Self in the Ghanaian Pentecostal Diaspora." In *Between Babel and Pentecost: Transnational Pentecostalism in Africa and Latin America*, edited by Ruth R. Marshall-Fratani and André Corten, 216–34. Bloomington: Indiana University Press, 2001.

van Klinken, Adriaan. "Male Headship as Male Agency: An Alternative Understanding of a 'Patriarchal' African Pentecostal Discourse on Masculinity." *Religion and Gender* 1, no. 1 (2011): 104–24.

———. "Queer Love in a 'Christian Nation': Zambian Gay Men Negotiating Sexual and Religious Identities." *Journal of the American Academy of Religion* 83, no. 4 (2015): 947–64.

Vertovec, Steven. "Migrant Transnationalism and Modes of Transformation." In *Rethinking Migration: New Theoretical and Empirical Perspectives*, edited by Alejandro Portes and Josh DeWind, 149–80. New York: Berghahn Books, 2007.

Vilaça, Aparecida. "Culture and Self: The Different 'Gifts' Amerindians Receive from Catholics and Evangelicals." *Current Anthropology* 55, no. S10 (2014): S322–32.

———. "Dividualism and Individualism in Indigenous Christianity: A Debate Seen from Amazonia." *HAU: Journal of Ethnographic Theory* 5, no. 1 (2015): 197–225.

Viswanath, Rupa. "The Emergence of Authenticity Talk and the Giving of Accounts: Conversion as Movement of the Soul in South India, ca. 1900." *Comparative Studies in Society and History* 55, no. 1 (2013): 120–41.

Vitrine. "Naturalização: Tudo o Que Você Sempre Quis Saber" [Naturalization: Everything you always wanted to know], n100 (August 2014), 14–18.

von Baeyer, Sarah LeBaron. "National Worlds, Transnational Lives: Nikkei-Brazilian Migrants in and of Japan and Brazil." PhD diss., Yale University, 2015.

Warren, Jonathan, and Christina A. Sue. "Comparative Racisms: What Anti-Racists Can Learn from Latin America." *Ethnicities* 11, no. 1 (2011): 32–58.

Watanabe, Hiroki. "Nihon no Shūkyō Jinkō" [Population of religious adherents in Japan]. *Journal of Institute of Buddhist Culture at Musashino University* 27 (2011): 25–37.

Watarai, Tamaki. "Can a Mestiça be a Haafu? Japanese-Brazilian Female Migrants and the Celebration of Racial Mixing in Contemporary Japan." *Journal of Intercultural Studies* 35, no. 6 (2014): 662–76.

Weiner, Michael, ed. *Japan's Minorities: The Illusion of Homogeneity*. London: Routledge, (1997) 2009.

———. "'Self' and 'Other' in Imperial Japan." In *Japan's Minorities: The Illusion of Homogeneity*, edited by Michael Weiner, 1–20. London: Routledge, (1997) 2009.

Werbner, Richard. "The Charismatic Dividual and the Sacred Self." *Journal of Religion in Africa* 41, no. 2 (2011): 180–205.

White, Daniel. "Affect: An Introduction." *Cultural Anthropology* 32, no. 2 (2017): 175–80.

White, Merry I. *Perfectly Japanese: Making Families in an Era of Upheaval*. Berkeley: University of California Press, 2002.

Williams, Philip, Timothy Steigenga, and Manuel A. Vásquez, eds. *A Place to Be: Brazilian, Guatemalan, and Mexican Immigrants in Florida's New Destinations*. New Brunswick, NJ: Rutgers University Press, 2009.

Willis, David Blake, and Stephen Murphy-Shigematsu. *Transcultural Japan: At the Borderlands of Race, Gender and Identity*. London: Routledge, 2007.

Wilson, Sandra. "Family or State? Nation, War, and Gender in Japan, 1937–45." *Critical Asian Studies* 38, no. 2 (2006): 209–38.

———, ed. 2002. *Nation and Nationalism in Japan*. London: Routledge.

Xiang, Biao, Brenda Yeoh, and Mika Toyota. *Return: Nationalizing Transnational Mobility in Asia*. Durham, NC: Duke University Press, 2013.

Yamada, Masanobu. "'Bestowing the Light of the Gospel in Japan': The Formation of an Ethnic Church in the *Dekassegui* Community." In *Transnational Faiths: Latin-American Immigrants and Their Religions in Japan*, edited by Hugo C. Quero and Rafael Shoji, 53–74. Farnham, UK: Ashgate, 2014.

Yamamoto, Lucia E. "Gender Roles and Ethnic Identities in a Globalizing World: The Case of Japanese Brazilian Migrant Women." In *Japanese and Nikkei at Home and Abroad: Negotiating Identities in a Global World*, edited by Nobuko Adachi, 187–206. Amherst, NY: Cambria, 2010.

Yang, Jie. "The Politics of Affect and Emotion: Imagination, Potentiality, and Anticipation in East Asia." In *The Political Economy of Affect and Emotion in East Asia*, edited by Jie Yang, 2–28. London: Routledge, 2014.

Yano, Christine R. *Tears of Longing: Nostalgia and the Nation in Japanese Popular Song*. Cambridge, MA: Harvard University Press, 2003.

Yarris, Kristin E. *Care Across Generations: Solidarity and Sacrifice in Transnational Families*. Stanford, CA: Stanford University Press, 2017.

———. "'Pensando Mucho' ('Thinking Too Much'): Embodied Distress Among Grandmothers in Nicaraguan Transnational Families." *Culture, Medicine, and Psychiatry* 38, no. 3 (2014): 473–98.

Yomiuri Shimbun. "Nihonjin: Shūkyōkan" [The Japanese: Views on religion]. May 30, 2008.

———. "Tension Between Brazilians and Right-Wing Extremists at a Housing Project in Toyota, Aichi. [In Japanese.] June 9, 1999.

Zigon, Jarrett. *"HIV Is God's Blessing": Rehabilitating Morality in Neoliberal Russia*. Berkeley: University of California Press, 2011.

———. "Moral Breakdown and the Ethical Demand: A Theoretical Framework for an Anthropology of Moralities." *Anthropological Theory* 7, no. 2 (2007): 131–50.

———. *Morality: An Anthropological Perspective*. Oxford: Berg, 2008.

———. "On Love: Remaking Moral Subjectivity in Postrehabilitation Russia." *American Ethnologist* 40, no. 1 (2013): 201–15.

———. "Within a Range of Possibilities: Morality and Ethics in Social Life." *Ethnos* 74, no. 2 (2009): 251–76.

INDEX

absorption, prayer as, 87–88, 170, 174
afastamento, 63–65, 104–6. *See also* families: separation and estrangement of
affective openness, 101
alterity, 170–72
ambiguous cultural identity. *See* cultural ambiguity
ancestral personhood, 148
ancestral veneration: belief and faith in, 138, 143–48, 157–58, 202n7, 202n12; blood ties and, 129–31; historical context for, 18, 20; nonreligious, 164; *obon* commemoration, 58, 138, 146, 202n7
appearance, ethnic or racial, 4, 13–14, 15, 21, 23, 30, 47, 72–73, 113, 120, 121
Argentina, migration to, 44
Asad, Talal, 136
assimilability, 16, 39, 47, 121–22
Association of Families Abandoned by Migrant Workers, 60

"backward" minority status, 40–43
baptism, 123, 137–41, 147, 148–49, 150–51, 172–75, 176
Beatriz, 55–56, 57–58, 62–63, 67–68, 71–72, 149, 186, 188–89
belief and faith, 133–53; ancestral veneration, 138, 143–48, 157–58, 202n7, 202n12; baptism and, 137–41, 147, 148–49, 150–51; communion based on, 151–53; conflicting, 145–47, 148; conversion and, 137–41, 147, 148–51, 184; cultural context for, 136–37; defined, 135–36, 150; embodied, 134–35, 136, 175–78; ethnic

and racial identity affecting, 141–48; in eye of the beholder, 133–35; faith beyond belief, 135–37; family ties and commitment in, 138, 141–51; interiority of, 136, 140–41, 150; language reflecting, 138, 141, 150–51, 158–59, 175–78; nonreligious views of, 164–65; overview of, 184; as relational commitment, 150–51, 153; self intersection with, 157–60, 175–78; sincerity of, 140–41, 148, 150, 157–59; as state of mind, 136–37
Bible study, 29, 83, 85–86, 191n2
Bielo, James, 150
bifocality, 45
blood, 113–32; body metaphors, 124–25; ethnic and racial identity and, 7, 8, 9, 30, 47, 113–22, 130–32; forms of signification, 118–19, 126–27, 200n13; generation and, 7, 30, 115, 117–18; gradation of Japaneseness, 121–22; kinship metaphors, 116–17, 118–19, 122, 123–25, 126–27, 130–32; names and, 121–22; national identity and, 7, 8, 9, 47, 115–20, 128–30, 131–32, 184, 200n1; overview of, 183–84; religious conceptions of, 114–16, 122–32, 183–84; return migration and, 7, 8, 9, 115–16, 117–18, 119–20; visa boundaries based on, 7, 115, 117–18; water baptism and, 123
body metaphors, 124–25
Bolivia, migrants from, 4, 193–94n33
Borges, Marcelo, 44
Borneo, religion in, 136
branqueamento (whitening), 16–17